I0377860

DISCOVERING THE MOVIES
IN NEW BRUNSWICK

DISCOVERING THE MOVIES IN NEW BRUNSWICK
A HISTORY OF CINEMA

DAVID FOLSTER

EDITED BY
MARION BEYEA

CHAPEL STREET EDITIONS

Appreciation of Place

Chapel Street Editions exists within the unceded and unsurrendered territories of the Wolastoqiyik, Mi'kmaq, and Peskotomuhkati people. The work we do is born from the stories carried by this land and its inhabitants. The animals, plants, soil, water, and air make this place home for the Indigenous people, who belong to this land, for the descendants of those who took this land and made it a belonging, and for those who have since come from away. Chapel Street Editions holds a deep appreciation for our place within this land and the stories it tells. We honour the land's Indigenous caretakers and offer our gratitude for their wisdom and guidance.

Copyright © 2021 by The Estate of David Folster

Published by
Chapel Street Editions
150 Chapel Street
Woodstock, NB E7M 1H4
chapelstreeteditions@gmail.com
www.chapelstreeteditions.com

ISBN: 978-1-988299-38-9

Library and Archives Canada Cataloguing in Publication
Title: Discovering the movies in New Brunswick : a history of cinema / David Folster ; edited by Marion Beyea.
Names: Folster, David, author. | Beyea, Marion, editor.
Description: Includes bibliographical references.
Identifiers: Canadiana 20210347961 | ISBN 9781988299389 (softcover)
Subjects: LCSH: Motion pictures—New Brunswick—History. | LCSH: Motion pictures—Production and direction—New Brunswick—History.
Classification: LCC PN1993.5.C3 F65 2021 | DDC 791.4302/3097151—dc23

Photograph of David Folster by Glen Ross. Copyright © 2006

Book design by Brendan Helmuth

Chapel Street Editions, Ltd. gratefully acknowledges the financial support of the Department of Tourism, Heritage, and Culture, Province of New Brunswick.

For my father,
Hugh Hammond Folster,
who took me to my first moving picture,
a Hopalong Cassidy western, a long time ago.

Other books by David Folster:

The Great Trees of New Brunswick, 1987

The Chocolate Ganongs of St. Stephen New Brunswick, 1990, 1991

Ganong: A Sweet History of Chocolate, 2006

Table of Contents

Preface i

Introduction: Coming Attractions. 1

   1. At the Doorstep of the Movies 7

   2. First Flickers 37

   3. Movie-making in the Land of Canaan. 49

   4. Itinerant Showmen and Nickelodeons 67

   5. The Spreading Picture Culture 85

   6. Backcountry Filmmakers 103

   7. End of a Dream 125

   8. A Movie Mogul Comes Home 147

   9. Technicolor Woman 165

   10. The Sun Shines on Campobello. 181

   11. Remembering the Movies 201

Epilogue: State of the Art 229

Publisher's Afterword: A Salute to David Folster . 243

About the Author 249

Acknowledgements 251

Bibliography 253

Illustration Credits. 261

Preface

David Folster's *Discovering the Movies in New Brunswick* was over thirty years in the making. When I first met David in 1978 at a movie night at the Provincial Archives where early footage from local education and tourism productions and National Film Board films in their holdings were screened, he was eager to talk of his interest in New Brunswick's connections with the movies. He had many references in mind and had done research following up on some of them.

The dedication of his book to his father, and his attributing his interest in pursuing the topic of movies and New Brunswick to him, reveals that David had a happy introduction to the movies and they remained an important part of his growing up in Grand Falls. However, it was the movie-related tales and references he came across as he worked on other writing projects and met the demands of his daily employment that convinced him there was a book to be written. A master storyteller, he had a passion for telling New Brunswick's stories and believed it was important for people to hear them to develop pride and interest in their home province. He believed that having our stories told in movies was as important as publishing them—perhaps more so—as it was a medium that touched many people.

He indignantly recalled the arrogance of an American producer in the early days of film, Lewis Selznick, whose view was that "If Canadian stories are worthwhile for making into pictures, companies will be sent to Canada to make them." As it turned out, the fate of Canadian films and a Canadian film industry was sealed with the control of distribution firmly in the hands of American companies. Big companies were in control of all facets of the industry and able to prevent an independent producer like Ernie Shipman, an early Canadian film producer whose movies met with success, from getting his movies distributed.

It was an issue that David did not give up on and he probed the potential of New Brunswick movies being made with film maker, Gilles Walker, and author, David Adams Richards, whose interviews are part of

Discovering the Movies in New Brunswick

the New Brunswick film story he presents. He was disappointed when Joe Medjuck, a movie producer from Fredericton, who graciously hosted us in the luxurious studio of The Montecido Picture Company in Santa Barbara (the former home of a Saudi princess), told him he didn't have a desire to tell New Brunswick stories but rather ones that would be popular and commercially viable.

At times it seemed that David was reluctant to finish his manuscript, wanting instead to track down an elusive detail or follow up on another movie-related lead. For him, the search was part of the fun. His journalistic approach made him want to see, touch, and taste what he was writing about and to talk with anyone who had a connection with the event or person or place. As he interviewed people around the movie stories and brought his questions to archivists and librarians, he made many friends. Being a great listener and communicator, people were very willing to help him, and over long exchanges, first by letter and phone and then by email, the people he interviewed or sought information from became friends who were vested in his project.

To familiarize himself with the sport fishing and hunting that brought many rich and famous people to New Brunswick he interviewed a number of people in the area of the Tobique River who had worked as camp cooks and hotel staff and recalled the men who guided the *sports*. He made a trip to the Proctor Free Library in Proctor, Vermont to consult the records of long time officers of the Nictau Fish and Game Club, father and son, Redfield and Fletcher Proctor. His particular interest was in the film footage these *sports* shot of their adventures, and in one of their guides who fashioned a homemade camera and became a cameraman himself. This took him to Silver Creek, California where he stayed several days with Donald Ryder Dickey, Jr., the son of an ornithologist, hunter and nature photographer who came to the Tobique from California a number of times, first to hunt, and then film.

He was interested in where people watched the movies and what impact they had and interviewed a number of classmates from his Grand Falls high school—mostly females who were very happy to renew the relationship.

In Los Angeles and Hollywood David reviewed the records left by Donald Dickey Sr. at the University of Southern California Archives and he searched for answers to a number of questions at the Archives of the Academy of Motion Pictures in the Pickford Center for Motion

Picture Study. At the latter it was sometimes difficult to tell fact from fiction as press releases and other publicity pieces were written for the purpose of showing an actor or actress in a good light and often did not jibe with information found in official records consulted earlier. He speculated on why their links to New Brunswick were downplayed or hidden. He visited the Autry Museum of the American West to check out Bob Nowlan of Springfield New Brunswick, a founding member of the Sons of the Pioneers. In San Francisco it was important to go to a branch of the Wells Fargo Bank where the photographic studio of W. H. Rulofson once stood. He drove to the Sonora Valley where Rulofson had been an itinerant photographer selling miners on the notion of having their photograph taken for family and friends back home. A chance visit to the County Court House there turned up very interesting details of the trial of Rulofson's, colleague Eadweard Muybridge, who shot and killed his wife's lover in a jealous rage.

Some of the links between place and movies were quite tenuous such as his visit to Cap Lumiere, New Brunswick. It was the Lumiere brothers who devised an early motion picture camera and made the world's first movie and David wondered if the place name had anything to do with them. It did not, but it was a lovely spot to visit.

There were reasons for the long gestation of his movie book beyond his disinclination to give up the search for a fact or detail. He needed to incorporate the newly uncovered material. He had to write and re-write and eventually eliminate some subjects and move others to be hinted at or told in short inserts. He vacillated between an academic treatment of his subject and the storytelling book, a kind of extended journalism, which he settled on.

Sadly, David's sudden death in 2010 meant he did not write the chapter he planned to include on movies and francophone New Brunswick. Similarly, David did not complete his intended final chapter that was to bring his investigation of movie making in New Brunswick to more recent times. The editors decided to include as an epilogue the brief part he had written of the last chapter he had planned and to round it out from his research notes and other sources and to include content on Acadian movie making.

The epilogue would have been where he linked the episodes that reveal the ways in which the movies touched New Brunswick, how they came here, how they were received, what impact they had on viewers, and the role individuals from actors to producers played in the larger film world. It also would have afforded him the opportunity to analyze the influence of these and, undoubtedly, he would have returned to his belief that it was important for New Brunswickers to tell their stories in film. Scholars who are turning their studies to the film industry in New Brunswick are now providing the analysis. And as David said, the stories that comprise *Discovering the Movies in New Brunswick* could be the subject of movies themselves. Perhaps they will be. David would be delighted.

He would also be delighted that his good and long-time friends at Chapel Street Editions have published his book. It is the outcome of his love for his home province, of happy years of uncovering documentation and meeting people who helped him tell the stories of New Brunswick and filmmaking.

Marion Beyea
Provincial Archivist New Brunswick
1978-2013

Introduction

Coming Attractions

Seated with my father in our hometown theatre, the Opera House, in Grand Falls, New Brunswick, waiting to see my first moving picture on a Friday night in the mid-nineteen-forties, I was a long way from imagining that I would ever write a book about the movies. The idea didn't occur to me, in fact, until many years later when a couple of pieces of local movie lore piqued my interest, and I began thinking about what else might lie hidden beneath the surface of this quiet little province down by the sea in Canada.

This book is the result of that cogitation. It is a cinematic history of one small corner of North America. It is a story of how the movies came to a place and how they affected individual lives in that place. It is an evolutionary tale of the cinema written from the perspective of a distinct locale.

New Brunswick, one of Canada's Maritime Provinces, is not the sort of place one expects to have much cinematic history. Tucked into the folds of the continent's northeastern edge, it sometimes seems the province, the rest of the country, not to mention the rest of North America, finds easiest to overlook. But fuelled by a certain amount of writerly ego—the notion that, if you dig deeply enough, you can usually find a good story, sometimes even a meaningful one—I went looking. My search took a long time, but what I discovered was a series of truly remarkable cinematic tales, each connected, in one way or another, to New Brunswick.

My first surprise was how quickly the movies came to the province. Just seven months after Thomas Edison introduced them to New York, in April, 1896, a road company brought a few pieces of jittery film to Saint John, on the Bay of Fundy, and showed them as a novel "specialty" between acts of a live Victorian melodrama. As images of people and animals moving "as in life" passed before their eyes, the audience at the city's Opera House, on Union Street, erupted in wild applause.

What ensued from that moment in New Brunswick was, in many ways, a microcosm of the general North American experience with the movies. As travelling troupes carried the first films to the province's small cities and towns, itinerant picture men began taking them into the deeper countryside. These men were genuine, if generally unheralded, moving picture pioneers, as were those who followed in the Nickelodeon era of five-cent "permanent" theatres. In New Brunswick, the latter included one of the most knowledgeable early picture men in the world, another who started one of Canada's earliest chains of movie theatres, and a woman who was reputed to be the first female editor of a daily movie page in the country. All three were in Saint John, which developed into a "good picture town" and one of Canada's early regional distribution centres for film.

Researching this topic also opened a window on the province's social history, which determined the precise nature of the cinematic experience and imparted a distinctive flavour to it. In 1905, a cameraman for the American Mutoscope and Biograph Company, of New York, came to New Brunswick to make a movie about moose hunting. This was because the province was known internationally for its prolific moose territories. The cameraman got his film, and today it is the oldest surviving film of New Brunswick. We also know what happened to the cameraman. He became the most innovative cameraman in the history of silent film and collaborated with director D.W. Griffith in making all the great classics of that period, including *The Birth of a Nation*.

As in this instance, the province regularly brushed up against larger film history, often without knowing it. It was like a cinematic variant of the six degrees of separation, and it was one of the things that made the subject so engaging. Another motion picture, shot in New Brunswick in 1922, became a semaphore for the rough road ahead for all Canadian-made films. It is notable for that reason, and also for the fact that one of its disillusioned actors later emerged as a Hollywood star.

The trails of some of these stories, of course, led well beyond New Brunswick. I went to the National Archives in Ottawa and the Library of Congress in Washington; the Beinecke Rare Book and Manuscript Library at Yale University and the library and archives of the Academy of Motion Picture Arts and Sciences in Beverly Hills; an ancient market town, Kingston-upon-Thames, in England; an old gold mining town in California; and a small village in Vermont. I found relevant material in all of these places, and many others. I'm also happy to report that not once did a bemused librarian, archivist or interview subject say to me in disbelief, "You're writing *what*? About *where*?"

A cinematic history of a place must also include men and women who left that place and found careers in the movies. The first from New Brunswick was probably Genevieve Blinn, a member of a Saint John theatrical family named Nannary. She supposedly appeared in films with the early screen vamp, Theda Bara. But Miss Blinn herself has been so eclipsed from memory that when I went looking on the Internet for more about her, I was immediately led to the website of a modern porn actress who'd obviously had no compunctions about appropriating the name of a long-dead silent film actress as her own.

Better known, and better used, were Louis Mayer and Walter Pidgeon, the former as the man who built Metro-Goldwyn-Mayer into the greatest studio of its day, the latter as a handsome leading man whose career in the movies spanned half a century. Both grew up in Saint John and have been much written about over the years. But, even after all this time, it was still possible to find fresh material—in Pidgeon's case, about the first twenty years or so of his life, and, in Mayer's case, about how the Depression-wracked University of New Brunswick brought him home in 1939 and gave him an honorary degree, with fingers crossed that he might reciprocate in some meaningful way.

A stranger tale is that of the pretty little farm girl from outside Fredericton who, having migrated to the so-called "Boston States," met and married the inventor of Technicolor. She is reported to have been the first woman ever filmed in Technicolor, but, more important, she also helped introduce the process to the movies and became one of the first highly paid female executives in the business. Her real story, at once both remarkable and bizarre, is told here for the first time.

Only rarely has Hollywood itself come to New Brunswick, but one occasion was June of 1960, when all the glamour and panoply of American movie-making descended on Campobello Island, just off the province's coast. For nine glorious days, this lovely isle in the outer Bay of Fundy basked in international attention as the movie-makers shot scenes for *Sunrise at Campobello*, the story of future U.S. President Franklin Delano Roosevelt's agonizing recovery from polio. Decades afterward, when I visited, the memory of those sweet days still lived in some island homes, as though it had all happened yesterday.

Discovering the Movies in New Brunswick

Movies insinuated themselves into the lives of New Brunswickers in many ways. Once a visiting road show or an itinerant showman had whetted the public appetite, and improving artistry and technology made longer "photoplays" possible, full-time picture houses sprang up. Outside the province's three cities, these initially were in towns (or, occasionally, irrepressible villages) where a local mill, fish plant, or nearby dam supplied the community, including the local theatre, with electricity. Another essential element was the railway. Because the roads were only marginally passable, (as a horrified editor from New York's *Moving Picture World* discovered when he tried to travel them in 1916), trains were the only practical way by which films could reach the distant theatres from the "exchanges" in Saint John.

The possibilities of film excited people. This included a clever fishing and hunting guide, Bert Moore, who worked the Tobique River country in northwestern New Brunswick. Inspired by a visiting California filmmaker, the New Brunswicker actually built his own moving picture camera with wood and scalped metal parts, and, with the camera, shot remarkable wildlife footage that Canadian Pacific's Associated Screen News turned into films. Terry Ramsaye wrote the scripts for Moore's movies (even silent films required them). Ramsaye, I discovered, wrote the first definitive history of the American film industry—another example of the six degrees of separation.

Which brings me back to my father. Besides his family and friends, he loved two things—gadgets and railways. For a long time, I thought of these as rather disparate interests, until I read *River of Shadows*, Rebecca Solnit's biography of Eadweard Muybridge, who was one of the fathers of modern motion pictures (and who also figures prominently in one of the stories in this cinematic history). Solnit's book makes the point that railways and moving pictures had something in common: railways shortened physical distance; moving pictures had the effect of shortening temporal distance, *making the past part of the present, and the present part of the future.*

In the middle of the Great Depression, my gadget-prone father somehow found cash to buy a small, eight-millimetre moving picture camera, with which he shot movies of family, friends, fires, ski-jumping at the nearby Danish-Canadian community of New Denmark, and, of course, passing trains. Thinking about this now, and about how I got started on this somewhat strange enterprise, I sometimes wonder if its roots don't lie there, with my father, on a snowy Sunday afternoon in the

Coming Attractions

Fig. 0.1 Ski jump scene from a movie taken by the author's father.

nineteen-thirties, pointing his camera upward at young skiers hurtling down a precipitous sluice on homemade skis, briefly imagining himself a cameraman for Movietone News.

    Whatever my motivation, the result is a cinematic history years in the making, with a cast of, if not quite thousands, then at least dozens, a history played out in an unlikely place and presented against the backdrop of the wider world of pictures. And it begins with a mysterious death. Just like in the movies.

Chapter One

At the Doorstep of the Movies

The cinematic history of New Brunswick begins nearly twenty years before the movies were invented.

It begins across the continent in San Francisco, where, on an afternoon in early November, 1878, one of the city's best-known citizens plunged to his death from a rooftop. As the news quickly spread along Montgomery and Sacramento Streets, people could scarcely believe their ears. The victim was a popular society photographer, William Herman Rulofson, who'd gone to the roof of his studio to inspect a new skylight. Then, suddenly, he was over the edge and on his way to the ground, his last words hurling out behind him; "My God, I am killed."

How had it happened? It was a question nobody could answer with absolute certainty. Years afterward, speculation persisted about whether it was an accident or a suicide; there were hints of both in the sparse evidence available. All people knew for certain was that this death, in the darkening late afternoon, brought to an abrupt and tragic end a career that had been quite remarkable, even for an era full of stories about young men achieving success against long odds.

Rulofson was from New Brunswick. Thirty years before, he'd joined the Gold Rush to California and made his first money travelling in a horse-drawn studio and taking daguerreotype portraits for lonesome miners to send to their families back home. He later settled in the gold country, remaining there for more than a decade, until finally moving to San Francisco, where he and a partner founded one of the great photographic studios of the Far West.

It was called Bradley and Rulofson, and under William Herman's hand (while his partner Bradley ran an associated supply house) it achieved international renown. Its clients included railway baron Leland Stanford, the Harvard naturalist Louis Agassiz, writers Bret Hart and Mark Twain. P.T. Barnum told Rulofson his portrait was "a better picture than I was even able to get in Paris, London, or elsewhere." The actor Edwin Booth paid a similar compliment. Rulofson became a friend and confidante of newspaper publishers, beautiful women, and, fatefully, of the man who would be a father of moving pictures.

His name was Eadweard Muybridge. Some readers will recognize him as the maker of those sequential pictures of a galloping racehorse that appear in books about the history of photography and about the history of the cinema. Those same pictures stand at the very beginning of the phenomenon that became the movies.

Long before that, Muybridge had been another of the thousands of migrants who surged into California in the middle of the nineteenth century, most hoping to find gold, the rest ready to benefit from the spoils of it. Muybridge was an English émigré, and he was first a bookseller, which is likely how Rulofson met him. Later, Muybridge turned to landscape photography, and when he went to the spectacular Yosemite Valley to take pictures, Rulofson was one of his sponsors. The photographic results were also spectacular, and in time Rulofson's gallery and studio became Muybridge's chosen sales salon. The two men came to know each other well, which is why, at a traumatic moment in Muybridge's life, William Rulofson would be called upon to try and help save his friend from the gallows.

Fig. 1.1 Obelisk in the graveyard surrounding St. Paul's Anglican Church at Hampton.

* * *

Another possible beginning for this story would be in the leafy cemetery that surrounds St. Paul's Anglican Church, at the village of Hampton, New Brunswick. It is where, in a plot marked by an obelisk, we find the graves of Rulofson's parents, William and Priscilla Amelia Rulofson, and two of his siblings, both named Stephen J., both having died as babies. His maternal grandparents are also buried here; Captain John Howard, a seaman from nearby St. Martins, and his wife, Patience, about whom an apocryphal story still surfaces from time to time, that she was the daughter of Hannah Lightfoot, mistress to England's King George III.

Colour and legend surrounded the Rulofson side of the family, too. Descended from an eighteenth-century Danish immigrant, William Herman's grandfather, Rulof Rulofson, was a British officer in the breakaway American colonies before he received a grant of land on the Hammond River in southern New Brunswick. On their way to a new home at Upham, near Hampton, he and his bride Mehitabel cut two willow twigs for riding crops, which they planted at the homestead. Years later, the Saxby Gale of 1869 brought down one of the trees, and its wood was made into furniture pieces that are still treasured by descendants of the family.

Rulof Rulofson became a respected member of his community. He was a justice of the peace, New Brunswick's first schools superintendent, and a warden of his church. But the family suffered a reversal when William Herman's father, a farmer, died within a few months of his son's birth in 1826. As a result, the family's straightened circumstances meant that eventually William and his two surviving brothers had to make their own ways. Relatives helped where they could, and James Melick, a relative by marriage and a watchmaker and jeweller in nearby Saint John, may have taken William Herman under wing. Melick had an interest in science and regularly attended lectures at the Mechanics Institute, where the subjects covered everything from astronomy and galvanism to a "Comparative View of the Male and Female Intellect." Another likely topic, after its invention in 1839, was daguerreotype photography, and presently Melick had a studio of his own above his shop at the city's bustling Market Slip.

This is probably where William Herman Rulofson began his photographic career, but the ultimate confirmation of that—from Rulofson himself—is missing, because afterward he never spoke of his early life. This apparently was an endemic condition among Gold Rush Californians, who simply chose to reinvent themselves in the new El Dorado. But Rulofson seems to have carried it to excess, casting an aura of mystery over those early years.

Sometime in the 1840s, he travelled to Europe, supposedly to learn more about daguerreotypy. Then, departing for home in 1846, he was shipwrecked in Dundrum Bay, on the coast of Ireland. After a night of terror for the passengers, Rulofson supposedly made his way to Liverpool, where he earned enough money from photography to buy another ticket. The trouble with this story is that the ship, the *S.S. Great Britain*, merely grounded in the bay and the ensuing scene was not nearly as chaotic as is described. The steamship company soon reimbursed its passengers for their fares.

What is definitely known is that, by early 1848, Rulofson was back in New Brunswick. In the little provincial capital of Fredericton, he rented rooms from a Mrs. Howden, at the corner of York and King streets, and set up a daguerreotype studio. Among those who sat for him was the province's chief justice, Ward Chipman Jr.

It was not, however, a propitious time for going into business. New Brunswick's economy was seriously ailing. Shipbuilding was down, the timber trade was off, and farm crops had failed three summers in a row. There was no money for capital works, no opening "for profitable employment of any kind." As a result, the very bone and sinew of the province—farmers, forest workers, mechanics and other tradesmen—were leaving, many sailing out of Saint John for Boston, with the Western states as their ultimate destination. William Rulofson soon joined them, although he had a different plan in mind. In Boston, he probably spent his time inspecting, and perhaps buying, new photographic equipment. Then he headed back north, this time to Newfoundland. His stay there would be relatively brief—just a matter of months—but they would be eventful ones.

In St. John's, Rulofson took rooms in the residence of one Archibald Currie, at the rear of the city's new Customs House, where he and a partner, a local chap named Wilder, advertised their facility to take daguerreotypes "of every size, with or without colour, and without regard to weather, in a superior style, and more life-like in expression than any ever before offered to the public." The partnership lasted until September, when William announced he was going it on his own. The following month, he again appeared in a newspaper announcement. He had just been married. His bride was Amelia Violet Currie, the daughter of his landlord. He was twenty-two, she no more than fourteen. She may also have been pregnant.

*   *   *

That December, telegraph wires were humming with news of another kind; gold had been discovered in California. The find had been made nearly a year before, and rumours had been flying for some months. But the American President, James J. Polk, had waited until he had an official report in hand before addressing Congress. "The accounts of the abundance of gold in that territory," he said, "are of such extraordinary character as would scarcely command belief were they not corroborated by authentic reports of officers in the public service." Polk based his remarks on a dispatch from Colonel R.B. Mason, the U.S. military commander in California. It told of fifty thousand dollars worth of gold being mined every day, of men becoming instantly rich.

Polk's announcement triggered one of the nineteenth century's greatest mass migrations. In the following months, thousands of hard-pressed men dropped what they were doing in various parts of the world and headed for California's gilt coast. In far-off Newfoundland, William Herman Rulofson wrapped up his affairs, then he, too, was off.

There were three possible ways to reach California from the East; "the Plains across, the Horn around, or the Isthmus over." The American Plains route was uncertain and dangerous, but crossing the Panamanian Isthmus seemed infinitely worse. It was a trek through an untracked, fetid and pestilential jungle rife with cholera, dysentery, and a wracking fever spawned in the slime-choked Chagres River. There was no guarantee that, in taking that route, you would ever see California.

That left a trip by sea, down the East Coast, round Cape Horn, at the tip of South America, and back up the Pacific Coast to San Francisco. Rulofson seems to have decided on this route, leaving Newfoundland in April aboard the brig *Osprey*, which took him at least as far as Baltimore. Passage from the Northeast to California cost about two hundred dollars, for which the traveller also got fifteen days' extra accommodation at the end of the voyage. But he was told to bring his own bedding, and that he could expect a few inconveniences, like the violent weather off Cape Horn, which sometimes trapped ships for weeks. And then there were those furry dead things they often found at the bottom of the drinking casks, and rats so brazen that they came to the bunks and nipped at the occupants' toes and fingers.

But there were also compensations. The birds of the Southern Hemisphere were spectacular in their variety and plumage, although some men saw this as an invitation to bring their guns on deck and let the lead fly. Rulofson, however, concentrated on picture taking, and later claimed that, during stopovers, he photographed "everything of interest from a Patagonian savage to a Brazilian emperor."

Nothing, however, could have prepared him for San Francisco, which he finally reached in the summer of 1849. The harbour was filled with ships, many of them abandoned, their crews off in the hills, looking for gold. From the waterfront, a sprawling city of tents and shanties spread up the slopes. At night, it was an "amphitheatre of fire," lanterns glowing against canvas. In a convulsion of garish, amoeboid growth, a once sleepy Mexican town, formerly called *Yorba Buena*, had been transformed into a Sodom and Gomorrah of the Pacific, with gambling salons, billiard halls, bathhouses, and whorehouses, all capable of deducting tidy sums from the profligate miners. One of the "lewd women" claimed she made fifty thousand dollars that year.

There was a bitter irony to all of this. Until just before gold was discovered, Americans hadn't shown much interest in California, which Hernan Cortes, the Spanish *conquistador*, had named after Calafia, a beautiful Amazon Queen in a sixteenth-century novel. For years, Spain used it as an exile for "idle, undesirable people," even while establishing a system of missions to convert and control the local Indigenous people. After newly independent Mexico quietly took over in 1822, the territory remained mainly a wretched outback suitable only for the *cholos* (rascals and mongrels) of society.

An important change was signalled when the new authority decided to secularize the Franciscan missions. The intent was to turn over the vast mission lands and huge herds of livestock to the Indigenous inhabitants, but they were so ill-prepared that it all wound up in the hands of retired military men and others with connections. And so was born California's so-called pastoral period, when no more than eight hundred families formed a new social order, living on huge *ranchos* in the midst of lovely, unfenced countryside, their every need met by armies of Indigenous servants and labourers, the first mythological era in a land destined to be known for mythmaking.

Americans began trickling into this bucolic paradise in the early 1840s, and, in 1846, President Polk manufactured a war with Mexico, with California as one of the prizes. Two years and many lives later, the Americans had it. Under the Treaty of Guadaloupe Hildago, the U. S. got more than five hundred thousand square miles, including parts of today's

Arizona, Wyoming, Colorado and New Mexico, and all of Utah, Nevada and California.

The treaty was signed on February 2, 1848. Ten days earlier, a carpenter building a sawmill on the American River in northern California had discovered the gold that would transform the Pacific West.

* * *

Eadweard Muybridge did not have gold specifically in mind when he landed in the United States in the early 1850s. Born a little more than two decades earlier in Kingston-on-Thames, not far upriver from London, he was a young man still trying to find himself, right down to the matter of his name. The family name was Muggeridge, and his given names were Edward James. But he made several revisions before finally settling on Eadweard Muybridge, the distinctive spelling of his first name probably derived from two Saxon kings who'd been crowned in Kingston. It also helped him to stand out a bit, something he seemed to crave.

Like Rulofson's, Eadweard Muybridge's early days are clouded by a shortage of documentation. His first years in America have large gaps, but, by about 1852, he was in New York, working as a commission agent for a London publishing company. He also travelled, visiting Atlantic ports as far south as New Orleans. Then, somewhere around mid-decade, he relocated to San Francisco. The bookstore he opened on Montgomery Street was one of forty in the city, an indicator of how much it had changed in the half-dozen years since William Rulofson first laid eyes on it.

Rulofson hadn't lingered long amid the sprawling confusion of those days, heading for the mining country as soon as he got his bearings. Back East, itinerant daguerreotypists had been travelling the countryside like tin peddlers; others had done the same thing during the Mexican War, offering weary soldiers on the line the chance to "send a keepsake home to your wife or sweetheart." To Rulofson, the gold fields presented a similar opportunity, with fewer bullets.

Heading east from San Francisco, he made his way to Stockton, a busy staging area on the San Joaquin River. In the *Stockton Times and Tuolumne County Intelligencer*, he ran a notice like those he'd used in New Brunswick and Newfoundland. Customers should "make an early call," he advised, because his stay would be "extremely limited." In the reciprocal journalistic style of the day, the editor responded with a similar appeal to all "who desire to behold themselves in California 'fixins'."

Rulofson picked his way through the gold country in his mobile studio, travelling woodland trails that were dotted with campfires at night. When he reached Sonora, he stopped. The town, which had been named by its original Mexican settlers, sat in a lovely valley of oaks, surrounded by the foothills of the Sierra Nevada Mountains. Recently, however, several thousand American and European gold-seekers had landed there, and tensions seethed between older residents and the newcomers. Fights broke out, people got murdered, mobs meted out justice.

But Sonora had gold, and perhaps a future, and for a young man like Rulofson, now in his mid-twenties, it looked like a place to make a stand. He would remain there for more than a dozen years, during which the town gradually returned to its former civility.

A contemporary observer had said of Sonora; "Every man carries arms, generally a Colt revolver, buckled behind, with no attempt at concealment." Rulofson wasn't exempt. In 1851, he got into a dispute with a man named William Smart, who accused him of trying to burn down his house. In a quarrel, Rulofson shot Smart in the arm, and the victim vowed revenge; "He has shot me, and I mean to shoot him." But before that happened, the combatants wound up in court, where both were found culpable. A frontier judge ordered each to post a five hundred dollar bond and to keep the peace for six months.

As Sonora prospered—that same year a vein of gold six inches to a foot wide was unearthed right in its centre, and much more gold lay nearby—amenities were added. It got a small theatre (attached to a saloon), a museum, a library, and a "Literary and Scientific Institute." Rulofson initially kept his mobile studio, which proved handy when a fire swept the town, and he was able to haul the wagon out of harm's way with a team of oxen. He later acquired property and gradually grew into a businessman well enough respected to be asked to collect contributions when fire struck another town.

He also assumed the mantle of a family man. In January, 1853, more than four years after their wedding in Newfoundland, his child-bride Amelia arrived by ship in San Francisco. With her was their son, who'd been named William Howard and was now a toddler perhaps just shy of four years of age. Before the year was out, they had another son, and there would eventually be several more children.

William's business grew as his talent for flair and innovation began to emerge. He advertised that, for fifty cents, he could take "the cheapest and best pictures in the State to send in letters to the friends back home." He also sold "stereoscopes," an early version of the three-dimensional photographs that later became popular in Victorian households. "We have invented our own plan for taking Stereotypes," Rulofson trumpeted, "and they cannot be equalled elsewhere."

The success of the Sonora business made it Rulofson's springboard for his move to San Francisco, although that didn't come until early 1863. When it did, his new city wasn't long in taking notice. Rulofson had learned the value of promotion as well as the importance of striving for excellence in his craft. He used the latest equipment and best materials. He hired, or otherwise drew into his professional milieu, the most talented photographers. San Franciscans responded.

* * *

One Sunday morning more than two decades ago, I caught a train out of London. At that point, I knew little about Eadweard Muybridge, other than that he had been born in Kingston-upon-Thames, which is where I was headed. I had no idea what I would do when I got there, but, within moments of my arrival, I spotted a man walking along the street, and something in my intuition told me he might be the one person about on this early morning who had heard of Muybridge. "Ah, Eadweard Muybridge," he responded, "Ah, yes"! And then he directed me to the local museum, which, he said, had a very fine exhibition about Muybridge.

It turned out that the Kingston branch of the English retail chain, Marks and Spencer, in observing the centennial of its founding in 1884, had decided to spend its celebratory funds on an exhibit at the Kingston Museum and Heritage Centre devoted to this native son "who won international fame as a photographer of movement and pioneer of cinematography." In panels and displays, it traced Muybridge's life from his beginnings in Kingston, through various triumphs and tragedies, to his semi-retirement back in Kingston, where he died in 1904. The exhibit paid homage to his landscape photography in San Francisco and Yosemite, noted problems in his personal life, and celebrated his photographic studies of the way humans and animals move, the work that ultimately brought him to the doorstep of the movies. It also contained his original zoopraxiscope, the machine that was, as the exhibit programme noted, "the first moving picture projector."

One of the remarkable things about Muybridge's progression from bookseller to becoming a father of motion pictures is that nobody knows exactly when or how he began the transition. This is because there are large gaps in the knowledge of what he did between the years 1861 and 1866—his "Years of Uncertainty," as the Kingston exhibit put it, his "Lost Years," as others have identified them. By 1860, he had evidently decided on some kind of change and had turned the book business over to his brother. He then set out for Europe, but on his way across Texas, suffered a grievous head injury in a stagecoach accident. He is known to have sought treatment afterward in New York and England, but for the most part the record of those years is a blank.

This has led to a certain amount of speculation, some of it quite tenuous, about how Muybridge learned the basics of photography. One day, at Canada's National Archives (now called Library and Archives Canada), in Ottawa, I was perusing microfilm of the early trade journal, *The Moving Picture World*, and came upon a full-page story under the headline, "Muybridge Motion Picture Experiments." The story, in the edition of October 14, 1916, was based on an interview with an old camera hand named Joseph Thwaite, who had arrived in San Francisco from New York in the early 1860s and had gone to work at Bradley and Rulofson.

"Mr. Rulofson, of this firm," Thwaite related, "had gotten acquainted with Muybridge when he first came to California as a book agent." Muybridge had later made a killing on "some famous book" and this had financed his return trip to Europe. Thwaite made no reference to the stagecoach accident, but he did say that Muybridge had visited London, Paris, and perhaps Australia. "In Paris, he had picked up some old cameras and had gotten interested in the picture taking game." When he got back to San Francisco, he was dead broke and had looked up his old friend Rulofson. Subsequently, said Thwaite, Muybridge "spent some months in our gallery learning the inside rudiments of picture-taking and development. I taught him myself how to make his first picture bath."

* * *

Within a few months of its start-up, the Bradley and Rulofson gallery and studio was on its way to becoming *the* outstanding photographic business on the Pacific Coast. The experience of trying to scrape out a living as a daguerreotypist in New Brunswick and Newfoundland had taught Rulofson the importance of getting his name before the public, and in San Francisco he applied this lesson assiduously. He gave pictures to the newspapers in return for photo credits, and he traded photographic sittings for advertising space. He produced innovative promotional items. One was a redeemable coupon equal in value to a one dollar gold note that a customer could apply to the price of his or her portrait. There were also advertising cards filled with montages of prominent clients. To one of these, labeled "Men of Mark," Rulofson saw fit to add his own picture.

His flair and brimming confidence earned him a sobriquet, "The P.T. Barnum of Photography." At the same time, he conducted the business of the studio with acumen, style and grace. Located above a billiards parlour on Montgomery Street, it was reached by elevator. Customers could step in from the street, seat themselves on a cushioned bench, and be whisked to the second floor. There, a courteous staff member, often Rulofson himself, greeted them in a well-appointed reception area. Its tasteful accoutrements included a Brussels carpet, floor-to-ceiling mirrors, damask and lace point curtains. Sofas were carefully positioned in the room. There was a grand piano. It was a space, a visiting newspaperman declared, "rivalling in luxuriance a European salon."

Elsewhere on this level, and on the third floor, were rooms devoted to developing, printing, and mounting the photographs; for storing negatives; for oil painting and drawing with India ink; and, most important, for taking the portraits. The last space, located on the third floor, was equipped with an immense skylight of ground glass, the better to soften and subdue the brilliant California sun and give the portraits a proper tone. There were also offices, one of which Eadweard Muybridge would come to occupy.

* * *

Unlike William Rulofson, who was always a businessman-photographer concentrating on lucrative portraiture, Muybridge had decided to become a landscape photographer. He gave himself a *nom d'artiste*—Helios, god of the sun—and, adopting one of Rulofson's old ideas, set himself up with a light, horse-drawn wagon that he called "The Flying Studio." Photography was now in its so-called wet-plate era. Glass plates were coated with collodion, a thick, yellowish mixture of nitrated cotton, alcohol, and ether, and then bathed in a solution of silver nitrate. To capture images on these glass negatives, they had to be exposed while still wet, which meant that everything—cameras, chemicals, plates, and the equipment for preparing and developing them—had to be carried into the field. Hence, "The Flying Studio."

Muybridge began with San Francisco. He took hundreds of images in the city, many of them stereographs. Then he turned his eyes toward Yosemite, which lay about one hundred and seventy miles due east. In 1864, President Abraham Lincoln had turned the valley over to California to be preserved in perpetuity. It was an other-worldly place of lofty peaks, hanging precipices, tall waterfalls, and huge granite domes, all the result of upsurges of molten rock millions of years before. During the spring and summer of 1867, Muybridge spent several months clambering through the rugged terrain by foot and by mule train. To finance the expedition, he had enlisted a coterie of "our best known connoisseurs and patrons of art" to subscribe to the photographic series that would be the issue from this adventure. Among these distinguished subscribers was William Rulofson.

His supporters were not disappointed. Muybridge produced photographs unlike any seen before, capturing the valley's surreal quality from unusual angles, creating mood with clouds photographed for that very purpose, and with mist and shadows and falling water. The pictures brought him public attention, and he began receiving photographic commissions. One for the federal government took him to Alaska, which the U.S. had just bought from Russia. He photographed the Pacific coast along the way, including parts of Vancouver Island. He also did photographic work for the western railways.

In the course of all of this, he met Flora Stone. She was a young employee of the studio where Muybridge was then affiliated, a competitor of Bradley and Rulofson's. She was blonde, attractive, and married to a saddlemaker named Lucius Stone, who seems to have been something of a lout. Muybridge may have counselled her to leave Stone, which she did, and then married Eadweard. She was twenty-one and ready to experience what life had to offer. Eadweard was twice her age and utterly committed to his art, no matter what sacrifices that entailed. It was not a formula for marital bliss.

* * *

William Rulofson's personal life had also taken a turn. In January 1867, his wife Amelia died. They had been married for more than eighteen years, and she had borne him three sons and three daughters. Her obituary reported her age as thirty-two.

William didn't waste much time in finding a new wife, nor did he have to look far. At his gallery, working as a receptionist, was a young woman,

Mary Jane Morgan. As an infant, she had crossed the American Great Plains in a wagon train, and now, at twenty-three, she was a striking beauty. Their courtship was brief, and they were married within six months of Amelia's death.

There was a substantial difference in their ages—William was now forty-one. But he was handsome at that age, with a pleasant face framed by distinguished mutton chop whiskers, and he had dash and style. They became one of the city's most attractive couples.

William parlayed his engaging manner into business and social success. Though diligent in his work habits, he sometimes seemed a kind of frontier boulevardier, presenting his card and compliments to visiting celebrities, whom he would then photograph in rooms he kept for that purpose at San Francisco's Palace Hotel. He met the Earl and Countess of Dufferin that way, and a host of other distinguished visitors to the city.

He had an eye for beautiful women and shared the confidences of a beguiling array of artists, actresses and adventuresses. All the while, he maintained an aura of strict respectability. He was a Mason, a member of several fraternal and charitable organizations, a regular communicant at Episcopal services. At home, he and Mary Jane settled into a happy life together, soon adding two children of their own to the four from his first marriage still residing with them.

Fig. 1.2   William Rulofson.

The studio and gallery prospered. It now had a professional staff of thirty-six and a weekly payroll of six hundred dollars. Having one's portrait taken at Bradley and Rulofson's became a fashionable thing to do, and an even greater compliment was to have it join others exhibited on the gallery walls. These were photographs "so life-like," said one enchanted visitor, "that you almost fear to speak, lest they hear you." It was the kind of ultimate praise that would endure until the photographic medium advanced to its next stage—moving pictures.

* * *

Flora Muybridge would have loved the movies. Her marriage to Eadweard Muybridge had finally released her from the yoke of her overbearing first husband. Now she was ready for entertainment and frivolity. But the movies, which Eadweard would help invent, were still a quarter-century away. So she chose the entertainments of the day: musical performances, stage revues, theatrical presentations. Unfortunately, she chose them in the company of the wrong man.

He was "Major" Harry Larkyns, a charming rascal who was a drama critic on a San Francisco newspaper. The tales he told of his past were beyond belief. He said he'd been a soldier of fortune under Garibaldi, and had once held the rights to the harem of an Arab potentate. Poor, unsophisticated Flora was smitten, and, rather indiscreetly, she became the Major's regular companion.

Eadweard, meanwhile, pursued his art with total commitment. In 1872, a year after he and Flora married, he returned to Yosemite with a new camera that allowed him to make much larger glass negatives. That summer and fall he spent several months in the valley, sometimes putting himself at considerable risk on the dangerous cliffs in order to obtain stunning new views. He took hundreds of stereoscopic pictures, and, with his new camera, made "mammoth" twenty-by-twenty-four-inch glass plate negatives. His compositions were innovative and adventurous, and they marked, says one of his biographers, Rebecca Solnit, "his first moment of artistic greatness."

Earlier that spring, Muybridge had taken an even more consequential first step. He had been hired by former California Governor Leland Stanford to try and settle a long-standing argument among racing buffs over whether, at some point in its stride, a trotting horse had all four hooves off the ground. Although getting an image of a horse moving at thirty-eight feet a second was a long way from landscape photography, Muybridge did it. The telling photo was probably no more than a silhouette, but it showed that, for a brief moment in its stride, the animal does "fly." That original image, preserved now only as the Currier and Ives lithograph it inspired, represented Eadweard's introduction to motion photography.

It was, however, his new pictures of Yosemite that created the greatest stir at the time, aided by William Rulofson, whose gallery Muybridge had at last chosen to represent him. In a fit of jealousy, a competing gallery sought to belittle the photographs, but against Rulofson's high dudgeon, and his promotional deftness, the rival owner had little chance. Muybridge earned another success, achieved by hard work and a long absence from home.

So it went, more or less, until one day, in the Fall of 1874, when Eadweard showed up at Bradley and Rulofson in a highly agitated state. Rulofson asked what was wrong. "You will find out soon enough"! shouted Muybridge. William steered him away from the customers. "Promise me, Rulofson," Muybridge continued, "that in the event of my death you will faithfully give my wife all that belongs to me." It sounded to William like a suicide threat. But Eadweard had something else in mind.

He had been aware that some sort of liaison existed between Flora and Harry Larkyns and had earlier threatened to kill him unless he left town. Wisely, Larkyns did just that, relocating to a mining camp north of San Francisco. The final straw for Eadweard, however, came when, at the home of a nurse who had assisted Flora when she'd given birth a few months before, he spotted a photograph of the baby taken at Rulofson's. He and Flora had named their new son Floredo Helios, a combination of their given names and his *nom d'artiste*. However, turning over the photograph, Eadweard found it inscribed with another name; "Little Harry."

Muybridge flew into a rage and, as the nurse, under pressure from him, revealed details of the affair, he collapsed to the floor. He then left the house for the gallery where, after his brief encounter with Rulofson, he went to his office and retrieved a pistol. As he was leaving, Rulofson, now aware of the circumstances, again tried to stop him.

"Many good women are wrongly slandered," he said.

"One of us will be shot," Muybridge replied.

"For God's sake, don't kill him," pleaded Rulofson, as Muybridge broke away and raced for the ferry. He caught it just as it was leaving the dock.

Well after dark, he arrived at a silver mine called Yellow Jacket. He headed straight for a cabin where lantern-light filled the windows. The men and women inside were having a party. He knocked on the door and asked for Larkyns. When he appeared, Eadweard said to him, "Good evening, Major. Here is the answer to the message you sent my wife." And he shot him dead.

At his trial, which began in February, 1875, Muybridge, heeding legal advice, entered a plea of not guilty by reason of temporary insanity. But, as the trial proceeded, he became increasingly uncomfortable when his lawyer paraded witness after witness who testified to his "mental aberration" and "eccentric habits." These, they said, had been the unfortunate result of the head injury he'd suffered in the stagecoach accident fifteen years earlier.

One of the witnesses was William Rulofson. Before the accident, he said, Muybridge had been a fine gentlemen and excellent businessman, but afterwards he became slipshod and exhibited tendencies that were, by Rulofson's standards, inexplicable. He would, for example, refuse to take a photograph, even a commissioned one, if it didn't conform to his artistic standards, the customer be damned. And there was that business in Yosemite, perching on the edge of a precipice three thousand feet above the valley floor, just to take a photograph. You had to have something wrong with you to do that, said Rulofson.

This testimony was intended to help an old friend, but it deeply offended Muybridge. Meantime, the prosecution countered with witnesses who maintained the defendant was in complete control of his emotions and faculties. It soon became obvious that the insanity plea wasn't going to work. So, Muybridge's lawyer, William Pendegast, switched tactics and argued for justifiable homicide. His two-hour summary was so eloquent and emotional that, at times, even Muybridge was in tears. "It is the weakness of the law that there is no adequate punishment for the seducer," Pendegast declared. After deliberating for thirteen hours over two days, the jury delivered its verdict; not guilty.

Soon after, Muybridge severed his connection with Bradley and Rulofson, moved to another gallery, and left on a photographic expedition to Central America. He was gone nearly a year, and when he returned, he learned that Flora had died. He made new arrangements for care of the boy, Floredo, and resumed photographic work. In San Francisco, he took a new series of historically significant photographs—large panoramic views that would be a valuable record of how the city looked, before the devastating earthquake of 1906. And then Leland Stanford beckoned him back to the racetrack.

* * *

Apart from losing his prized landscapist, William Rulofson did well at business in the mid-1870s. In 1874, he and Bradley undertook a major renovation at the studio, and William, the inveterate promoter, made sure it received a big spread in *The Philadelphia Photographer*, the journal of the National Photographic Association. The studio also won recognition for having taken the best photograph in the United States, a portrait of a comely young woman—Flora Muybridge. That same year, Rulofson became president of the national association, and, finding that it had incurred a substantial debt, proceeded to eliminate it with an auction in which he served as a donor, buyer, and entertaining auctioneer. People remembered the event afterward, not just for its success, but for its great fun, too.

Rulofson may have been a hale fellow well met, but he took his photographic profession seriously. He'd taken a lead role in organizing West Coast photographers before taking the national association by storm. He liked to welcome visiting photographers to his studio. When an Australian amateur arrived with an impressive collection of landscape prints and negatives, some of them huge, Rulofson, taking a swipe at Muybridge, said they far surpassed anything previously done. He kept up with the latest technology, and his ruminations about arcane aspects of his craft sometimes appeared in publications like *The Philadelphia Photographer*. From all this hard work, he gained professional respect, social standing, financial success, and assorted honours.

He was still very much at the top of his game when he turned fifty, in 1875. His home life, though, was less sanguine. As long ago as 1867, the year Amelia died and Mary Jane became his wife, he'd felt it necessary to order William Howard, the son he'd fathered in Newfoundland, to go to sea in order to escape a designing actress. Another son chose a similar escape to avoid his father's stern discipline—the ship's captain later adopted this lad. As well, one of Rulofson's daughters married badly, and two others defied his wishes in picking their mates.

He also carried another familial burden, one he kept entirely to himself. Across the continent in New York State, his brother John Howard, who had changed his last name to Rulloff, had become a notorious criminal. Because his crimes were widely reported, William had to know about his brother's tragic turn. But the relationship remained his secret, even when the law finally applied the ultimate penalty, hanging John Howard for murder in 1871.

Then, a half-dozen years later, came the hardest blow of all. In the midst of planning a party to be held at the Palace Hotel, Mary Jane wrote a note concerning the arrangements and asked thirteen-year-old Matilda, or "Mattie," as she was known in the family, to deliver it to the hotel. She was William's last child by his first wife. The weather was rainy, and it was a long walk. Mattie came down with pneumonia and died. After that, things were never again quite the same.

Having established that trotting horses could fly, Leland Stanford now wanted equine photography applied to a more serious purpose. He wanted Eadweard Muybridge to see if he could capture the precise gait of the fastest horses. If that could be done, Stanford reasoned, perhaps other horses could be trained or even bred to mimic that gait. Muybridge's first task was to improve on his earlier racing images. In July 1877, he did that with a photograph of Stanford's prize trotter, Occident; newspapers hailed it "astonishing." But it was only a first step. There remained the necessity of somehow extending this single image into a rapid-fire series of them that would show the horse's full gait.

Fig. 1.3 Plate from J.D.B. Stillman's The Horse in Motion, *showing Muybridge's arrangement of 24 cameras for instantaneous photography.*

It was the following summer before Muybridge was ready to try. An elongated shed was built on one side of a racetrack, inside of which twenty-four high-quality cameras were installed. Light threads, attached to electromagnetic switches were stretched across the track. When the chest of the galloping horse snapped the threads, the switches flipped, triggering the shutter of each camera in sequence. Another important requirement was that the background should be as purely white as possible. So, sheets were hung from a fence on the opposite side, and lime sprinkled on the track.

It took some trial and error, but ultimately the experiment worked. It took less than half a second for the horse to race past each camera, a blur to the naked eye, but not to the cameras. They recorded twenty-four tightly sequenced, distinct photographs of a racehorse in motion. Such a thing had never been done before, and it created great excitement.

There was one notable dissenter; William Rulofson. That August, he wrote a letter to *The Philadelphia Photographer* in which he assailed this latest accomplishment of Muybridge's. "None knows better than yourself," he began his letter to the editor, "that the country is full of photographic quacks vending their nostrums, deceiving the credulous and defrauding the ignorant." The Muybridge horse photos, he said, were another example. They were nothing more than "diminutive silhouettes," and, as for the experiment itself; "Photographically speaking, it is 'bosh'; but then it amused the 'boys,' and shows that a horse trots part of the time and 'flies' the rest, a fact of 'utmost scientific importance.' Bosh again."

The easy explanation for this outburst—that Rulofson still deeply resented Muybridge's abrupt dismissal of him after the trial—hardly seems adequate. After all, William could have interpreted the dismissal as more proof of his erstwhile friend's instability. Was he jealous of Muybridge's success and acclaim? Perhaps. But a more sympathetic explanation is that Rulofson himself had succumbed to irrationality, and understandably so. His family problems, especially Mattie's death the previous year, surely left him in emotional turmoil; and he was under financial duress. A series of poor business decisions forced him to curtail family expenditures.

He did another strange thing in 1877. He published a book, *The Dance of Death*, under the barely disguised pseudonym, "William Herman." It was a moralistic attack on the waltz, written in language that was itself rather prurient. He blamed the upper echelons of society for embracing the dance. They were the very people who made up his most important clientele and whose companionship he had often sought. It was not the act of a well man.

But he was still a talented, technically adept photographer, and, as if to draw attention to his own considerable abilities, he undertook something quite remarkable. He created a life-sized photograph. His subject was one of his young daughters, and according to the legend that grew up around the picture, he took it by poking his camera lens through an opening in the door of a darkroom and capturing the image on a large glass plate inside. The resulting print was called the largest ever made. Rulofson had an artist paint over it to make it look more like an oil portrait. Then he had Mary Jane, who was pregnant, take it to France, where it became a hit of the Paris Exposition of 1878.

* * *

Discovering the Movies in New Brunswick

Fig 1.4 Sequence of a race horse galloping. Eadweard Muybridge 1887.

Eadweard Muybridge's "diminutive silhouettes" may not have produced faster racehorses, but they certainly were not "bosh." Not only did they change the course of his own life, they set him on a path that led directly to moving pictures.

In that same summer of 1878, he began using the photographs in illustrated lectures. He would flash a single sequential photo on a screen and then, with another projector, simultaneously show an artist's depiction of a horse at the same point in its stride. Audiences laughed when, aided by his commentary, they saw the discrepancy between the real and the imagined. The comparison vividly illustrated the value of motion photography. Also that year, Eadweard published a series of photographic cards, each showing sequential positions of a horse in motion. These boosted his reputation further, both at home and abroad.

He continued his motion studies, first with Leland Stanford's ongoing support and then, after the two had a falling out, under the auspices of the University of Pennsylvania. The artist Thomas Eakins helped him gain the university position. Renowned for the realism in his paintings, Eakins saw Muybridge's photographic studies as a means to achieving greater artistic accuracy. Although he'd been fired from an arts academy for his insistence on using undraped models in student drawing classes, Eakins wielded enough influence to persuade the university to bring Muybridge to Philadelphia. Here, in a carefully secluded outdoor studio, Muybridge took hundreds of sequential photographs of male and female models. These studies, along with others he made of a great many different animals, were published in a seminal work, *Animal Locomotion*. It contained seven hundred and eighty-one separate photographic plates, and its importance as a scientific and artistic reference has lasted into the twenty-first century.

* * *

In Paris, in February, 1878, Mary Jane Rulofson received a disturbing note from her husband. He said he'd spent the previous day worrying about her, and that night, while heavy rain was deluging San Francisco, he'd dreamed of Mary Jane and their ten-year-old son Charlie, who must have accompanied his mother to Paris. "I wish you to understand," he told Mary Jane, "that if anything happens to me before your return, that all my property belongs to you..." There had been hostility between the children of William's first family and those of his second, which Mattie's tragic death had only worsened. So he further instructed his wife that, in the event of his demise, she should not attempt to bring two daughters from the first marriage, twenty-one-year-old Emma and eighteen-year-old Isabel, back into her home, or to treat them as her own children. He closed the letter with; "I am your devoted husband."

Although Mary Jane did not immediately rush home (she, in fact, remained in France to have her baby) and William did not die for another several months, members of the family were convinced the letter's poignant instructions were evidence that he was contemplating suicide. That was why, according to Robert Haas, who in the 1950s wrote about Rulofson in the *California Historical Society Quarterly*, its contents were kept secret for seventy-five years.

Rulofson plunged to his death from his studio roof on November 2. He struck a pile of tin before landing on the sidewalk. He was carried to a nearby apothecary and then to the office of his own doctor, who pronounced him dead. He was fifty-two.

The newspaper *San Francisco Alta* reported the circumstances of the death as follows; William had been standing on a firewall, watching workmen lowering lumber with a pulley. His foot slipped on the precarious perch, and "he instantly lost his balance and was precipitated to the sidewalk, a distance of about 55 feet." Although an inquest ruled the death accidental, the incident was never quite put to rest. Long afterward, a story surfaced that a photograph of his "secret" brother Rulloff, the New York State murderer, had been found on William's body, which may have strengthened the suicide theory. Later, Ambrose Bierce, the curmudgeonly author of *The Devil's Dictionary*, who had known William, muddied the waters further by observing; "Rulofson himself executed a dance of death by stepping off the roof of a building."

After her husband's demise, Mary Jane worked at the gallery for a time. Then, in 1883, it was sold, and presently the new owner began disposing of items he judged to be superfluous. They included Rulofson's carefully preserved glass plate negatives of "every person of note" who'd come to the Pacific Coast in his time. The buyer was Joaquin Miller, a poet and aspiring mentor, who was building a grand retreat for literary types in the Oakland Hills. He wanted to add a greenhouse to the estate, which required rectangular pieces of glass. Miller put people to work scraping the images from Rulofson's studio plates, and, in a flurry of gray-black shavings, one of the great photographic collections of the early Pacific West disappeared.

* * *

Having deconstructed the motion of a running horse, Eadweard Muybridge proceeded to put it together again. He did it with the zoopraxiscope, the name he gave to a machine whose principle was based on an earlier device called the zoetrope. In the zoetrope, the illusion of motion was created when sequential images placed inside a cylinder were spun past vertical viewing slits in the outer wall. Muybridge's zoopraxiscope took things a step further. It lighted images on a revolving glass wheel and *projected* them onto a screen.

Muybridge had his projector ready soon after he took his first sequential photographs in that highly eventful year of 1878. Later, he carried the device to Europe, where he was repeatedly celebrated as a genius and a wizard. People sensed that something marvellous was at hand. No observation, however, was more perceptive than that of a newspaper reporter who'd watched Muybridge demonstrate the zoopraxiscope at an art gallery in San Francisco. "Mr. Muybridge," he wrote, "has laid the foundation of a new method of entertaining the people, and we predict that his instantaneous, photographic magic lantern zoetrope will make the rounds of the civilized world."

As predictions go, this is one of history's better ones.

The World's Longest Zoetrope

Years ago, when our family went to visit relatives in Woodstock, New Brunswick, our trip took us through the village of Hartland. It was just one of several villages on the road from Grand Falls, but Hartland was distinguished by its covered bridge, which ran for nearly a quarter-mile across the St. John River, making it the longest covered bridge in the world. What really excited my younger sister and me was the phenomenon we observed as our car slowly crossed the bridge. "Look!" we'd shout from the back seat. "It's just like the movies."

Fig. 1.5 Zoetrope. Invented by Horner William George.

We were right. The flickering and continuous image of the river we saw as we gazed out the side of the bridge *was* very much like a motion picture. But how could this be, since the side was enclosed with wooden boards? One reason was because the vertical boards had small gaps between them; another was because we were watching from a moving car; and a third was something called "persistence of vision."

Persistence of vision is the idea that the retina of the human eye retains each image it sees for a split second. According to this theory, the images we glimpsed through the gaps, as we made our way across the bridge, melded together to form a continuous picture. Scientists have long debated the validity of the theory, but it was used to explain an ancient novelty device called the zoetrope. In a form popular during the nineteenth century, it consisted of a cylinder with equally spaced vertical slits in its sides and a series of sequential images on its inner wall. When the cylinder was spun on its axis, and the images were

Discovering the Movies in New Brunswick

Fig. 1.6 At the dawn of the cinematic age, New Brunswick covered bridges sometimes served as impromptu "theatres" for itinerant picture men. But the covered bridge at Hartland, the world's longest, had another connection to the movies. Though they may not have known, people crossing by horse-drawn carriage or automobile were also passing through the worlds longest zoetrope.

viewed through the vertical slits, they appeared to be moving. At first, the toy was called the "wheel of the devil," but later got its classier, Greek-inspired name, zoetrope, or "wheel of life."

It is another of the devices that lies at the evolutionary beginning of motion pictures, and when Eadweard Muybridge first unveiled his projector, the zoopraxiscope, it was sometimes called a "magic lantern zoetrope." People are still inventing zoetropes. In 1980, a filmmaker built a "linear zoetrope" at a former subway stop in Brooklyn, New York. Consisting of two hundred and twenty-eight slits in a wall, with a hand-painted image behind each slit, it offered passengers a colourful animation as the subway train sped by. The animation lasted about twenty seconds. Since New Brunswick once had more than four hundred covered bridges, there were, in fact, linear zoetropes all over the countryside. But the one in Hartland, which has been there since 1922, has always been the longest. Its "show" lasts about a minute, the time a car should take to cross.

'The Dance of Death'

In publishing his 1877 polemic against the waltz, *The Dance of Death*, William Herman Rulofson used a thinly disguised *nom de plume*; William Herman. He did it, he said, so as not to divert attention from the book's essential message.

There wasn't much danger of that. Rulofson expressed his concerns in language that was unmistakable. The waltz, he said, was "an open and shameless gratification of sexual desire and a cooler of burning lust." While others might declare the dance merely "suggestive," Rulofson said that to its most ardent male practitioners—the "perfect dancers," he called them-—"it is an actual realization of a certain physical ecstasy which should at least be indulged in private, and, as some would go so far to say, under matrimonial restrictions."

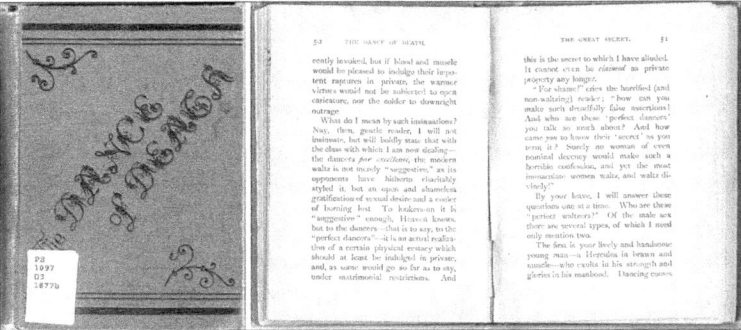

Fig. 1.7 Book cover and two-page spread of William H. Rulofson's book The Dance of Death.

The waltz had been the target of attacks almost from the time it emerged from its roots as an Austrian peasant dance in the eighteenth century. Introduced to the English court at a ball in 1816, it drew a blast from *The Times*, which said its "voluptuous intertwining of limbs and close compressure on the bodies" added up to an "obscene display." Naturally, the salacious language only increased the dance's popularity.

> With *The Dance of Death*, Rulofson started another firestorm. Religious publications rallied to his support, while critics of the book imagined its possible effect on impressionable young people. Why had he written it? Was it some late-blooming manifestation of a Loyalist moral code? Or was he indeed becoming unhinged as a result of family and business pressures? His answer, given to a newspaperman not long before he died, was that he had once lost a fiancée to the waltz. He had seen her dancing with another man, and it so offended him that he promptly walked out of her life. While the tale may seem rather far-fetched, it was, at least, one of the few times Rulofson ever unburdened himself about his life before he reached California.

The Evil Brother

William Herman Rulofson had two older brothers who were, in their own way, as clever as he was. One, Rulof Isaac Allen Rulofson, became a millwright at Milltown, Maine, and built the first sawmill in the United States equipped with a "live gang" saw, a cutting system in which a cluster of saws passed through logs simultaneously. Later, he moved to Strattanville, Pennsylvania, where he became a prosperous lumberman and a pillar of the community.

The oldest brother was John Edward Howard Rulofson, who literally had a big brain. Unfortunately, it directed him into a life of crime. His bad turn began in Saint John where, while serving as a young clerk in a prestigious law firm, he was convicted of robbery and spent two years in jail. Leaving the city, he landed in the Finger Lakes District of Upper New York State and found work as a teacher. Now calling himself Rulloff, he married one of his pupils and had a daughter. When mother and child both disappeared, he came under suspicion. He escaped across Lake Erie but was brought back to Ithaca, N.Y., and convicted of his wife's abduction. He served a prison sentence and, upon his release, was re-arrested and tried again, this time for his child's murder, although police still had not found a body. On appeal, his lawyer argued that the "mere absence" of somebody was not enough to prove death and won the case. He was free again, though he did have to escape an angry mob at the Ithaca courthouse.

Fig. 1.8 *Murderer John Edward Howard Rulloff, formerly Rulofson.*

The close call should have taught him a lesson, but Rulloff had an unfailing faith in his ability to outsmart authority. He was convicted again for robbery, but managed to talk his way out of other tight situations. A consummate conman, he was also brilliant. His passion was philology, the study of linguistics, and he became an ardent advocate for a universal language, a pursuit that brought him to the attention of important people, not least Horace Greeley, the New York publisher.

But Rulloff couldn't stay away from crime, and one summer evening in 1870, he and two companions tried to rob a store in Binghamton, N.Y. Two clerks were standing guard, waiting for them. Rulloff shot and killed one of the clerks. Trying to escape, Rulloff's two henchmen drowned in the nearby river, and he was captured shortly after. Brought to trial, he was sentenced to death. Supporters of his petitioned the governor to commute his sentence to life imprisonment so that he could continue his philological work, but were turned down. In his last hours, a visitor arrived to commiserate with him, an emissary from Greeley. Then, on May 18, 1871, he went to the gallows.

When I visited Ithaca, one of the first things I saw was a bumper sticker that read, "Meet Me at Rulloff's." It turned out to be a pub just outside an entrance to Cornell University, and inside the pub, a glass case mounted on a wall held items purportedly left over from his time. Ithaca knows about "the notorious Rulloff," partly because the local DeWitt Historical Society occasionally marks anniversaries from his strange saga.

They also knew about him, I found, in Uris Hall at Cornell. I saw his preserved brain there, a survivor from a once large collection of human brains started in the nineteenth century by a professor of animal biology named Burt Wilder. Wilder believed much could be learned from examining the human brain, and his collection included the brains of common and uncommon people, including a suffragette, assorted professors and economists, journalists, and one notorious murderer. Rulloff's was among eight pickled in formaldehyde and on display. It was flat on top, and large—the second largest known, I was told. No connection had been found between brain size and intelligence, but Rulloff's was the one that still attracted the most attention.

From the Zoopraxiscope to the Cinographoscope

By the last quarter of the nineteenth century, quite a few people were trying to invent a moving picture projector. They included Thomas Edison, who had already created a machine that played music and hoped to develop another that "did for the eye what the phonograph does for the ear." One night, in 1888, he attended a lecture in New Jersey by Eadweard Muybridge. Newly enthused, Edison returned to his laboratory and instructed an associate, William Kennedy Laurie Dickson, to see what he could do.

At the Doorstep of the Movies

Fig 1.9 Muybridge's zoopraxiscope and disc from the collection of the Kingston Museum in Kingston upon Thames, southwest London, England.

Later, after a trip to Paris for the 50th anniversary of Jacques Mande Daguerre's invention of photography, Edison came home to a pleasant surprise. Dickson showed him a little film in which he, Dickson, came toward the camera and said, "Good morning, Mr. Edison. Glad to see you back. I hope you are satisfied with the Kinetograph." Impressed by this, and by a rapid-fire "photographic gun" another scientist, Etienne Jules Marey, had shown him in Paris, Edison urged his researchers forward on two fronts—to develop a camera, the Kinetograph, that took pictures in a vertical line, and another machine, the Kinetoscope, that allowed one to view them.

But the researchers couldn't come up with a truly practical means of merging sight and sound, and Edison's interest waned; he couldn't imagine that moving pictures by themselves would be anything but a short-term novelty—to the great frustration of Dickson, who eventually left his employ.

Edison's interest revived, though, when, during the economic depression of the early 1890s, the only part of his phonograph business that grew was building coin-operated machines for arcades, and he decided that maybe the same thing could work for moving pictures. This is why, in 1894, two Canadian brothers, the Hollands, were able to open the world's first "Kinetoscope Parlour" in New York. It was a place where individuals could peer into bulky pine cabinets to watch a few seconds of performing animals, western rope tricks, hootchy-kootchy dancers, and women's skirts being lifted by sudden gusts of wind. Coin by coin, the arcade earned one hundred and twenty dollars on its first day.

The phenomenon spread quickly. When it reached Paris, photographer and businessman Antoine Lumiere decided Edison was charging too much for his films. He asked his son Louis to find a solution. With his brother Auguste, Louis decided to take the idea beyond the peep show machine. Why not a machine that projected the films for an audience? A stumbling block was the need for something that would stop each film frame for a millisecond as it passed before the projector's lens, long enough to register on the human eye. The solution finally came to Louis during a night of nightmares and fitful sleep—the drive mechanism of a sewing machine could give exactly the intermittent movement he needed. "In one night," Auguste Lumiere said later, "my brother invented the Cinematographe."

Its public unveiling, before thirty customers in the basement *Salon Indien* of the *Grande Café* on the *Boulevard de Capucines*, Paris, was on December 28, 1895. When word reached the States, Edison went into panic mode. Still lacking an operating projection system of his own (mainly because he hadn't pushed the research), he got a stop motion device from another inventor, Thomas Armat, and built a projector named the Vitascope. When it was used for the first time at Koster and Bial's Music Hall, on April 23, 1896, Edison put it in a booth fitted with a double lock "lest somebody steal his first principles," said *The New York Times*. It was a futile exercise.

Chapter Two

First Flickers

Sixteen years after the California newspaper reporter's prescient observation, moving pictures arrived in Saint John, New Brunswick. At that point, they bore some resemblance to the form we know today—images captured on film threading their way through a projection device that cast them onto a screen. Each film lasted only a few seconds, each was limited to a single scene: a train pulling into a station, a dancer, or (gasp!) a kiss. But they were the movies.

Not that it had occurred to anybody yet to call them that. Instead, they were simply identified by the machines that projected them, giving those machines an anthropomorphic character. In Saint John, it was the Cinographoscope, or, as the newspapers preferred, the "great Cinographoscope." The local *Globe* called it "the famous picture machine by which human beings and animals can be shown on a screen, and walk and act as in life." It was "one of the most wonderful discoveries of the age."

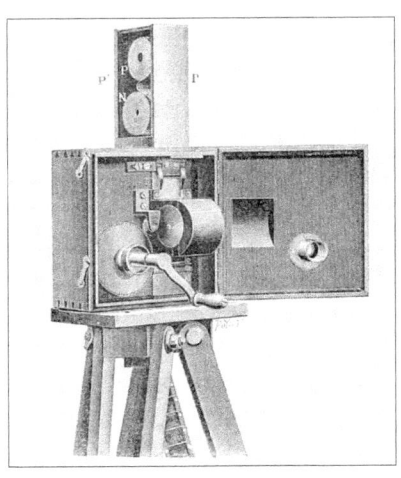

Fig. 2.1 Cinematographe camera in projection mode, 1897.

The Cinographoscope was the lineal descendant of Eadweard Muybridge's "magic lantern zoetrope," and its arrival in Saint John, in November 1896, came only months after Thomas Edison introduced his projector, the Vitascope, in New York. A plaque near one of the entrances to Macy's Department Store, where Koster and Bial's Music Hall once stood, marks the location and the date, April 23, for this first showing. Precisely seven months later, on November 23, the sensational new technology reached Saint John.

The good rail and boat connections that existed between Saint John and the American East Coast partly explained the technology's rapid progression north into New Brunswick. Another important factor was Saint John's long tradition of theatrical entertainment. And then there was the fact that, once the Vitascope had been used publicly, and despite Edison's extravagant efforts to keep the projector hidden from prying eyes, the genie was out of the bottle. It was only a matter of weeks before imitative machines began to appear.

That's what the "great Cinographoscope" was—a clone. It had become available just weeks earlier that fall, with one its first purchasers the Ethel Tucker Company, out of Boston. The Tucker Company, named for its star, knew she was popular in Saint John, and had already visited once in 1896. The company had a wide repertoire of Victorian dramas and light comedies, which made it feasible to consider a return to the city in the same season. For insurance, though, they added moving pictures as a "specialty" to be shown between acts of their live presentations.

Nineteenth-century audiences in Saint John were quite sophisticated. Theatregoing had begun in the city more than a hundred years earlier, when a "company of gentlemen" broke up the monotony of a long colonial winter by presenting a pair of British satires. So appealing was the idea that a British colonel, Edward Winslow, stationed upriver in Fredericton, drove sixty miles on the ice covered St. John River in an open sleigh to see them.

Over the decades, Saint John became home to resident repertory companies, its newspapers and audiences closely followed stage happenings in Boston and New York, and it was an important stop for touring companies on the eastern circuit. All of this ebbed and flowed, of course, according to the state of the local economy, which certainly had its ups and downs. Two catastrophic occurrences in the nineteenth century were the collapse of the wooden shipbuilding industry after mid-century, and an 1877 fire that destroyed hundreds of buildings and put thousands of people out of their homes.

But there was always a gritty resilience to the place, and, after rebuilding, the city began a process of regularly trying to reinvent itself. One idea was to enhance Saint John's standing as a manufacturing centre by getting a shorter, faster rail connection through the forests of Maine to the blossoming markets of Central Canada. So local leaders lobbied hard, and they got the line built.

Opening of this so-called "Short Line" took place in 1889, and it was marked by a summer-long festival that included an "Electric Exhibition" dedicated to Thomas Edison, whose grandparents had once lived just across the Bay of Fundy, in Nova Scotia. Unfortunately, the Short Line confirmed the old adage that what goes up must also come down; in providing access to Central Canada, it also exposed the Saint John market to a rash of new competitors. Coupled with a general economic depression, the effect was devastating. Local manufacturers closed, hundreds lost their jobs.

Saint John, nonetheless, kept certain dreams alive, one of which was to build a first-class theatre. The project was delayed several years because the proposed location, on Union Street, was home to an array of saloons and worse distractions. Patrons of the arts insisted it was hardly the right neighbourhood for a house of high-minded entertainment. Finally, a convenient fire took care of the problem, and the theatre that rose from the ashes was indeed a splendid building.

Named the Opera House, as were many theatres in those days because the name conveyed respectability, it opened in 1891. It could accommodate an audience of more than twelve hundred, the most affluent of whom, dressed fine and laved fragrant, occupied crimson seats made of plush and oak on the main floor. Others sat, according to their means or

Fig. 2.2 1906 photograph of the Opera House which opened in Saint John on Union Street in 1891. The City's first movie was screened there in 1896.

preference, farther back, or in the balcony, or, above that, in the distant gallery. Standard admissions were, respectively, thirty, twenty and ten cents. A cascade of light fell from a handsome electrolier, a moulded proscenium arch framed the stage. Taking it all in, a besotted observer said the new theatre filled his imagination with "long vistas of pastimes" yet to come.

Magical evenings did follow. One show replicated a full-masted schooner on stage, another, a two-hundred-foot steam train. The renowned prestidigitator, Marco, appeared with an up-and-comer named Harry Houdini. Not only did the future Great Houdini steal the show, bursting free from an assortment of handcuffs, ropes, and shackles, he also, according to a story that later made the rounds, learned his greatest trick—escape from a strait jacket—during a goodwill visit to the local institution known as the lunatic asylum.

And now the "great Cinographoscope" was coming.

The first show was scheduled for Monday, November 23, the first day in what promised to be a busy and pleasing week in Saint John. On Thursday, it would be Thanksgiving, a holiday not yet fixed to its present-day October date in Canada. Local hotels were advertising sumptuous dinners in salons decorated with harvest themes, and the railways were promoting family excursions to visit relatives in the country. For those remaining in the city, there would also be the possibility of taking in the Cinographoscope show, which had just completed a "phenomenally successful run" at Boston's Keith Theatre, and would be playing all week in Saint John.

These new picture machines, it must be said, were marvels of ingenuity—assemblies of gears, wheels, pulleys, driving belts, and friction discs that somehow guided a piece of volatile nitrate film frame-by-frame past a lens and a white-hot lamp to project a flickering image on a screen. It followed that they were also fragile, and could be a horror to operate. Just the month before, another company had publicly unveiled a projector called the Biograph. The job of operating it had fallen to a young employee, Billy Bitzer. He later remembered it as one of the most frightening experiences of his life. Encased with a machine noisy as a trolley, in a projection booth he likened to a coffin, he needed his hands, a foot, his forehead and his nose to keep and the machine running and the film from igniting. Bitzer never forgot being "scared stiff and almost desperate."

Naturally, none of this inherent drama was known to Saint John's theatregoers as they strolled down the long entrance to the Opera House auditorium that Monday evening in November, 1896. They were simply looking forward to the performance of a popular comedy, *Mr. Potter of Texas*, and to seeing, as a bonus, their first-ever moving pictures.

Imagine their disappointment when, after the house lights dimmed, the manager of the Opera House appeared on stage to announce that the Cinographoscope had been damaged in transit. It could not be made to work.

The manager was profoundly embarrassed. It was he, after all, who had promoted the projector, and what it could do, as nothing short of a miracle. And now it wouldn't work. Damnation!

Late that night, after the audience had gone home, their disappointment having been somewhat assuaged by a good performance of *Mr. Potter of Texas*, and by a pair of sweetly melodic sisters who entertained at intermission, the manager climbed to the balcony where stood the offending machine on its spindly legs. He stared at it a long time. And then, somehow, he fixed it.

Before going home, he walked the dark streets in the chill early morning hours to deliver the word to the newspapers that the vital repairs had been made, and that the Cinographoscope would absolutely make its debut in Saint John at that afternoon's matinée.

And so it did, seven months and one day after Edison had brought the first moving pictures to New York. That night, a *Globe* man came to the theatre, and, in the next day's paper, he restored some of the aura surrounding the Cinographoscope, calling it "the feature of the evening."

> It was much appreciated by the audience, as was shown by the frequent applause. A street in New York with the street cars, horses and people all moving along was fine, and the circus parade, with the elephants with their clumsy motion as they walked past, looked quite natural. The review of the horses and all the other pictures were very pretty and called forth much applause.

In December, The Greater New York Comedy Company brought another picture show to Saint John, and in the following year several troupes, including Ethel Tucker's, came to town with an assortment of projection machines. They included the Edison Vitascope and the Lumiere Cinematographe and others called the Cinephotograph, the Veriscope, the Projectoscope, and so on. The *faux* scientific names gave them a certain better-than-a-novelty aura, and each was, in its turn, proclaimed to be the "best yet." For the first time, too, Saint Johners had the experience of seeing events they'd read about months before. These included Queen Victoria's Jubilee Parade in London, and an outdoor boxing match in

Las Vegas where, also for the first time, one of the fighters had insisted the start be delayed until noon, "when the light for the picture was best."

In small ways, the cinema was taking hold, but it probably still seemed no more than a passing fancy, which is what Thomas Edison had thought of it. Life itself went on, in the usual proportions of joy and sadness. The bicycle craze was upon Saint John, and many "Black Birds," "Red Birds," and "Ruby Reds" were on the streets. It rained steadily, and a merchant on King Street advertised "freckle soap" for boys afflicted with rust. Handsome young Fred Spencer dashed about in pursuit of a career as a theatrical impresario.

A man heroically shot an eagle on Paradise Row. Another swore on Sheffield Street, was fined eight dollars, and got his name in the paper. So did certain people who attempted suicide, or were charged under the Bastardy Act, or were involved in delicious divorces, all of which the *Globe* reported with the zeal and avidity of a Hearst newspaper. It was the stuff of people living out the dark side of their convulsive lives, and, though they couldn't know it yet, subjects for thousands of moving pictures to come.

An invisible cinematic paradigm had fallen over the unsuspecting city. Down at the docks, an American agent boarded an immigrant ship and demanded to see the thirty dollars each passenger needed in order to proceed to the United States. From their bosoms and stockings and other unmentionable hiding places, they fished out the pocketbooks and kerchiefs that held their fortunes. Some, including a pregnant woman, were rejected. There was much weeping and wailing. The scene was familiar. Some years before, a man named Jacob Meir had arrived at the same docks with his family. Their prospects seemed dim, but a son, named Lazar, would become the highest paid executive in the United States. He did it in the movie business.

Even the minutiae of daily life held unsuspected links. One day, a Mrs. C. B. Pidgeon of Cedar Street, in the city's North End, took out a newspaper advertisement seeking "A GIRL for general housework." Some weeks later, the paper reported that Mrs. Pidgeon had taken a spell, perhaps while attending ceremonies for Canada's natal day, and was carried into the City Building "in a faint." Then, in September, the reasons for Mrs. Pidgeon's previous appearances in the newspaper became clear. She gave birth to a fine baby boy. Hannah and Caleb Pidgeon named their boy Walter, and he grew up to be a Hollywood star.

A Road Company and its Movies

One of the films brought to Saint John by The Greater New York Comedy Company, the second troupe to reach the city with moving pictures in 1896, was *The Kiss*. It featured a lingering (forty-seven second) sealing of the lips between two stage actors, one of them an ostensibly hot-blooded Canadian, May Irwin. Although the pair repeated this scene every night on Broadway, in a musical called *The Widow Jones*, it immediately achieved notoriety when it became a film sequence.

If any sensibilities were aroused in Saint John, though, they did not get mentioned in the *Globe*. The newspaper focused instead on the technology behind making a film, and on the Comedy Company's manager, a "Colonel" P. H. Clafin, who made it all seem absolutely astounding. "The negatives are put on a celluloid strip one hundred and fifty feet long," said the colonel, "and each strip has upon its surface a total of 2,400 pictures, which pass before the lenses at an astonishing rate of forty per second." Some of the pictures were in colour, and these were "painted by hand by an expert in Mr. Edison's factory at Orange, New Jersey."

Fig. 2.3 *"The Kiss" starring Canadian theatre star May Irwin an 1896 film was one of the first ever shown commercially to the public. It depicts a re-enactment of the kiss between May Irwin and John Rice originally from the final scene of the stage musical* The Widow Jones. *The film was directed by William Heise for Thomas Edison.*

The Rayoscope, the Comedy Company's projector, was "the latest and most perfect of the few animated picture machines before the public." In a tour that began in Lowell, Massachusetts, in October and had continued profitably in most of New England's larger centres, the machine had never failed "to create a sensation." And just ahead were Halifax, Quebec, Montreal, Toronto, New York State and Washington, D.C. "The Rayoscope," said the colonel, "is really one of the wonders of the world."

The *Globe*, evidently convinced, put the story on its front page.

"The Handsomest Man in Hollywood"

Movie fans of a certain age knew Walter Pidgeon well. He was that tall, distinguished actor who first appeared in movies when they were still silent. By the early forties, he was a star, sharing billings with the biggest names in Hollywood. Some of his films became minor classics; some are still shown on television. On the screen, he personified integrity, decency, and urbanity. A gossip columnist once called him "the handsomest man in Hollywood." He was twice nominated for Academy Awards and had a film career that lasted half a century.

The Saint John family he'd been born into was moderately well off. His father, Caleb, ran a men's clothing, shoe, and boot store and was choir director at his Baptist church. The family lived at 30 Cedar Street, in the city's North End, not far from the riverboat landing at Indiantown. Caleb had his share of personal troubles. His first wife, Amanda, died in childbirth in 1880, leaving four young children, and his second wife, Amanda's sister Maggie, succumbed shortly after they wed in 1891. Walter's mother was Caleb's third wife, Hannah Sophronia Sanborn, a young woman originally from Prince William, in rural York County, New Brunswick, whom he married in 1896.

Their son was only six when his father died, a sudden victim of Bright's disease, but Caleb left a will, signed on his deathbed, providing a modest trust income for the family, which by now also included two younger brothers. Walter attended school and, by 1914, was in Grade Ten at Saint John High. That was the year his formal schooling ended. A story, often repeated, that he attended the University of New Brunswick before joining the army is not supported by the university's records. He did sign up during the First World War, but contrary to the legend conjured up by Hollywood press agents, he did not go overseas. He was injured in a horse-riding accident while training at Ontario's Camp Petawawa in April, 1917. He appeared to be recovering well after

Fig. 2.4 Walter Pidgeon with Greer Garson in Mrs. Miniver, *the 1942 movie that starred both. Garson and Pidgeon were nominated for best actress and best actor respectively.*

a hernia operation when he suffered an attack of acute pleurisy and was subsequently transferred to the Nova Scotia Sanatorium in Kentville. He remained under that institution's care for a year, before getting a medical discharge from the military at the end of August 1918. A year later, he married Edna Verna Pickels, from a prominent merchant family in Annapolis Royal, N.S.

Walter made his start in show business in Boston in the early nineteen-twenties, but supposedly almost gave it up after

Edna died while giving birth to their daughter. Friends finally persuaded him to continue. Blessed with a rich baritone voice, he was known as a singer for several years, including after he moved to Hollywood. What he really wanted, though, was to be an actor, and he gradually made the transition.

Under contract to Metro-Goldwyn-Mayer in the late nineteen-thirties, he mostly appeared in so-called 'B' pictures, until the studio loaned him to Twentieth Century-Fox to appear as the village cleric in the Welsh coal-mining drama, *How Green Was My Valley*. By 1942, he was back with MGM and co-starring with the English actress Greer Garson in *Mrs. Miniver*, a story about how the Second World War came home to a middle-class British family. His role as husband and father brought him an Academy Award nomination. He received another in 1943 when he again teamed with Miss Garson in *Madame Curie*, and he would ultimately appear in eight movies with her. So well matched that they were easily mistaken for a real-life couple, Walter was always, to some of his fans, simply "Mr. Miniver." Off-screen, he was indeed considered quite a catch, but when he remarried, in 1931, it was to a woman with no connection to the movies. She was Ruth Walker, his secretary, and they remained together until his death in 1984.

The nineteen-forties were the peak of Walter's career in movies, but he was still getting roles in the nineteen seventies. His last film appearance was as the impresario Florenz Ziegfeld in *Funny Girl*; it was his one hundred and first movie. He also appeared many times on the stage, beginning in the nineteen twenties, and many more times later on television. One appearance Saint John never forgot was when he came back to the city for a Victory Bond rally during the Second World War. It was a classic return of a hometown movie hero; autograph seekers jammed Union Station, and there were fans all along the route to the Admiral Beatty Hotel.

To an extent, he kept up with his old hometown through letters with former acquaintances. One was a boyhood pal, Allan Beatteay. Once, in 1980, Beatteay wrote to tell Walter about recent changes in the city. A square had been refurbished in the old neighbourhood, and new buildings were rising all over the place, including one put up by Irving, New Brunswick's big corporate family. Walter replied that he was pleased to hear of the changes, but who, he wanted to know, was Irving?

Fig. 2.5 Promotional photograph for the 1943 film Madame Curie *From left: Walter Pidgeon, Greer Garson, Margaret O'Brien, 1944.*

Chapter Three

Movie-making in the Land of Canaan

The first flecks of autumn were appearing in the woodlands of southern New Brunswick when a party of American hunters rode an Intercolonial Railway train out of Saint John on a September day in 1905. Six people were in the party, two of them moving picture men. One was Billy Bitzer.

This was the same Billy Bitzer who had timorously operated the Biograph projector during its harrowing debut in New York nine years earlier. Now he was a full-fledged Biograph cameraman who'd already made cinematic history. He'd filmed the Spanish-American War in Cuba and the first boxing match shot under artificial lighting, on Long Island, New York.

He'd come to New Brunswick to make moving pictures about moose hunting and salmon fishing, two sporting activities in which the province had a growing international reputation. The New England Forest, Fish and Game Association had commissioned the films for the big Sportsmen's Show it organized each year in Boston. This year's would open on Christmas Day.

Bitzer worked for the American Mutoscope and Biograph Company of New York, a company he'd joined when it was still an outfit selling magic tricks and gadgets. Its direction changed when W. K. L. Dickson, the disgruntled Edison employee, arrived, shortly after Bitzer. Dickson brought with him the Mutoscope, a machine that showed pictorial sequences with a system of flip cards instead of film; by turning a crank, viewers could watch a short moving or "mutating" picture.

Working closely with Dickson, Bitzer came to admire him greatly, even to the point of growing a moustache so that he might more closely resemble his mentor. When the Biograph projection system was ready, he and Dickson went to Ohio to film presidential candidate William McKinley receiving a telegram at his home informing him that he was the Republican Party's nominee. The film, an early newsreel of a sort, was another little piece of cinematic history, which Bitzer showed on the night he introduced the Biograph to New York.

And now, here he was in New Brunswick, on his way to making moving pictures about men and moose and salmon.

The province was a sportsmen's paradise. Its wild lands were full of "big game," meaning moose and caribou, plus the encroaching white tail deer. And its rivers were teeming with game fish, none more alluring than the flashy and fleshy Atlantic salmon. Another advantage was that the rivers and game fields were relatively easy to reach. "There is no ground in eastern America that is so easily accessible as New Brunswick," boasted the province's chief game commissioner.

Foreign sportsmen had discovered the province during the last quarter-century. They came mainly from the United States, although a royal party from England came to the same hunting ground as Billy Bitzer in 1905, a prolific area known as the Canaan Woods. Another indicator of the sporting types being attracted was the desk register at the Queen Hotel in Fredericton, which regularly bore the names of Carnegies, Whitneys, and Vanderbilts, scions of American fortunes on their way into the Big Woods. "Mr. Vanderbilt goes annually to the game districts of New Brunswick," reported the local paper in a typical item, "and spends two or three weeks enjoying the sport which the shooting season affords."

An excellent chronicler of the sporting scene was Fredericton's Frank Risteen. His day job was as a court and legislature recorder, but, a sportsman himself, he contributed regularly to newspapers like *The New York Sun* and to magazines like *Outing* and *Forest and Stream*. A typical dispatch from the literate and light-touched Risteen:

> Just three days' hunting in the Canaan country enabled Dr. J. G. Van Vechten, the genial coroner of Oneota, N.Y., to make the acquaintance of the biggest moose that has been seen in that region for some years. The Doctor, being licensed to officiate as coroner in the moose woods of this Province, at once proceeded to hold an inquest. By means of a timely combination of [guide] Jim Paul's birch horn and a .45-70 rifle, the Doctor was able to ascertain that the antlers of the

moose contained eighteen points and measured just 52 in. across. It has always been the proud boast of Jim that he could call a moose 'half a mile furder off' than anybody else. In this declaration he would seem to be quite justified, for the Doctor relates that this moose was so far away that from his first answering grunt until his arrival at the inquest an hour elapsed.

A group of Baptists, migrating east from the St. John River Valley in the eighteenth century, had given Canaan its Biblical name. They may not have had the fruitful moose exactly in mind when they named their new land of hope and promise, but it *was* a Baptist preacher who later posited a theory about why the animals were so big and abundant. The Reverend W. C. Gaynor, pastor of St. John the Baptist Church, in Saint John, and also a sportsman, said it was because the moose were migrants, too—they'd come down from northern New Brunswick to escape that territory's harsher winters. Such a trek, extending diagonally from the chilly headwaters of the Restigouche River, was long, but with few hazards for a travelling moose, save an occasional hunter's camp or lumberman's shanty. "Doubtless it came from these northern feeding grounds," Pastor Gaynor declared, "that the wilds of Canaan, with their lighter snowfall, have drawn their inexhaustible supply of moose. The country itself is low, grassy and well-watered, the ideal home of the antlered monarch of America."

Few hunters would disagree, and especially not Dr. Heber Bishop. A Canadian now practicing medicine in Boston, he had once hunted the Miramichi region of the province. There was lots of game in that district, but the hunting grounds were far from the railway (it was all relative, as we'll see), which meant a long, time-consuming and expensive haul by horse and wagon. So he'd switched to the Canaan Woods, with no regrets.

Bishop, described by Frank Risteen as "one of the most widely known and deservedly popular of American sportsmen," was the natural leader of the moving picture expedition. Others in the party included the New England Forest, Fish and Game Association's manager, Richard Follett, an artist and lithographer, C. Everett Johnson, and a railway man from Maine, Harris Coe.

The other movie man on the trip was Frank Marion, Bitzer's boss at the Biograph company and a rarity in the business, a college graduate. A former newspaperman, he'd started with flip card Mutoscope productions and then progressed to making Biograph films; one of them was called *The Escaped Lunatic* and was said to be the first American film featuring a chase scene. Marion loved crime stories, and just before leaving for New Brunswick, he and Bitzer had filmed one called *The River Pirates*, shot near his home in Connecticut. He had also just put in a hard several months rebuilding the Biograph company, after a hiring raid on his employees by Edison, and, as much as anything, his trip to the sporting grounds may have been therapeutic.

Riding the Intercolonial train to the village of Petitcodiac, in southeastern New Brunswick, the group then switched to a rickety little branch line, the Elgin, Petitcodiac and Havelock. By now, after a thirty-year existence of hauling farm goods to market, the EP&H was reduced to a single train consisting of a wood-fired steam engine, a passenger coach, a flat car, and a boxcar doubling as a baggage car. It was nicknamed The Bull Moose Special.

The first things the Americans noticed were the weeds and tall grass growing between the rails, a sign of a neglected roadbed. Sure enough, no sooner was the train under way than passengers were being thrown about in their seats. One of the bemused hunter-travellers said the trip was already becoming memorable, and Billy Bitzer thought so, too, but for a different reason.

Less than a decade after moving pictures began, the demand for new films had become insatiable, and it would only accelerate as the five-cent theatres called Nickelodeons began springing up in North America. When he joined the Biograph company a few years later, the soon-to-be-famous director, David W. Griffith, called the place a "sausage factory" because of its frantic production rate. The films of moose-hunting and salmon-fishing Bitzer would shoot in New Brunswick, for example, were just two among forty-eight he would work on in 1905.

Even so, when a cameraman was on field assignment, he had to be, like a newspaperman, always on the lookout for yet another story. On the rollicking Bull Moose Special, Bitzer sensed he'd found one.

Only a few months before, the concept of Hale's Tour films had been born. Named for the retired fireman who came up with the idea, they were travel films shot from moving trains and shown in "theatres" made to resemble passenger coaches. The best of these theatres added railway sounds and imparted a rocking motion to the parked coaches. Cameramen did crazy things to make Hale's Tour films. In Norway, an Englishman, risking frostbite and worse, sat outside on the front of the engine to shoot the newborn country's mountain scenery in winter.

Bitzer didn't have to go that far on The Bull Moose Special. Rounding up the hunters, he had them go out on the tender, where the wood fuel was stored behind the engine. Outfitted in their Abercrombie and Fitch hats and breeches, and looking like the gentlemen "sports" they were, they clambered round the tender while Bitzer, with his bulky Biograph camera fixed to a tripod, filmed them and the passing scenery. The film later became a novel entry in the "Hale Tour Runs" listed in the Biograph catalogue.

Reaching the end of the line at Havelock, on the edge of the Canaan Woods, the group found guides from the James Ryder sporting operation

Fig. 3.1 William Ryder (left) and his brother, James Ryder (right), guides from the James Ryder sporting operation in Cannan Woods, NB who hosted the group filming there in 1905 for the New England Forest, Fish and Game Association.

waiting for them. Ryder was a veteran outfitter with a stellar reputation. Heber Bishop called him "the mentor of the Canaan Woods." No need to shoot the first moose you saw, he said, Jim would always deliver a bigger one.

But first you had to get to Ryder's hunting establishment, which lay deep in the woods. The province's game commissioner said New Brunswick had been chosen for the filming—the first ever of a moose hunt—because of "the ease with which the picture making outfit could be got to the home of the moose." Now came the specifics of what he meant.

It started with an eighteen mile trek, by horse and wagon, to a spot known as The Forks, on the Canaan River. Next, the little wagon train had to take to the edges of the stream that, according to one of the American hunters, had to be forded fifty-two times in seven miles, including once when they had to climb onto the backs of the horses to keep dry. This was followed by a long stretch called the Bad Lands, where a forest fire had left the area a tangled mess of stumps and charred tree trunks interspersed with a scattering of small new trees. Slowly and carefully, the wagons picked their way across this terrain. About halfway, they came upon a so-called "moose barren." This was one of those grassy, well-watered plains that Pastor Gaynor wrote about, where the earth, softened by bubbling springs, was rife with cloven hoof prints, and where the skeletons of dead trees, called rampikes, bore swatches of moose hair. Bitzer called a halt and shot film.

Finally, late on a Sunday afternoon, they reached Jim Ryder's camp, perched above a small lake on a ridge that formed the divide between the watersheds of the Canaan and Salmon rivers. The lake, and another nearby, were rich in the moose diet of aquatic plants, and the surrounding forest offered excellent cover for the animals. Ryder maintained that it was the best moose territory in all of Canaan.

At first light the next morning, they heard the splashing of a moose feeding in the lake. The territory would more than live up to its reputation. It was Bitzer and Marion's intention to film as many aspects as possible of a classic moose hunt. Moving pictures had changed. No longer were they mere, single-shot glimpses of daily life; now they were using several different scenes to tell more complete stories. In America, the breakthrough had come in 1903 with *The Life of an American Fireman*, which told the story of a brave fireman rescuing a mother and child from a burning building. The same cameraman soon followed with *The Great Train Robbery*, which used twenty separate scenes to tell a tale of treachery on the rails. These were fictional productions—what would shortly be called "photoplays'—but an "actuality" could be filmed in the same way, which is what Bitzer and Marion were about to do in the Canaan Woods.

They wanted to film not just the killing of moose, but also some of the peripheral activities of the hunt—leaving Ryder's wilderness cabin and setting out for a day in the bush, gathering wood and building a fire for lunch, clinking cups and wishing each other luck, and so on. These were the things that would convey to the viewer a greater sense of what a big game hunt was like.

It also had its exotic aspects. One day Ryder gathered his guests together to instruct them on the arcane act of "calling" a moose. This was done with a "horn" made of birch bark that resembled a small megaphone. The idea was for a human to use this device to mimic the mating call of the female moose. This was a strange, guttural mixture of sounds that began with a low moan, built to an inharmonious middle, and ended with a come-hither whelp, which, from a moose cow, came out as a kind of snort. Done properly, it was, to a love-starved bull, irresistible.

Ryder, a man in his early fifties with a full moustache that flowed across his upper lip to meet flourishing mutton-chops at the sides of his face, told the hunters the technique worked best during the oestral season—late September to mid-October—when cow moose were in heat, which, he explained, was right about now.

So, at dusk that evening, two of the hunters—Follett, the game association man, and Johnson, the artist—made their way to one of several elevated "blinds," or "crow's nests," that Ryder had in the trees throughout his territory. They spent the night there. At dawn, Follett raised the birch horn to his lips and delivered his version of the siren song of the cow moose. Unbelievably, a response came from somewhere in the surrounding trees, and moments later a massive bull with a huge set of antlers came crashing through the brush. Follett promptly shot him.

Word was then sent back to camp, and soon Bitzer arrived with his camera and tripod.

> [T]he picture machine was set up and the two men in the crow's nest went through the identical motions which they had gone through only a short time before in shooting the big animal. When Mr. Follett fired his rifle the Biograph was turned on the moose and a picture was taken of the two

men running up to the fallen animal and cutting his throat. The moose was an immense one, its antlers having a spread of 54 inches and its weight being 1,200 pounds. *Newcastle Union Advocate*, October 11, 1905.

Reenactments like this were fairly commonplace in the making of pictures. As in this instance, they were the only practical way of getting something on film, and even then, there were limitations—the hunting party could hardly be expected to prop up a dead, 1200-pound creature so that it could be toppled over for the camera.

It was also still a time when the early men of the cinema spoke in terms of how many "pictures"—meaning individual frames—they shot during a filming. Inevitably, it was always an impressive number. Bitzer estimated he shot forty-to-forty-five thousand "pictures" in Canaan; for the record, it added up to about a mile of film. Included was the premier sportsman, Heber Bishop, notching the twenty-eighth moose kill of his career, which he shot from a canoe after coming round a point of land and spotting the animal on shore.

After a few days of this, the party split up, most of the sports heading back to the States, while Bitzer and Follett, emerging from the woods, caught a train north to the town of Bathurst, at the mouth of the Nepisiguit River. The Nepisiguit was an angling stream celebrated for being abundant with two species of game fish not normally found on the same river. What made it possible on the Nepisiguit was a natural barrier, a waterfall at the upper end of a narrow canyon about twenty miles in from the sea. The waterfall prevented Atlantic salmon from progressing any farther upstream, which meant the river above the falls belonged to trout. In their respective domains, both species swam in carefree profusion. Richard Follett called the river one of the best in North America for angling. Follett was an expert fly-caster, and he and Bitzer came to the Nepisiguit to make a film about salmon fishing. Although the season was over when they arrived, they got permission from the New Brunswick Government, which was keen to promote the sport, and they also caught a break from the weather. The early-October days turned warm and sunny, and the salmon rose to the fly as though it were June or July.

After about a week on the Nepisiguit, the pair started for home. In the railway centre of Moncton, New Brunswick, a newspaperman from the local paper, *The Transcript*, caught up with them. Or perhaps *they* haled

Movie-making in the Land of Canaan

Fig. 3.2 Moncton Transcript *story highlighting movie making in the Cannan woods.*

him. In any event, his story ran at the top of the next day's front page. "New Brunswick," it said, "is going to get well advertised as a great territory for hunting and fishing as a result of the visit of these gentlemen with their Biograph Machine, which takes the scenes right from the forest and reproduces them with full details of life and action."

When the Boston Sportsmen's Show opened on Christmas Day 1905, it occupied two main halls of Boston's Mechanics Building. Everything had been done to simulate the sensuous attractions of the wilderness experience. Log cabins stood in groves of real trees—birches, spruces, fragrant pines, and firs—along with two large ponds, one with a thousand trout swimming at the base of a waterfall and rising occasionally to snap at bits of twig on the surface. In the other pond were two thousand waterfowl, representing seventy-five different species, all joined in wondrous cacophony. There were also exhibits of live game birds, including an entrancing show of pheasants, property of a New York cartoonist.

Among wild animals on display was a calf moose named Pete, from New Brunswick. Pete had been a star attraction at the annual Fredericton Exhibition earlier that fall, and now the province had dispatched him to the Boston show, under the care of guide Jim Paul. Before leaving

Fredericton, Paul had received specific instructions from a government minister about what to do with Pete when the show was over—sell him. The minister didn't want to encourage the idea that New Brunswickers could keep moose as pets, as Jim had done. Jim made two hundred dollars on the deal.

On opening day, ten thousand patrons came to the show. They looked at the birds and fish, watched the comic antics of two bear cubs, gazed at displays of wigwams, portable camps, motor boats—and automobiles; "With the automobile the sportsman is practically independent in his movements, and it has been found that for hard travel on bad roads they will stand the wear as well as horses," said an advertisement.

At an appointed hour on opening day, a guide paddled a canoe bearing Ernest Seton Thompson to the centre of the fish pond, and the famous

Fig. 3.3 The New Brunswick government and the guides association were active in promoting the province to potential hunters and fishers, and attendance at sportsmen shows was an important part of their effort. By train they sent trees and plants, stuffed and live animals and birds, and even a camp to be erected as part of their exhibits. A live moose was a major attraction to newspeople and the public, and Pete, Jane, and Miss Shepody each made an appearance in shows from 1905 to 1931. It is impossible to know which moose is pictured here. She was identified as Jane by Fred Phillips who was working with the Travel Bureau of New Brunswick at this time. He tells the story that "Public life was to prove disquieting to Jane to such an extent that she became the only one of her species ever to be treated at Veteran's Hospital in Philadelphia. It was a shrewd piece of NB Travel Bureau exploitation."

naturalist-writer stood and acted out one of his stories, "Spearing the Big Sturgeon." Later in the show, the pond was used for a fly-casting tournament, and one of the nine entrants was Richard Follett. The moving pictures, meanwhile, were shown after the daily lectures. They had been well advertised, and the Canaan Woods film, titled *A Moose Hunt in New Brunswick*, had been previewed earlier for a sporting crowd at Boston's Copley Square Hotel. They had pronounced it very fine, and the day after Christmas the *Boston Transcript* newspaper echoed those sentiments more generally. "The Biograph pictures of the chase, made in the hunting field and on the most famous game fish waters, give the show the flavour of the real thing, and are already much talked about."

By this time, Billy Bitzer and Frank Marion were back at their jobs with Biograph in New York. Bitzer kept up his pace of nearly a new film a week, and Marion resumed his duties as the company manager. Then, in 1907, Marion left Biograph and joined two others to form a new company, Kalem, which became one of the first moving picture companies to locate in Hollywood. Marion did well for himself. After the First World War, during which he had an American presidential appointment in Spain, he sold his interest in the company and was able to retire in early middle age. He travelled widely and gave money to Syracuse University for a building devoted to photography.

Bitzer, meanwhile, had remained at Biograph and was there when a newcomer joined the company, a writer trying to earn a little money as a moving picture actor. He was terrible at it, and decided that maybe he'd be better at directing. Bitzer tried to talk him out of that, but the company let him make some risqué Mutoscope productions, and then allowed him to progress to actual moving pictures. In 1908, he and Bitzer made *A Calamitous Elopement*, and with that, though it was hard to recognize at the time, the greatest director-cameraman duo of the entire silent era was born.

Fig. 3.4 G. W. "Billy" Bitzer

Fig. 3.5 Cameraman G. W. "Billy" Bitzer and director D. W. Griffith on location in the snow filming the American film Way Down East (Griffith, 1920). Bitzer stands behind a Pathé camera.

The writer-turned-director was David Wark Griffith, and he spent the next few years earnestly cranking out short features for the Biograph "sausage factory." He had bigger ideas, though, and a compelling desire to make films more complex and ambitious in their scope. In 1913, in California, he got his chance. He and Bitzer, who left the Biograph company with him, began work on a film called *The Clansman*. "You get that old camera of yours to photograph this right, Billy," Griffith said, "and we won't be eating at Childs any more. We'll give them pictures that will blow off the tops of their heads." The elaborate production ran way over budget, and Bitzer later claimed he had to loan Griffith seven thousand dollars to keep it going. But when the film was finished and retitled *The Birth of a Nation*, it was both a commercial and artistic success, despite the racist overtones of the story, and it changed forever how films were made.

Working together into the 1920s, Bitzer and Griffith continued to experiment with technique. As Billy later described it, "What Mr. Griffith saw in his mind we put on the screen." But the motion picture industry was changing, and both would wind up in places far from where they had once been. Griffith made his last film in 1931, and by the time he died, in 1948, he was living, alone and embittered, in a Los Angeles hotel room.

As for Billy Bitzer, he enjoyed the perks of the creative life for as long as he could, but a return trip he made to New Brunswick, in 1906, may have been revealing for what lay ahead.

We might not know about this trip back to the province, except for another of those pesky newspapermen who showed up at the riverboat wharf in Fredericton one evening early that August. A chartered steam yacht named the *Hudson* had just pulled in, and aboard were Follett of the Boston Sportsmen's Show, an assistant to the president of a steamship company, two other men from Boston, and Bitzer. Billy had his Biograph machine with him and was taking moving pictures of the entire trip, reported the newspaperman. The party had missed the Star Line riverboat out of Saint John that morning, and so had chartered the *Hudson* for the trip to the capital. They had arrived as "one of the happiest parties of visitors ever to strike Fredericton," which sounds like turn-of-the-century journalistic code for a group well into its cups.

Their intention was to film a canoe trip that would take them up New Brunswick's Tobique River, followed by a portage round Mount Carleton in the province's north-central highlands, and then back into the canoes for a plunge down the racing Nepisiguit River to the ocean. Frederic Ireland, a Congressional reporter and freelance writer in Washington, had probably provided the idea for the film after making the same trip and writing about it in *Scribner's Magazine* a couple of years earlier.

But no moving picture was ever completed. An entry in the old Biograph Company logs, at the Library of Congress, shows that some film from the Follett-Bitzer trip was processed later in August, 1906, and that its quality was "good." But there is no record of a completed film, nor does one appear in Bitzer's filmography. Maybe the trip turned into too much of a good time. Or maybe the problem was the weather. Weather records indicate the late summer of 1906 was exceptionally dry in that part of New Brunswick, and it's possible low water levels made the rivers too difficult to navigate.

By the early thirties, Billy Bitzer had fallen on hard times. After some very difficult years, he got a job at the Museum of Modern Art in New York and spent his days annotating his films and recording his experiences as a film pioneer. Eventually he moved back to California and to a retirement home lately established by the film community for people like him. He died there in 1944.

But earlier, in the thirties, his situation had been extremely dire, his desperation poignantly described in a letter I found in the small Bitzer file at the Archives of the Academy of Motion Picture Arts and Sciences. The letter had been written in February 1931, when Billy was living in a "cold furnished room" in New York City. He'd had his "liquor disease" under control for five years, he told an old friend, but he had no job and even had to think about whether he could afford a stamp for the letter. "But I'm going to take a chance. I have a good landlady. I am penniless, and I just thought if you are working and could give an old pioneer just a little helping hand, you can't realize what it would mean to me right now."

Bitzer's New Brunswick Movies

A Moose Hunt in New Brunswick and *Salmon Fishing—Nepisiguit River*, the films Billy Bitzer shot in New Brunswick in 1905, are the oldest surviving motion pictures of the province. Preserved as part of the Bitzer materials at the Museum of Modern Art in New York and the Library of Congress in Washington, and at the Provincial Archives of New Brunswick in Fredericton, they show parts of the province at a time and in a way no other medium can quite match.

They are not extensive in their views, nor do they betray any exceptional talent in cameraman Bitzer at this early stage of his career. But they are engaging in their own way. We look sharply at the little steam train, The Bull Moose Special, and at the rigours of the wagon trip into Jim Ryder's camp. We watch the way people moved and the clothing they wore, including that of a woman who, dressed in vintage finery—a broad-brimmed hat and a long white dress—came to watch the Nepisiguit River salmon fishing from the shore. We speculate about these things. Was the woman, who took an animated interest in the proceedings, there to demonstrate that this was a sport that could interest females, too?

The wonder and beauty of old films is, after all, in the eye and the soul of the beholder, a lesson that came home one night in 2005 when the Provincial Archives of New Brunswick put on a "Hollywood in Havelock" night in the very village from which the moose hunters had entered the Canaan Woods a century earlier. Villagers, young and old, watched Bitzer's film of the hunt in rapt attention. During tea and coffee afterward, the talk was all about moose and subjects the movie stimulated. A daughter and her mother said they were going home to see if they could find a photo of an ancestor who'd been in vaudeville. (It had been mentioned that, early on, films had been vaudeville "acts."). A man remembered somebody who'd kept a pet moose with which he hauled a sleigh. And another, an obvious gun buff, had been fascinated to see that the hunters were still using black powder, even though smokeless powder had been available since the Boer War. He thought perhaps it was because these sports didn't want to take a chance with the new-fangled stuff when they were deep in Canaan Woods, miles from civilization.

Fig. 3.6 Billy Bitzer was here. Lakestream Lake, Cannan Woods.

One Sunday almost a hundred years after Billy Bitzer went to the Canaan Woods, two descendants of Jim Ryder, their outfitter in 1905, led me to the spot where, based on an old newspaper account, they believed their ancestor's cabin had stood. Although forest still covers much of New Brunswick, logging roads run everywhere now, and we actually drove to within sight of the place. It was a small clearing just above an adjacent lake. No log cabin was there now, indeed no visible signs that one had ever been there, and, though I listened ardently, no epiphanic murmurings came from the surrounding trees. But the place did fit the newspaper description, more or less. The lake was sheltered and shallow, its surface broken here and there by patches of sedge and other aquatic plants. There were boggy areas close to the shore, and behind them the autumn woods blazed with colour. It still looked like a wilderness lake, a place still fit for moose.

The Iconic Moose

One fall before the turn of the twentieth century, Henry Braithwaite, a legendary New Brunswick hermit-guide, and Harry Chestnut, soon to be a legendary canoe maker, killed a huge moose in the Tobique River country. The provincial government promptly bought the animal and arranged for it to be sent to a taxidermist in Saint John so that it could be displayed at that winter's Boston Sportsmen's Show. This may be taken as the symbolic beginning of New Brunswick's love affair with the moose as a provincial icon.

Previously, the province's glories had flowed from the great days of sail. But as the iron men and wooden ships faded from blessed memory, a rustic new image of New Brunswick began to emerge. It was the home of big game, and nothing represented it more spectacularly than the primordial bull moose. Never again, right up to the present, would the external perception of the province, or indeed its sense of itself, be as sharply defined as it was then.

Not that New Brunswick didn't have competition, the adjacent state of Maine also had moose, and, periodically, arguments erupted over which jurisdiction had the larger animals. Size mattered. Once, a newspaper in Bangor, Maine, had the temerity to suggest that a big moose head hanging in the Crown Land Office at Fredericton had actually come from the state of Maine. The province's chief game commissioner bristled. "New Brunswick is unquestionably the best ground in eastern America for moose hunting," he declared. It had "no need to go to Maine for moose heads."

By the twentieth century's second decade, moose symbols were rampant, not least on government brochures. Then, in the 1920s, a brewery in Saint John began making Moosehead beer, and now people could raise a glass to the splendid beast. Still, if one wanted to pick a single Year of the Moose in New Brunswick, it probably would have to be 1905. Not only did Billy Bitzer shoot the first movie of a moose hunt, it was also when Prince Louis of Battenberg (Prince Philip's grandfather) came to the Canaan Woods. The prince wasn't successful in bagging a beast, but never mind. The alert mayor of Fredericton, hearing this disquieting news, caught up with the prince's train as he was leaving New Brunswick and presented the startled royal with a mounted trophy head. It was the mayor's contribution to maintaining New Brunswick's image before the world.

Fig. 3.7 Cover of Crown Lands pamphlet promoting the attractions of hunting in New Brunswick.

Chapter Four

Itinerant Showmen and Nickelodeons

> "A local man is getting ready to start out on the road with a moving picture show. 'Teddy Voye,' who has had a good deal of experience in the theatrical business, is in tow with several American thespians, and they will now play the small towns throughout the Province, opening next week at Burtt's Corner. A local pianist will go along with the show and their friends wish them good luck."
>
> – Fredericton *Daily Gleaner,* June 9, 1906

Teddy Voye, a young man from a village outside of Fredericton, was smitten with show business at an early age. When he was just six, a theatre company manager, parading his troupe through the city to promote that night's show, spotted the lad's "black curly hair and fine features" and hired him on the spot. Teddy never recovered. In time, he did just about everything the business had to offer. He travelled with acting companies, minstrel shows, carnivals and circuses. And then, in his late twenties, he hit the road with a movie show.

The itinerant motion picture man is part of movie folklore. Appearing on the scene soon after theatrical troupes and vaudeville companies brought the first films to the cities and larger towns, he lasted into the era of the dedicated movie house. In New Brunswick, a few of his kind even enjoyed a revival in the 1930s, when the movies first began talking.

The earliest among these peripatetic showmen were models of frugal efficiency, arriving at villages and country crossroads with no more than a battered valise, a projector, a few canisters of film, and a bed sheet or piece of canvas to show them on. Nevertheless, they played a particular and important role in the evolution of the cinema. They extended its reach beyond the cities and towns, and thereby sowed the seeds of a movie culture in places that would otherwise have waited much longer for it to arrive.

In 1906, New Brunswick had a population of about three hundred and forty thousand, the majority of whom lived in coastal fishing villages, riverside mill towns, and small farm communities. This made the province a promising prospect for picture men like Teddy Voye, but there were challenges. One was electricity, or, rather, an absence of it. In the case of the little milling community of Burtt's Corner, for example, electrification did not come until the 1930s, although the village was just a few miles from Fredericton, the New Brunswick capital. How, then, did Teddy Voye show moving pictures there in 1906?

Fig. 4.1 Gas illuminated projector in the holdings of Kings Landing.

A vintage projector in the collection of artifacts at New Brunswick's Kings Landing Historical Settlement holds the answer. The projector's source of illumination was not an electric bulb, but a bright gas lamp. Since early movies used volatile nitrate-based film, this apparatus obviously required careful handling, but it was the only choice a picture man had as he ventured into the province's non-electrified precincts.

Itinerant Showmen and Nickelodeons

A man named Clark, who lived in the border community of Milltown, just across the St. Croix River from Maine, had built the machine now in possession of Kings Landing. He'd assembled it from parts acquired in the States. The machine had probably used acetylene, a gas produced from water and calcium carbide in a portable generator. Clark was also a peripatetic picture man, visiting nearby communities in New Brunswick and Maine around the turn of the century.

Teddy Voye's projector was undoubtedly similar but had likely been purchased already assembled. By 1906, such machines were available from amusement supply companies and mail order houses. Sears, Roebuck, for one, advertised "complete outfits" for moving pictures. According to a 160-page "special catalogue," this included projectors, stereopticon machines, gas making outfits, illustrated song slides, sets of views for lecturers, and motion picture film. Promising that "travelling exhibition work" was more popular than ever, the catalogue copy also gave helpful hints on how to run a successful business.

A collection of posters, handbills, and tickets has survived from Teddy Voye's days on the road. They suggest his career in the movie business had several incarnations. One handbill promotes "Voye and Crangle's Big Moving Picture and Vaudeville Company," another advertises the "American Biograph Company and Their Famous Motion Pictures," and an old ticket shows Voye as manager of "Hall's 20th Century Animated Show." It is stating the obvious to say that being able quickly to reinvent his presentation was a key to Teddy's survival as a turn-of-the-century roadie.

Fig. 4.2a Handbills advertising shows presented by Teddy Voye who had a stage career touring with theatrical shows. When movies became popular he travelled with a projector system until 1931 when he became manager of the community theatre in Minto.

Discovering the Movies in New Brunswick

Fig. 4.2b *Additional handbills and ticket for shows by Teddy Voye.*

Itinerant Showmen and Nickelodeons

A commonality of his New Brunswick movie tour was that most of the places he visited could be reached by rail, which was lucky because the province's roads fell somewhere between a cow path and a stagecoach run. Automobiles were rare, delicate, and not very speedy. The experience of a group of drivers who ventured out from Saint John in July 1906 was typical. They found part of the road strewn with large boulders. "It was rough riding, indeed," one reported, "and the occupants of the cars had all the jolting they wanted."

By train, though, Voye and company could travel in reasonable comfort across much of the province. They went from the towns of Newcastle and Richibucto in the East to the railway junction of McAdam and the border town of Calais, Maine, in the West. Local legend holds that, in the absence of a suitable hall, New Brunswick's picture men sometimes set up in wooden covered bridges, of which the province had many. Voye, however, seems to have had no trouble finding venues. In Richibucto, he presented "all the latest New York successes in Pictures and Vaudeville" for two nights in the local Temperance Hall. In McAdam, his "strictly moral and refined" show played in the Orange Hall.

Fig. 4.3 McAdam Theatre – the Orange Hall, also called the Temperance Hall, built in 1907, destroyed by fire in 1948. Movie posters are apparent on the side of the burning building.

Besides showing several short films, Teddy usually had along a singer to lead a round of "illustrated songs." Sometimes it was a chap named Harry Mayo, other times one of those inevitable road show "colonels" or "professors." As the words of familiar ballads on painted slides were projected on the screen, Mayo or Professor Arthur LeBarion conducted a sing-a-long, rousing the audience during a night of filmed vignettes with titles like *The Lost Collar Button* and *Please Help the Blind*. It was the novelty of the new entertainment that brought out the villagers. Voye's advertisements assured them that, "Our Pictures are positively steady. Our latest machine does away with all that quiver." To the movies themselves, he added sound effects: a few beats on a trap drum to heighten a dramatic moment, drumsticks on leather for gunfire, a few turns of a ratchet as a building collapsed.

But even as Teddy Voye began his touring in 1906, a profusion of full-time moving picture houses, which would ultimately chase his kind from the road, was already looming. Just the previous year, the nickelodeon had been born in the States. It was a type of theatre where a customer put down a five-cent piece and entered a small hall, often a modestly reconstituted storefront, to watch a series of short films. As soon as the cycle of films was completed, it started again, and the customer could stay as long as he wished. The idea spread quickly, thanks to the minimal investment required. All a bare-bones operator needed was a rented small hall or storefront, a few dozen wooden chairs, a projection machine, a screen, and a piano. Total cash outlay—about six hundred dollars.

The nickelodeon craze reached Saint John in the spring of 1907, following on the heels of a local failure that was itself a harbinger of changing times. A few months earlier, the Keith-Albee theatrical circuit had teamed with the American entertainment pioneer, F. F. Proctor, to operate the York Theatre in the Mechanics' Institute as a vaudeville house. The idea failed. So, on a Saturday night in mid-April, the York closed, to reopen the following Monday as the Saint John Nickel.

Over the weekend, the new Keith management had hastened to repaint the hall in theatrical tones of red, green, and gold, and to relocate the box office. But the biggest change was the conversion to moving pictures. "Come when you will. Remain as long as you please," was the promotional cry. "Nothing Cheap But the Price." It was the siren call of the nickelodeon, and the man who sounded it, in this instance, just happened to be one of the most knowledgeable people anywhere about moving pictures.

F. Guy Bradford had worked in the Old Country with an American named Charles Urban. Urban invented a projector called the Bioscope, and Bradford ran the London Bioscope Company, supplying film programs to the big English music halls. He arrived in Canada, early in the 1900s, part of a team the Canadian Pacific Railway hired to make a series of scenic films about this country. The team also included Joseph Rosenthal, celebrated for his camera work during the Boer War, and Bradford's brother-in-law, Cliff Denham. The CPR wanted the "scenics" to promote British emigration to Canada, and one of the railway's instructions was that there should be no pictures of winter. The films, always accompanied by a lecturer, were later shown at town halls, corn exchanges, and theatres throughout the British Isles. Thousands did migrate over the ensuing years; nobody knows how many felt hornswoggled about the climate.

Bradford and Denham stayed in Canada after the job was finished, and for a while they toured, showing the films to Canadian audiences. Then Denham left for New York, and Bradford joined the Keith organization. It was a propitious time—just as the nickelodeon phenomenon was gathering steam. Bradford launched nickelodeons in Montreal and Quebec City before heading for Saint John, where the prospects were also promising. This was because the nickelodeon was the workingman's theatre, and Saint John was still a workingman's town.

You would be sure of that, had you seen the Labour Day parade of 1902 in the city. Hundreds of workers, all nattily dressed, took part. There were five hundred longshoremen wearing black pants, blue shirts, white belts and bowties, and fifty printers decked out in frock coats and silk hats; two hundred teamsters astride horses, and fifteen cigar-makers rolling stogies aboard a float and tossing them to spectators; and many more. The parade wound through the streets for four hours and, in its colour and exuberance, celebrated the continuing importance of the workingman to the life of the city.

There was no doubt the city was ready for a workingman's picture house. Having it in a Mechanics' Institute was a happy coincidence. Mechanics' Institutes had been founded decades earlier to further the technical education of workingmen. Saint John's, built in the 1840s, was a grand, columnar building on Carleton Street where many lectures, discussions, and scientific demonstrations were held over the years. After the Great Fire of 1877, the building achieved particular importance as a theatre, since most of the city's other entertainment venues had burned. And now it would be home to one of the scientific wonders of the age.

The Nickel's first motion picture program, on April 15, 1907, consisted of five short films: *Robbing His Majesty's Mail*, *How Jones Lost His Roll*, *Adventurous Auto Chase*, *Canoe Sports*, and *Impatient Customer*. There was also an illustrated song, *Violette*. The program was a hit, and so, evidently, was much that followed, with the predictable result that the Nickel soon had competitors.

One was the Cedar, which opened as "the North End Picture Palace" at a union hall in an immigrant and working class part of the city. (Billy Bitzer claimed the explanatory, between-scenes "intertitles" of silent films helped immigrants learn English.) Next, after a brief springtime trial,

NICKEL

MONDAY and TUESDAY

MR. and MRS. JIM BALES — Good Singers

Newcomers to St. John in the Opening Numbers "Mary of Argyle," "When The Dew Is On The Rose" and in duet "Life's Merry Morning."

A NEW DICKENS' COMEDY — "MRS. LARRIPER'S LODGERS"

With Bunny, Mrs. Maurice, VanDyke Brooke and other Vitagraph favorites in the cast. Very highly referred to in dramatic journals.

PATHE WEEKLY No. 47 - Photo Newspaper

President-Elect Woodrow Wilson; Servians Leaving for the Balkan War; Funeral of Vice-President Sherman; Russian Imperial Family; Old-Fashioned Barbecue.

===COMEDIES AND THE ORCHESTRA===

WEDNESDAY and THURSDAY

ANOTHER MULTIPLE-REEL MELO-DRAMA

"THE LION TAMER'S REVENGE"

The Thrilling Story of a Menagerie, in which a Perfidious Clown meets his fate in a den of ferocious South African Lions.

A DASH OF INTENSE REALISM FOR A CHANGE!

FRIDAY and SATURDAY

THE MUCH TALKED-OF BIOGRAPH DRAMA

"THE PAINTED LADY"

A Study in Social Conditions that will grip your attention and set you thinking.

A BIG BUMPER WEEK!

Fig. 4.4 Handbill advertising movies being presented at the Nickel that opened in April 1907, one of the earliest Saint John nickelodeons.

in which the featured moving picture dealt with a great scandal of the day (and one with a New Brunswick connection), the St. Andrews Rink became a summertime picture house called The Happy Half-Hour, "the largest and coolest amusement resort in the city." Then the venerable Opera House switched to full-time pictures, with its former sing-along leader as manager, and, just like that, there were four full-time movie houses. Considering that there had been none only months earlier, this was cornucopic, and it marked the beginning of Saint John as a hot little moving picture town.

Towards the end of the year, competition intensified to the point that a pair of theatres—the Cedar and a newcomer called Princess— decided to invade the long placid waters of Sunday. Controversies were already raging in many places over Sunday showings of moving pictures, and it was very much within the character of the old Loyalist city that the local constabulary should be on high alert for *any* intrusions upon the sanctity of the Sabbath. A poor widow woman could certainly testify to that. She ran a small store where, according to the two busybodies who turned her in, she allowed Sunday School children to buy candy with their pennies "instead of placing them on the collection plate." Thus alerted, a constable observed one such transaction from behind a telephone pole, then swooped down on her.

Nevertheless, management of the Cedar and Princess theatres cooked up a stratagem they thought could beat the odds. For a Sunday just before Christmas, both scheduled the same religious film, Pathe's *The Life and Passion of Jesus Christ*, and promised that the proceeds would all go to the Protestant and Catholic orphanages in the city. Who could argue with that?

The police, that's who. On the appointed Sunday evening, large crowds appeared at the theatres, certain they would see *something*, either a show inside, on the screen, or a live one outside, featuring the law. Sure enough, just before the doors opened, a detective named Killen showed up. He charged both theatre managers with advertising a Sunday performance, and cited one for "causing circulars to be thrown on the sidewalks."

In court, the defendants argued that, when General William Booth, the Salvation Army founder, visited Saint John, *he'd* been allowed to show a Sunday film at the Opera House. That was different, said the magistrate. The Salvation Army did good work, while the picture men were simply trying to establish a devilish precedent. He fined both, then suspended the fines in return for their promises that there'd be no more attempts at Sunday showings, no more casting of handbills upon the streets.

At the Nickel, Guy Bradford had mapped out a higher road to success. Described by a colleague as "a very fine type of cultured English gentleman," he had immediately sought to broaden his audience by taking his film programs beyond the usual run of curios and trivial vignettes. He showed moving pictures of such things as the Prince of Wales visiting Lahore, India, and "various incidents of the little known whaling industry," and the building of a tunnel under the Hudson River at New York. His operating credo; "To amuse and entertain is good. To do both and instruct is better."

The sudden appearance of competition had not fazed Bradford—he had surely anticipated it—and he did not feel compelled to linger in the city. His assignment with the Keith organization was simply to get a theatre on solid footing, then move on to the next city in the company's sights; he did more than anybody else to spread the popularity of moving pictures in Canada, according to his colleague.

What undoubtedly eased Bradford's departure from Saint John, after about three months in the city, was finding the right man to succeed him. The chap had no prior experience in the moving picture game, which was not surprising, given that these were still early days in the business, but he was a former newspaperman, and that was not a bad background for a picture person to have.

His name was Walter Havelock Golding; his middle name the surname of a British general who'd fought during the India Mutiny. For years, later on, a portrait of the general at the siege of Lucknow would hang in Golding's office at the great picture palace he would play a key role in having built in Saint John. By 1907, he'd been advertising manager of the *Star* and *Sun* newspapers in the city, and also a reporter for the Saint John *Globe*. But most of all he was a publicist in the classic mold. He even looked the part. Short and wiry, he measured about five feet and weighed no more than one hundred and twenty pounds. He was thirty years old, energetic, verbose, and, when he wrote, the words gushed from his typewriter in a torrent.

He probably faced his first challenge as the new man at The Nickel on July 1, 1907, Canada's Dominion Day and the Fortieth Anniversary of Canadian Confederation. Patriotic Saint John had scheduled a consuming round of outdoor festivities and activities, and the only possible way the

Nickel, housed in what could be a painfully stuffy hall, could meet the competition was by opening at 10 a.m. for a children's program featuring a nine-hundred-foot "pictorial adaptation" of *The Three Bears* and promising "ventilation will be particularly looked after." It apparently worked.

From that moment on, Golding emitted a clear sense of a man discovering his *métier*. He was engulfed by the possibilities of moving pictures, especially as improving technology allowed films gradually to stretch into feature-length "photoplays." It was a "privilege," he declared, for audiences in Saint John "to witness the art of a celebrated actor through the medium of faultless photography." (True to his calling, he also had the gift of hyperbole—motion picture photography was certainly not yet "faultless.")

He percolated with ideas, and only occasionally did they exceed corporate limits and land him in hot water. Once, he hired a seven-piece orchestra for the Nickel. It was popular with audiences, but when the bosses in New York got wind of it, they made him fire the musicians. The setback was only minor, though, and the Nickel grew into a "klondike," the trade's word for a box office goldmine.

Some of the city's other theatres were not so blessed. One day, outside the Bijou Theatre on Charlotte Street, a lineman for the Saint John Street Railway Company came upon a bit of chicanery that smacked of desperation. Somebody had installed an illegal "jumper" connecting the railway's service wires directly to the theatre's house wiring. The Bijou was owned by the Canadian film pioneer Louis Ernest Ouimet, of Montreal, but it was his local manager, Charles Kerr, who got charged with "fraudulently and unlawfully consuming electricity."

Kerr denied any knowledge of the theft and, at a preliminary hearing for the case, blamed his "operator," a man named Chapin, who ran both the projector and a so-called "film testing machine" at the theatre. So where was Chapin? He had suddenly opted for the salutary delights of a Boston springtime, having been given a rail ticket paid for by an unnamed benefactor. The witness relaying this information was then asked who had put up the cash for the ticket, but, as delicately reported by *The Globe*, "Witness was not inclined to unbosom himself on this point." And that was that. Without the vanished key witness, the case soon fizzled. All Charles Kerr got was a few days in the slammer while awaiting trial, and he and the Bijou got away with just a few days of bad press.

A constant concern of theatre owners and operators during the nickelodeon era was the danger of fire. Some of the most basic of these early theatres were makeshift affairs, and the volatility of nitrate film was well known; it had a low combustion point of 284 degrees Fahrenheit. In parts of the United States, the incidence of fires was high, especially in places where the sudden mushrooming of nickelodeons had put a lot of inexperienced operators in projection booths. In 1907, the number of nickelodeons in the U.S. was estimated to be twenty-five hundred, and by the end of that year, it was thought that as many as a thousand had experienced a fire; fortunately, most were minor.

There was no reason that Saint John should be exempt from this threat, and it wasn't. The risk of calamity was illustrated one day at a local storefront theatre, the Wonderland, when a reel suddenly ignited during a show. Grabbing it, the projectionist threw it to the floor, where who-knows-what might have happened, except that audience members promptly kicked the reel into the street like a flaming hockey puck and "averted what might have been a serious fire." The only casualty was the projectionist, who singed his hands.

The incident was reported in *Moving Picture World*, a weekly trade publication begun in New York, in 1907, which for years diligently reported on motion picture happenings in New Brunswick. Virtually alone among trade journals, most of whom considered fires bad for business, *Moving Picture World* did not shrink from the subject, nor from pointing the finger at the parties responsible.

In 1909, a fire broke out at a nickelodeon in Carleton, just to the west of the city centre. Three hundred people were in the theatre when a spark ignited a film and set the projection booth ablaze. As people rushed for the door, a woman fainted, and a boy was pushed over a banister. Led by the manager, the nickelodeon's staff actually extinguished the blaze before the fire brigade arrived, but that was beside the point. "There is no excuse for such gross stupidity and carelessness," said *Moving Picture World*. "Every machine ought to be supplied with proper safeguards, and the manufacturers of machines should see to it that none are sold without fireproof cases."

The author of these pointed comments was probably the "projection editor" of the *World*, F. H. Richardson, who was sympathetic to the plight of projector operators. These men, and boys, laboured long hours for poor pay amid conditions that were inherently dangerous. Booths were poorly ventilated, hot, and filled with carbon dust from the projectors' arc lamps. In 1908, Richardson wrote a letter to *Moving Picture World* arguing for

Itinerant Showmen and Nickelodeons

an operators' union. "What is needed," he wrote, "is a bona fide union of operators, affiliated with the electrical workers' union, whose avowed and only purpose is to protect the operator." Not long after, he became the magazine's projection editor, from where he continued to campaign for industry improvements.

It isn't too far-fetched to imagine that copies of *Moving Picture World* reached the projection booths of Saint John, where they might even have caught the attention of a teenage boy named James Whitebone. Son of a cigar maker in the city, he'd gone to work in 1907 as an assistant projectionist and stage electrician in one of the city's theatres. He was thirteen and toiled ten hours a day for a weekly wage of four dollars. Later, he went overseas during the First World War, and when he came home, he began organizing Local 440 of the International Association of Theatrical Stage Employees. Then, for forty-eight years he was the Local's secretary and business agent, and was prominent in the labour movement provincially and nationally. It's hard to imagine that some of his motivation didn't come from youthful days and nights spent in the sweaty confines of a nickelodeon projection booth.

Fig. 4.5 Projection room at the Lyric Theatre in Saint John, New Brunswick in 1910.

By 1911, it was estimated that between twenty-five and thirty thousand people were going to the pictures every week in Saint John, a number that amounted to three-quarters of the city's population. The estimate came in an anonymously authored story in *The Globe* that was actually written by Walter Golding, whose enthusiastic prose was by now instantly recognizable by discerning readers, byline or not. Moving pictures, he wrote, had "become the most popular form of indoor entertainment Saint John and the rest of the world has ever known." And, after several years on the job at the Nickel, this meant but one thing to him; his hometown was ready for "a playhouse worthy of the city."

Despite many setbacks and disappointments over the years, and even as it watched Halifax surpass it as Canada's biggest Atlantic port, Saint John has always buoyed itself with optimism and the determined conviction that it stands in destiny's doorway, a mere step away from a return to the greatness it knew when it traded on "iron men and wooden ships." Part and parcel of this attitude was boosterism, and, in his time, there would be no greater booster of Saint John than Walter Golding. It may have started with his campaign for a theatre that would be both a showplace and a symbol of the city's new emergence.

He began lobbying his New York bosses. By the spring of 1912, his campaign was showing results; Keith-Albee had begun accumulating land on the south side of King Square. Then, as spring turned into summer, a strange thing happened; Golding abruptly left the city for British Columbia and a job promoting a new townsite along the Grand Trunk Railway. Had he had a falling out with Keith-Albee? Were negotiations for the new theatre not proceeding the way he'd expected? Was he stretched to the breaking point after five years of running the Nickel? Nobody today knows, including his modern-day descendants. And, in the end, it didn't matter, because, by autumn, he was back on the job in Saint John.

As December approached, he spent time composing a large newspaper advertisement, which finally appeared December 13, prominently splashed across the top of an inside page, a prime positioning that might explain the obsequious "cordial felicitations" the ad contained for *The Globe*'s "Venerable Editor." The advertisement announced that a "splendid showcase" would be built on King's Square, on a site once occupied by another cherished institution, Lanergan's Dramatic Lyceum. The new playhouse would be "a modern theatre for the exposition of all that is cleanly wholesome and educational in up-to-date amusements." It would open in late 1912.

It was a big moment for Saint John, a triumphant one for Walter Golding, and he couldn't let it pass without celebrating his precipitative achievements at the Nickel.

> The wonderful new era of Motion Picture drama, comedy, spectacle, research and travel has been thoroughly exploited in this house, and children and adults who before had been barred from higher-priced amusements have enjoyed their benefits. Vocalists of merit and instrumental music have been introduced, further widening cramped minds and conveying pleasure. It is no fiction to state that St. John's people—particularly the families of small wage earners—are happier and better informed today than they were when the Nickel was opened five years ago. The house has surely proved to be the rich man's rest cure, the poor man's happy hour, the whole family's inexpensive entertainment. (source unidentified, ed.)

Golding said that moving pictures had taken on "the aspect of permanency" in Saint John, and they did seem to signal another new beginning for the city. It was during this time that Saint John began to imagine itself as a regional service centre, and the picture business was demonstrating the possibilities. Production companies were setting up distribution offices in the city; by the end of the decade, there would be ten such offices, from which films could be dispatched to theatres in the three Maritime Provinces and Newfoundland.

This meant that any community in the region could theoretically have a moving picture house to call its own, and entrepreneurs weren't long in realizing that. Mostly, the theatres went up in cities and along the dusty main streets of the larger towns, although, once in a while, the cinematic dream would get the best of some earnest villagers, too. When, in 1916, a second theatre opened in the agricultural centre of Woodstock, in the St. John River Valley, the total for the three Maritime Provinces reached nearly one hundred, according to *Moving Picture World*. That was when the projection editor decided it was time he headed north to take a look, and he set out, on a circuitous path, for New Brunswick. It was a trip he never forgot.

Miracle in Moncton

The threat of fires did not disappear with the end of the nickelodeon era. On Saturday afternoon, February 7, 1948, Kent Theatre in the railway centre of Moncton, NB, was filled with young children. The manager, L.R. Conrad, thought he smelled smoked. In the basement, he found a fire already burning briskly. Racing back upstairs, he told an employee to call in the alarm and ordered ushers to key locations, including the balcony. Then Conrad went to the stage and calmly told the audience the show was being interrupted for a fire drill. When the fire department arrived five minutes later, the auditorium was full of smoke. But children and adults had already exited, some so quickly that they left behind scarves, coats, and gloves. Long afterward, one child, Eva MacDonald, remembered tripping over a woman in a fur coat lying on the floor as she made her way out of the theatre, but there had been no panic and no casualties. As the Kent burned to the ground, people were reminded of the worst movie house tragedy in Canadian history. It had occurred 21 years earlier, when Montreal's Laurier Palace Theatre burned, and 78 children died, most by asphyxiation. In Moncton, an assistant fire chief called the narrow escape in his city "miraculous."

Fig. 4.6 Fire at the Kent Theatre, Moncton, 1948.

Itinerant Showmen and Nickelodeons

New Brunswick and the 'crime of the century'

As the nickelodeon craze was bursting upon Saint John, in the spring of 1907, the St. Andrews Curling Rink showed a moving picture, *The Unwritten Law: A Thrilling Drama Based on the Thaw-White Tragedy*. It may have been a trial run and, if so, it was successful, for that summer the rink operated as The Happy Hour Theatre.

The Unwritten Law dealt with a story by then familiar to much of North America—the sensational murder of the famous architect, Stanford White, by Harry Thaw, ne'er-do-well son of a Pittsburgh steel tycoon. White had an affair with Thaw's wife, beautiful Evelyn Nesbitt, and Thaw achieved his revenge by shooting the architect on the rooftop garden of Madison Square Garden in New York. Newspapers called it the "crime of the century," though it was only 1906 when it happened.

Fig. 4.7 New York American, *Tuesday, June 26, 1906.*

There was a New Brunswick connection to the story. Stanford White had, for years, been coming to the province's famous Restigouche River to fish for salmon. He had designed fishing lodges on the river system and opulent homes in New York and Newport, Rhode Island for some of his fellow club members. Another of his creations was a salmon fly called "Night Hawk," well named for this consummate *bon vivant*.

Harry Thaw's eventual trial had echoes of Eadweard Muybridge's murder trial thirty years earlier. Thaw's lawyer wanted him to plead insanity, but he said no. The lawyer then switched to the argument that, in certain circumstances, a husband's actions were justified—the "unwritten law" of the movie's title. Thaw was finally found not guilty by reason of insanity and spent several years in an asylum. Evelyn Nesbitt later had what might fairly be called "a hard life." One break, though, was the $50,000 she got as a consultant for the 1955 movie, *The Girl in the Red Velvet Swing*, in which the sultry British actress Joan Collins appeared as Evelyn.

Fig. 4.8 Evelyn Nesbit Thaw, 1913.

Chapter Five

The Spreading Picture Culture

In the summer of 1916, the Projection Editor of New York's *Moving Picture World* decided to visit New Brunswick. He chose to go by automobile. It was a trip he probably never forgot.

The editor, Frank Richardson, could have chosen to travel up the East Coast by boat or train. But, perhaps because he also wanted to visit Quebec, he elected to use his car, which he later nicknamed "Nancy Hanks", after a famous racehorse, for the way the vehicle literally bounced over the primitive backcountry roads.

The trip began well enough. With his young daughter, Nellie, along for company, they headed up the western side of New York's Hudson River. The valley, whose beauty artists of the Hudson River School had already made famous, was resplendent with pastoral loveliness in the August sunshine, and the road wasn't bad, either.

When they reached Montreal and started across Victoria Bridge over the St. Lawrence River, they encountered a startling site. The bridge was crawling with soldiers armed with guns and fixed bayonets. They were standing guard. Only then did it dawn on Richardson that a country at war, even one in Europe, had to watch over the home front, as well. The sight, he admitted, gave him "the shivers."

But he had come to Canada to gain a sense of the state of moving picture exhibition in this country and to meet some of the theatre "operators," or projectionists. Montreal was a good place to start. It was Canada's cinematic birthplace. Twenty years before, on June 28, 1896, the country's first moving picture show had been presented in the city with a Lumiere *cinematographe,* and from that a pioneering picture culture emerged. In 1907, a young electrician, Leo Ernest Ouimet, started

North America's first "palatial" movie house, the Ouimetoscope. He also establishes Canada's first film exchange, and, incidentally, placed its first branch office in Saint John, New Brunswick.

From Montreal, the Richardsons headed east for Quebec City, one hundred and sixty miles down the St. Lawrence, and en route blew a tire, the first sign it wasn't all going to be smooth riding. By the time they got back on the road and reached the Quebec capital, Sunday had arrived, and theatres were closed.

Continuing along the river, Richardson drove steadily eastward onto the Gaspé Peninsula, a giant, sparsely populated thumb of landscape jutting into the sea at the far northern edge of the Appalachian Mountain Range. The Mi'kmaq called it "the place where the land ends." It had breathtaking scenery, but a highway hadn't yet been completed all the way round. Richardson went anyway and eventually reached the community of Gaspe, at the end of a narrow bay.

Seeing a moving picture show advertised, he and Nellie decided to take it in. It was an experience Richardson decided was worth recounting later in *Moving Picture World*. The seating in the local hall was on hard, pine benches. When the show started, the projector ran only in slow motion, and the film still broke seven times. The interruptions pleased no one, except possibly an antic young man at the front whose job was to find the right music for the player piano; he spent most of his evening frantically searching for, and switching, piano rolls.

The next day brought another experience. Leaving the Gaspé town, they soon motored into a stretch of hills that Richardson described as "eighteen miles of almost straight up and down. . . with rocks of all kinds and descriptions, ranging in size from a pebble to half a good-sized hill, with ruts, and real cute mud holes two to six inches deep, just to keep up the excitement." It was more than Nancy Hanks could handle, and she shredded a tire.

This wasn't something that should happen to a 49-year-old city man travelling with his daughter on a primitive road at the edge of the continent, and it got worse. Still fifty miles from the New Brunswick border, they couldn't find a replacement tire. But then a train came along (a rail line had been completed along the southern edge of the peninsula five years earlier), and they were able to get the car and themselves aboard. In this humbling way, they finally reached the northern New Brunswick town of Campbelton where Richardson purchased a tire from the local dentist.

Campbellton had been a boomtown. Situated in the estuary of the Restigouche River, it had, by the end of the new century's first decade, fourteen mills producing lumber and other wood products. Then, on a windy day in August, 1910, a spark from one of the mills started a fire that swept the town. In the aftermath, scenes of devastation were everywhere, none more poignant than the one captured by a photographer named J. Y. Mersereau. He was a police magistrate in another town where he was known as "Six Days Mersereau" because of the light sentences he handed out, and his feeling for the human condition shines through in this photograph; a group of men, several wearing suits and bowlers, are gathered outdoors round a table having coffee or tea amid the devastation. A makeshift shelter stands in the background. The incongruity of the clothing on their backs suggests it may be all they have left.

Fig. 5.1 Roseberry St., Campbellton, ca. 1920, rebuilt after the devastating 1910 fire. The town had a movie theatre by 1916 when Frank Richardson of the Moving Picture World *visited.*

But Campbellton soon bucked up and rebuilt, and, as one sign of its recovery, it had, by August, 1916, a moving picture theatre. So did the community of Athol, next door, and so did Dalhousie, just down the estuary. All three were owned by one S.M. Dimock, who also had one of the area's first automobiles, which was probably handy for getting films to and from the railway depot.

Dimock employed three "operators" for his theatres. Their names were Eddie Esliger, Albert LeBlanc, and J. R. Ellsworth Suthern. Frank Richardson was interested in meeting them, as he was other projectionists, because he was, in a very real sense, their champion on matters that ranged from safety in the booth to projecting the best possible picture. He was a technical man who could talk expertly about manipulating the carbons in an arc lamp, and the right slope for a theatre floor, and a thousand other esoteric subjects. He wrote about film projection every week in *Moving Picture World*, and he had, in 1910, produced a book, *Motion Picture Handbook for Managers and Operators*, in which he covered every conceivable question that could pop into an operator's mind. So valuable was the book for picture people that it came out in a third edition, in 1916, and there would eventually be seven editions. He was, as one admirer said, "the grandfather of modern projection."

So we should imagine this moment in 1916, on the North Shore of New Brunswick, when Frank Richardson—a picture man from New York—gathered together Messrs. Esliger, LeBlanc, Suthern, and maybe Dimock, too, to talk about the raw science and subtle art of silent film projection. A favourite topic was projector speed. It was a tricky business, Richardson said, because, in shooting a film, hand-cranking cameramen often didn't maintain the standard rate of sixty revolutions of the crank—they were sometimes off by as many as ten turns per minute. So operators, said Richardson, should be prepared to make adjustments when they showed the films. By varying the projector speed according to the screen action, Richardson said, they could present a film the way "the musician renders a piece of music." The operators must have liked that. The average backcountry operator probably hadn't thought of his work in such ethereal terms, so the visits were memorable for everybody, including Richardson, who approached all subjects with determined zeal.

Leaving Campbellton and headed for Chatham in the summer of 1916, Richardson and his daughter Nellie ran into more trouble. The roadbed on which they travelled was mainly made of sand and the noble flivver sometimes sank in as much as eight inches. And when it wasn't sand, it was rocks and ruts and mudholes. "Poor old Nancy Hanks probably would have bit us had she had teeth," Richardson said later.

Dusty, dirty, and tired, he and Nellie were greatly relieved when, at last, Chatham loomed on the horizon. It was a bustling little seaport town in the estuary of the Miramichi River. The first thing they sought as they chugged into town was a hotel. Finding one and approaching the desk, Richardson was encouraged when the young clerk asked whether he wanted a room with bath.

"Yes"! he almost shouted.

"I'm sorry, Mister, we don't have any of those," came the reply.

"Well, do you have public telephone"?

"Yes sir, we do. It's under the staircase." Then, after a pause; "But you can't use it, Mister, 'cause it's broke."

* * *

The picture business was growing fast in New Brunswick. One sign was the fact that, in 1912, the province decided to bring it under legislative control, and the provincial Legislature that year passed An Act to Regulate Theatres and Cinematographs. There was still general befuddlement over what to call the new medium, and so the word "Cinematograph," (*merci*, Lumieres) was adopted in many jurisdictions, not just New Brunswick, as a term embracing all matters cinematic.

The New Brunswick legislation required theatres showing moving pictures to be licensed at a fee rate of one hundred dollars for cities and fifty dollars for towns and villages. Projectionists, then known as operators, also had to be licensed. In 1913, the first full year with the legislation in effect, there were twenty-seven picture houses in seventeen different New Brunswick cities, towns and villages; an additional thirteen licenses were issued for what apparently were occasional, part-time, and seasonal operations. By the time of Frank Richardson's visit, three years later, the number of licenses had climbed to fifty, spread over twenty-nine communities.

One of those who paid the two-dollar fee for a projectionist's licence was Harry B. Camp of Woodstock, who was the father of Dalton Camp, the future renowned political operative and national columnist. As related by author Geoffrey Stevens in *The Player: The Life and Times of Dalton Camp*, it was in a Woodstock projection booth that a revelation came to Harry Camp—the voice of God telling him to leave his tawdry job and become a minister. This moment, writes Stevens, "saved Harold from a certain obsolescence as a movie projectionist and his family from a probable life of hardship, even penury."

Another projection licensee was William Richards, manager of the Opera House at Newcastle. An accomplished pianist from England, he had been swayed by Canadian promotional films and emigrated in search of a fresher, healthier climate (he suffered from diabetes). Reaching the Miramichi River town of Newcastle in 1911, he soon met a local girl, Janie McGowan, and they married a couple of years later. Presently, William, a graduate of the Royal Conservatory in London, became the accompanist for silent films at the Newcastle Opera House. Later, he became the theatre's manager, helped immeasurably by the feisty Janie. Their hard experiences in the moving picture business, including an attempt by a competitor to dynamite the Opera House, might have remained just another story within the family, had not a grandson of William and Janie's, some seventy-five years later, decided to build a novel around them. The grandson is the author David Adams Richards, and the novel is *River of the Brokenhearted*, published in 2003.

And then there was Carle Neilson, a Danish immigrant who had come to Canada with his widowed mother and a sister around the turn of the century. They settled in the colony called New Denmark near Grand Falls. The first Danish colonists had arrived in the area in 1872 and, amid an overarching wilderness of trees, had somehow managed to turn their hilltop lands into beautiful and promising farm country. What emerges from the artifacts of Carle Neilson's professional life—a flyer for Nelson's All Talking Pictures printed on peach newsprint, his old roadshow equipment, a few photographs, notices in the local paper, and government records—is a portrait of a Danish immigrant who, needing to find work, and perhaps having to support his mother and sister, is drawn to the burgeoning moving picture business. He makes a small bid for assimilation by dropping the "e" and the "i" from his Old Country name and takes up a life that is a mix of dreams and opportunism, hard reality, and a struggle to survive.

Nelson's name appears in the first list of licensed projectionists following the passage of the Cinematograph Act in 1912. He is, in 1913, a projectionist at Perth, NB. On the same list is Sanford Jamer, across the river at the Specialty Theatre in Andover. Both men were about thirty-two at the time, and it's hard to resist the idea that Jamer, an electrician, taught Nelson the projectionist's trade. In 1914, Jamer left for the military, and Nelson, still living at Perth, carried on at the Specialty, even as he started up a picture show of his own some miles away in the village of Centreville. He continued to operate there, probably part-time in a rented hall, into 1916, when he also began running the show at the Star in nearby Hartland.

The Hartland venture did not work out. In July 1918, a classified advertisement appeared in *The Canadian Moving Picture Digest*. "For Sale. A whole project booth of moving picture equipment: projectors, lenses, dynamos, and engines, all in excellent condition, and will be sold at a bargain." The contact is C.A. Nelson of the Star Theatre. Just above this ad is another—"Position Wanted by a licensed projectionist." That's C.A. Nelson, too.

He hung on, though, and the next year had a license to operate, in a limited way, likely because of the flu epidemic, in the villages of Centreville, Florenceville, and Bath. Later, a new category of license appeared— "Travelling"—and Nelson got one of those. The arrival of sound in the movies, in the late 1920s, had stirred a rebirth of the fabled itinerant picture men of yore. Nelson set up as a travelling picture man who called his show "Nelson's All Talking Pictures." His advertisements claimed he had "Positively the Best Talking Picture Equipment on the Road."

Fig. 5.2 Carl Nelson operated a travelling audio, motion picture show in the 1930s in New Brunswick and Nova Scotia.

Most of the letters and papers that survived Nelson were from the thirties and forties, when he lived, first, in Dorchester, near Moncton, and later in Parrsboro, Nova Scotia. About the time the Great Depression was settling in, he ordered two "Educator" portable projectors and a sound system from the Holmes Projector Company of Chicago. The cost was $1150. He put half down, promising to pay off the rest at the rate of $60 a month. His Ford truck, with NELSON'S MOVING PICTURES painted on its sides, became a familiar sight on local roads, as did he, neatly combed and spiffily dressed in a dark suit and bowtie, the very model of an itinerant country impresario. The movies were one of the things people permitted themselves in those austere days, and Nelson, meticulously managing to pay his bills (he once wrote a cheque to Holmes for forty-four cents), stayed with it for much of the decade. Then, in the early 1940s, he ran a theatre in Parrsboro, before moving back to New Denmark.

The second decade of the twentieth century was when moving pictures venues of one kind or another truly seeped into every corner of New Brunswick; they reached oceanside resort communities like St. Andrews and Shediac, the coal mining village of Minto, and the Bay of Fundy islands of Grand Manan and Campobello, among many other places in the province. In the dairy town of Sussex, the Pickwick Club began operating a picture show, and in company run villages like Black's Harbour and Plaster Rock it was, respectively, a fish packing outfit and a lumber mill that ran the pictures. The story is told about Plaster Rock that if lumberman Donald Fraser deemed a picture inappropriate, or if the crowd became unruly, he'd simply cut off the electricity which came from his mill to the hall. Within the decade, Annie Coutts of St. George and Emma Davidson of Moncton joined Janie McGowan as the first women in the picture theatre business.

In 1916, the year of the Richardson visit, pictures were being shown with some regularity in as many as forty venues in the province. These were not all conventional theatres, to be sure, but expansion of the picture culture was nevertheless clearly evident. Every community of any size had a space that could be rented. Carl Nelson took out moving picture licenses for both Hartland and Centreville in 1916. Fred C. Torrie, who, in 1913, had a modest fifteen-dollar license in the beach resort of Shediac had, by 1916, partnered with someone named McNeil and their business now rated a thirty-five dollar license. Even better as an indicator was the way the exchange business grew. In 1913, there were three exchanges, all based in Saint John, distributing moving pictures. Three years later, there were eleven.

At the local level, the picture business evolved according to community type. A good example was the town of Woodstock, a prosperous agricultural

The Spreading Picture Culture

and manufacturing centre of about four thousand residents situated in a lush part of the St. John Valley that people called "the garden of New Brunswick." Settled by United Empire Loyalists, Woodstock had the look and feel of a classic New England town, a place of stately, well-appointed homes, conservative attitudes, and just enough eccentric characters to make it interesting. As a by-product, it also had a lively theatrical tradition. A theatre called the Graham Opera House had opened as long ago as 1885, and, in 1908, two local businessmen, Albert Hayden and George Gibson, had built their larger Hayden-Gibson Theatre.

Long after it burned, in 1920, people fondly remembered the Hayden-Gibson for its spectacular ornamentation and its backdrops of beautifully painted canvas scenery, and also for the variety of its entertainments, which included road shows as well as local productions by the likes of the Valley Farm Dramatic Company and the Woodstock Tennis Club.

Neither the Graham Opera House nor the Hayden-Gibson Theatre leapt immediately into motion pictures when they arrived. Instead, other local entrepreneurs, sensing a rare, if passing, opportunity, opened

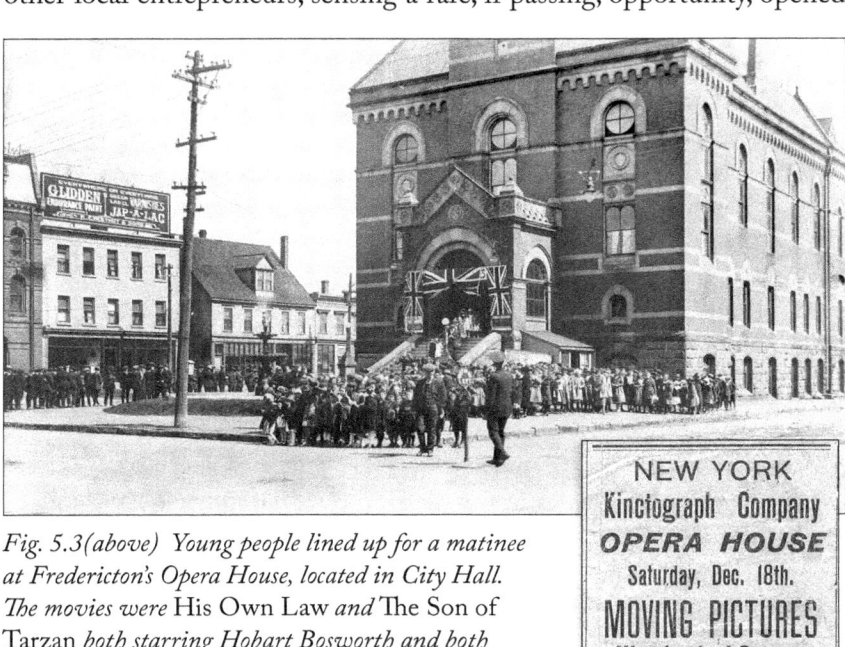

Fig. 5.3(above) Young people lined up for a matinee at Fredericton's Opera House, located in City Hall. The movies were His Own Law *and* The Son of Tarzan *both starring Hobart Bosworth and both released in 1920.*

Fig. 5.4(right) Poster for shows at Fredericton's Opera House

two separate "cinematic parlours" whose charms included the popular unmitigated wooden benches and long waits while the projectionist changed film reels and a live soloist filled the time with popular songs. Even at that, it was debatable who ran the better parlour, the Woodstock operators or a funeral director a few miles across the border in Smyrna, Maine who showed pictures in his funeral parlour when his normal business was slow, if not quite dead.

In any event, as moving pictures caught on, and a growing number of exchange offices in Saint John ensured that more and more films were available, both the Graham Opera House and the Hayden-Gibson began showing them, even as they continued to stage live shows. Then, in 1916, the Opera House was leased to Fred G. Spencer of Saint John who renamed it the Vogue and made it a full-time picture house.

Frank Richardson ended his tour of New Brunswick in Saint John. A meeting of theatre owners and managers had been hastily called so that they might meet Richardson, who had a message for them; they should form a regional association so that they could speak with a single voice in an industry that was headed in a bad direction. The largest players in the industry—the companies who made the pictures—were taking control of it and charging outlandish prices for their films. Theatre men had to organize, said Richardson, and they had to do it quickly. Saint John's theatre men agreed and so did their counterparts elsewhere. The Motion Picture Exhibitor's League of the Maritime Provinces was formed a month later in Halifax, with Walter Golding as its first president.

Industry control was still very much an issue when the Exhibitors' League gathered for a convention in Saint John in September 1917. Apart from the important business at hand, it was a moment when the motion picture community could proclaim what a vibrant part of the city's life it had become. Banners and bunting hung from the theatres and exchange offices, newspaper advertisements welcomed delegates, special events were planned, and two actresses of the silent screen arrived from New York as special guests. Frank Richardson came, too, this time by steamboat.

In Saint John, Walter Golding had got his splendid new picture house built. Construction started shortly after the announcement from Keith-Albee in December 1912, and the job had been completed, remarkably, in just nine months. The finished building was everything a theatre manager could hope for. The street in front was paved with concrete and lined by ornamental light standards. The façade of the high building itself featured polished granite and terra cotta, and its cornices and corbels and pedimented windows gave it an Italianate look. The lavish auditorium inside was coloured in old rose and old ivory and in Moorish tints. Frosted lamps formed the striking electrolier that hung from the ceiling. There were eight hundred leather-upholstered seats on the parquet main floor, one hundred more in six side boxes, and nine hundred in a balcony that was divided by a horizontal cross aisle. Every one of the eighteen hundred seats had an unimpeded view, and the acoustics—there would still be live shows, too—were perfect. It was a long way from The Nickel or, for that matter, from the city's Opera House, now twenty-three years old.

The new theatre got a nice spread in *Moving Picture World*, which called it "undoubtedly

Fig. 5.5 Imperial Theatre opening in Saint John.

the finest house of entertainment in the far Eastern section of America." The *World* noted, too, that the projection booth was made of "the Johns-Manville asbestos pattern"—the last word in fire protection. Overall, the house was nearly identical, save for seating capacity, to the New Imperial built by Keith-Albee in Montreal, and, perhaps for that reason, Saint John's was called the Imperial, too. And, of course, the man who moved into the manager's living quarters was Walter Golding.

A Village Movie House

Naturally, not every place could have a picture palace like the one about to rise in Saint John. At the other end of the spectrum was the country theatre earnest villagers decided to build far upriver, in a place called Andover, in that same buoyant autumn of 1912.

Andover was the shiretown of the farm and forest communities of Victoria County and had about five hundred residents. Directly across the river, and connected by a bridge, was Perth, with another three hundred and fifty citizens. A total population of eight hundred and fifty hardly seemed enough to support a daily picture show, but the villages did have two of the elements essential for a hometown movie house. They had a railway, which could deliver films from distribution offices in Saint John, and they had electricity, thanks to a hydroelectric dam on the nearby Aroostook River. A small cadre of interested villagers also had determination, and when no individual entrepreneur appeared to take on the job, they elected to build their movie house as a community project, much like they might build a local golf course.

They were a polyglot group, this little band of rural cinematic enthusiasts. They included a village doctor, a lawyer, an accountant, an insurance man, a railway station agent, and the local sheriff. Apart from a shared interest in moving pictures, their other common characteristic was that they were the sorts of people who knew lots of other people. So they formed a company and began to sell shares. Within four days, they'd sold seventy-one shares and raised fourteen hundred and twenty dollars. That was enough to buy land in Andover, at the very end of the bridge from Perth, and to start construction.

By Christmas, the theatre was ready. There was nothing fancy about it. In architectural style it was Carpenter Basic, country plain, and utilitarian. It had an Edison Model "B" projector and a large room with four hundred chairs. The chairs cost forty-five cents each and the entire building went up for seven hundred and fifty dollars. But it was infused with enthusiasm.

Before the opening, on Christmas Day, the company directors gave themselves sensible, hands-on jobs: the accountant became the ticket-seller, the insurance man the ticket-taker, and the sheriff, usher and implicit keeper-of-order. Their choice of a theatre name was equally inspired. They might have chosen one of the currently trendy names, like Unique or Peerless or Ideal, but instead picked one from the cinema's first days, calling their house the Specialty.

They probably could have called it the Dark Abyss and still drawn a crowd. Moving pictures were quite a change from Andover and Perth's usual entertainments of church suppers and socials and maybe the occasional amateur or touring company theatrical. Having a nightly picture show in the villages was almost beyond imagining, and, in the first nine-and-a-half months, the Specialty made a profit of nearly four hundred dollars.

It was the happy beginning of a story that, unfortunately, soon turned sour. Perhaps because of the onset of another winter, or maybe because the novelty simply wore off, the theatre began losing money. By the beginning of 1914, the company was one hundred and fifty dollars behind in interest payments on a mortgage and had other bills "that should be paid at once."

Then the First World War broke out and was soon subtracting young men from the villages. One who enlisted was Sanford Jamer, a good-looking lad stylish enough to have taken his best girl to his graduation from Andover Grammar School in a horse-drawn carriage. He'd become an electrician and, with ten shares, was the largest initial investor in the Specialty. In Europe with the Canadian Expeditionary Force, he twice survived enemy gas attacks. Back home, he moved to Nova Scotia after the war and married lovely Sadie Romans Parker of Halifax. In their handsomeness, they looked like they *belonged* to the cinematic age, and, sadly, their story did play out something like a moving picture. Working at an oil refinery in 1928, Sanford and a co-worker ran into poisonous gas. The co-worker died the next day,

Fig. 5.6 Sandford Jamer, shown here in a wedding photo with his wife, Sadie Romans Parker, had movie star looks himself. Of the original subscribers to Andover's Specialty Theatre, he was the largest with ten shares. An electrician, he was a valuable tradesman to have on board the venture.

Sanford lasted another week. Then the gas claimed him, too.

By the start of 1915, the Specialty's debt had reached six hundred dollars. In January, the theatre stopped running during the week, opening only on Friday and Saturday. The most persistent of the directors was the insurance man, Noble J. Wootten, who now leased the theatre. He couldn't have imagined what lay ahead, could not have guessed that the war would drag on for another three years. Or that, as it neared its end, an epidemic of Spanish 'flu would erupt so virulent and widespread that it closed theatres everywhere, and was so feared that, when a meeting of the Specialty's directors was called, in October, only Wootten and one other showed up; the rest were either too ill or too afraid to gather in a group as the contagion raged.

Wootten did everything he could to keep going. He saw to it that the editor of the *Victoria County News* got free passes for himself and his lady so that he might favourably mention the Specialty in the next edition. He sold tickets out of his insurance office for "the sweetest love story ever told," a First World War propaganda film called *Hearts of the World* that D.W. Griffith and Billy Bitzer had cranked out. He arranged an excursion train to the movies from Plaster Rock, a mill village on the Tobique River.

Some nights it must have worked—summer evenings, when Perthians strolled across the bridge, and Andoverites walked from their homes, and farm couples rode in from the country, when the film was pleasing, and the piano player in the corner struck chords that were right for the picture on the screen, when life was momentarily good, and so was the box office.

Otherwise, Wootten could not have lasted as long as he did. He finally quit in 1920, and somebody else took over. He lasted about a year. Back came Wootten, the relentless village businessman, offering to find whatever use he could for the building, in return for half the proceeds. But a fire interrupted that plan, and to the directors, it was like a Biblical injunction. They put the Specialty on the market "for the best price obtainable." It was The End.

But it wasn't. The theatre would last another half-century. Renamed the Capitol, it was where, in the nineteen-thirties, a talented chap, Bert Moore, brought remarkable wildlife films he'd shot on a homemade camera and thrilled audiences with them. Generations of villagers not only saw their first pictures there, but some received their high school diplomas on its stage, when it was still the best venue available.

It can be said that the theatre had a useful life, and when, finally, television imposed an inglorious decrepitude upon it, it was hardly the only picture house to suffer that fate. It burned to the ground one night in the nineteen-seventies, and one of the last things remembered about it was the sight of rats escaping the flames and racing across an adjacent parking lot.

The Second Coming of the Imperial Theatre, Saint John, NB, 1982-1994

From its opening in 1913, the Imperial Theatre flourished under the management of Walter Golding, who successfully brought the biggest names in North American show business to its stage. By 1929, however, "talking" movies were rapidly replacing live performance as the best attended form of public entertainment. The Imperial was leased to Famous Players and RKO, renamed Capital Theatre, and became primarily a "picture house" although live performances continued to be offered.

With the coming of television in the 1950s, movie attendance began to wane and eventually the Capitol closed its doors. In 1957, two sisters from the United States bought the building for $166,000 and donated it to the Full Gospel Assembly Pentecostal Church. The Church occupied the grand old theatre

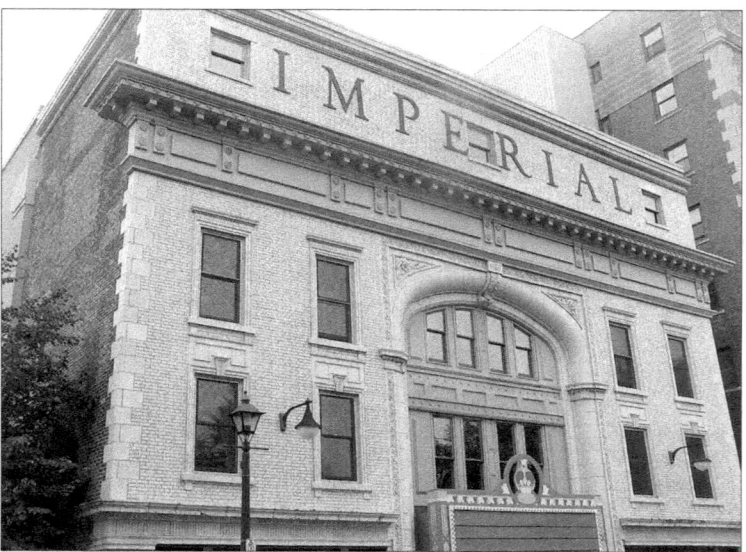

Fig 5.7 Exterior of the restored Imperial Theatre.

Fig 5.8 Interior of the restored Imperial Theatre.

building until a small group of Saint John heritage enthusiasts offered to purchase it in 1982. In what may be one of the strangest real estate transactions in the history of the city, the Church accepted a $1.00 down payment from Jack MacDougall with the understanding that the balance of the one million dollar purchase price would be paid on the same date the following year.

Jack MacDougall, the erstwhile owner of a taxi business, and currently between employments, was pressed into service for the cause of saving the Imperial by a band of friends. The media loved it; an "unemployed taxi driver" had put a dollar down on a million-dollar deal to save an icon of the city's cultural heritage and proposed to fund-raise the balance in a year's time. As it turned out, MacDougall was a bit more than an unemployed taxi driver. He was an organizer. (He later served as a chief strategist in Frank McKenna's election campaign in which the Liberal Party took every seat in the New Brunswick Legislature.)

As he tells it, he was pressured, goaded, and essentially forced into taking the lead on raising the money by the intrepid committee that quickly formed to save the Imperial. But, by his own admission, he had fallen in love with the building on his first visit and exploration of the interior. He could see what it had been and was captivated by the vision of what it could be again and what that would mean for the city of Saint John. MacDougall credits the committee and the thousands of Saint Johners who rallied to the cause. It was all those good folks who pitched in, he said, that enabled him to write a cheque for $999,999.00 on the due date and take possession of the Imperial Theatre in all its faded glory*

But then began the decade plus of restoration led by Tom Condon and the assembling of funds needed to bring the project to completion. In addition to ongoing fund raising, this required the coordinated financial support of the city, provincial and federal governments, which was no mean feat and in which Jack MacDougall was again a key player. The second coming of the Imperial Theatre, in all it's restored architectural elegance and enhanced utility, came to fruition in 1994 and has been the flagship of theatrical and musical performance in the city ever since.

Everyone who has attended performances at the restored Imperial will have observed the "angels in the architecture" but may not know that we now enjoy this splendid cultural facility because of the many "angels" in the city that gave generously to bring it back to life. When it comes to community, the province of New Brunswick is at the head of the parade, and the city of Saint John has this story to prove the point.

*Editor's Note: In 2017, a lively and at times hilarious memoir was published of what it took to save the Imperial Theatre. See *The Unemployed Taxi Driver* by Jack MacDougall.

Fig 5.9

Chapter Six

Backcountry Filmmakers

The old silent film spins out a flickering woodland vignette; a wiry New Brunswick guide on snowshoes boldly approaches a large bull moose stuck in the snow. Taking the animal's photograph, the guide then indulges in a showy bit of 1920s bravado, deftly enrolling the creature in "the famous order of the Bachelor Button" by sticking a boutonniere on the moose's ear.

They surely loved this little film in the United States when it was shown to sportsmen in New England, New York, Philadelphia, and in towns as far west as Chicago. To the eager sportsmen, it made palpable their best dreams about a pristine piece of the Canadian wilderness. Even better, it was about as *vraisemblante* as cinema could get; it had been made by a real-life, flesh and blood New Brunswick guide and outfitter.

Burton Stanley (Bert) Moore had, you might say, grown up with New Brunswick's Tobique River country. Born at a place called Scotch Lake, near Fredericton, in 1883, he had first followed his father Adam into the Tobique region in the northwest of the province in August, 1900. Years later, he still remembered that rugged introductory trek—the overnight walk from the railway station at Plaster Rock, followed by two days of poling a canoe upstream against a strong current. But he also saw his first moose on that trip, eight of them at once, and he was hooked.

The Tobique is one of the shorter and, at the same time, most fabled rivers in the province. Named for a Wolastoqiyik chief, the river rises back in the higher hinterland in little springs like the one that tumbles, sparkling and burbling, over iridescent green moss beside a hiking trail on the flank of Mount Carleton. Because the mountain, whose craggy top is barely above tree line, is the height of land here and the highest point in New Brunswick, the water on one side flows toward small lakes and the start of the Tobique, while the opposite side—offering a kind of mirror image—nurtures the springs and brooks that gravitate toward another set of lakes and the birth of the Nepisiguit River. From the top of Mount Carleton, you can see the beginnings of both river systems as you peer over a forested vista that resembles a great, rumpled, green quilt that historically has been rife with wild game.

In the decades that followed that first trip, Moore would spend a lot of time on the Tobique as a hunting and fishing guide, an outfitter, a sporting club manager, and as a maker of films about wildlife. These films, with their close-up shots of moose, deer and birds, thrilled sportsmen wherever they gathered and also went into general theatre distribution through Associated Screen News, the motion picture company owned by the Canadian Pacific Railway. More than three-quarters of a century after they were made, they still seem remarkable, revealing Bert Moore as a patient, creative and innovative pioneer in nature films.

The genre of nature films, today so abundantly represented on television, first emerged in the late 1910s and 1920s. Among its earliest practitioners were Canadians Byron Harmon, who made films about the Rockies, and Evelyn Cherry and Dick Bird, whose focus was on the Prairies. Perhaps the best-known early film of this general environmental field was *Nanook of the North*, released by an American, Robert Flaherty, in 1922; its portrayal of Inuit life, however, was more about anthropology than nature. Another early entrant was the legendary writer and conservationist Grey Owl, who made his first nature movie in 1927, several years after Moore began shooting his films.

Some of the early nature films, including a few made for the Canadian Government Motion Picture Bureau—forerunner of the National Film Board—were of the where-to-find-the-best-hunting-and-fishing kind. Moore's movies also served that purpose, but there was more to them than that. His films were primarily about nature, and he sometimes went to extraordinary lengths to get the sequences he wanted. Specifically, they were about the abundance of nature in New Brunswick, and they projected an image of the province that was captivating and alluring.

The Moore family, whose forebears emigrated to North America from the British Isles early in the nineteenth century, had a lineal interest in nature. Bert Moore's uncle, William H. Moore, was a dedicated amateur naturalist who amassed a considerable collection of mounted birds, animals and insects. These he displayed behind glass in a building with a little stream running by it on the homestead at Scotch Lake. William Moore recorded sightings of many bird species in New Brunswick, and what was perhaps the province's last sighting of a passenger pigeon.

Adam Moore, Bert's father, first went to the Tobique, which lies about one hundred and seventy kilometres due north of Scotch Lake, as a lumberman, about 1890. In the country's wooded hills and shallow rivers, he quickly perceived opportunity of another kind; this was the sort of raw territory that could attract sportsmen, especially well-heeled ones from the United States. He'd joined another man in a partnership that continued until 1902, when they divided hunting and fishing rights at the height of land between the Tobique and Nepisiguit river systems. After that, the Tobique side of the mountains was Adam's. He'd been correct is discerning its sporting potential and fortunate in his timing. New Brunswick was becoming known as the place where you could find the best fishing and biggest game in all of eastern North America.

Glowing reports from traders had started it all, as far back as the beginning of the nineteenth century. One concerning the Restigouche River spoke of Mi'kmaq fishermen netting three thousand salmon in two nights. A man arriving on the Tobique in 1863 said, "The trout are so numerous and voracious as to jump at the canoe paddles." Before long "shoals of Yankees"—the phrase belonged to a disgruntled English traveller—appeared beside the rivers. An 1883 article in *The Manhattan* enthusiastically described New Brunswick, as "a very paradise for the sportsman," and portrayed it as populated not by people but by "the long-lipped moose, the antlered caribou, the 'grim, taciturn bear' and other royal game."

In the United States, at the end of the last century, people were decrying the demise of their own frontier. Settlers and railroads had pushed into the country's nooks and crannies and, to some degree at least, had tamed them all. But here, barely an overnight train ride from Boston was a place still wild. Of no small symbolic significance was the fact that Gifford Pinchot, the advisor behind much of President Teddy Roosevelt's conservation legislation, was a member of the Tobique Salmon Club.

New Brunswick, as the writer, Frederic Irland, wrote in *Scribner's* magazine, had preserved "its perpetual youth." Coming north in the mid-1890s, Irland spent two autumns wandering through the interior wilds of the Miramichi River with guide Henry Braithwaite. Despite Braithwaite's subjecting him to all the best horrors of a pristine wilderness—trackless swamps, bog-riddled barrens, dense, tangled woods and a fifty-seven day stretch without sight of another human—Irland concluded he'd had a transcendent experience. "If life on earth had no more for me," he said, "I should feel that the recollections of those two seasons in the New Brunswick woods had made it worth living."

Hastened by such, the Yankees flowed north. "Our forests are, figuratively speaking, alive with Americans," reported a bush correspondent to a Fredericton paper one fall soon after the turn of the century. At the city's Queen Hotel, you could find Carnegies, Whitneys and Vanderbilts on the register, sportsmen awaiting the guides and wagons that would take them into the Big Woods. The prospect of securing a trophy was what motivated many of the sportsmen, and the proof was in the statistics. In the fall of 1905, for example, the customs department reported that no fewer than one hundred and twenty moose heads, twenty-five caribou heads and twenty-four deer heads, all taken by American hunters, mostly in the Tobique country, had passed through the rail centre of McAdam Junction on their way to taxidermists in Maine. And New Brunswick's largest taxidermy outfit, Emack Bros. of Fredericton, said they had orders to mount another one hundred moose and caribou heads, all for American sportsmen.

Fig. 6.1 Famous New Brunswick guides at the 1901 Chicago Sportsman's Show.

Backcountry Filmmakers

Two photographs from that era exist that classically illustrate the beginning and end of the commercial enterprise that was the New Brunswick game season. One features a veritable pantheon of the province's outfitting establishment. It is March, 1901, and standing on a street in Chicago are: Will Chestnut, soon to start a canoe business with his brother that would become a piece of Canadiana; George Armstrong and Harry Allen, already becoming woodland legends; Henry Braithwaite, considered the dean of New Brunswick guides; and standing slightly forward and at least a foot taller and wider than the others, Adam Moore. These men, gussied up with Stetsons, bowlers, suits, ties and topcoats, have been temporarily let loose from the eastern forest to pitch the province's attributes to the Windy City's sportsmen show. Their apprehended pose implies that, as soon as this damn photograph has been taken, they'll be pleased to get on the train and beat it back to the bush.

Fig. 6.2 Adam Moore (2nd from left) at train station in Perth, New Brunswick, seeing off sports with their bounty.

The second photograph brackets the game season at its conclusion; a trio of sportsmen has made the trip north, done the wilderness safari, fulfilled their dreams. Now, pressed back into suits, they are on the station platform at Perth, NB, waiting for the train with Adam Moore, who looks perfectly suited to the role of a sahib of the north. If you examine the photograph closely, you can see two skinned trophy heads wrapped in their furs, the whole point of this extended exercise.

If ever there was a legendary figure of the New Brunswick woods, it was Adam Moore. A huge handsome man with broad shoulders and massive hands, he looked like he could have come out of Central Casting, the very personification of a northern woods guide and outfitter. All of this, and his knowledge of woods and wildlife, imbued him with an aura and a reputation that carried down from the hills and reached far beyond the Tobique. Fredericton scribe, Frank Risteen, writing once of distant "earthquake rumblings from the vicinity of Bald Mountain on the Tobique," attributed them to "Adam changing his mind."

American sports regularly sought him out when planning a trip to the Tobique. Among them was Emerson Hough, a Chicago-based writer for *Forest and Stream* magazine. In December, 1901, Moore and Hough set out on a month-long wilderness trek across the top of New Brunswick on snowshoes to pay a visit to the reclusive outdoorsman, Henry Braithwaite, ensconced somewhere in the Miramichi country. Hough produced a series of magazine articles about the trek, and William Francis Ganong, a prodigious New Brunswick historian and cartographer, later commemorated it by naming a lake in the area Hough Lake. It sits in the province's northern highlands, just south of the Christmas Mountains. In 1922, Hough, who continued an occasional correspondence with Moore for some years after their trip, published a novel called *The Covered Wagon*. The following year it was made into a motion picture, the first epic western.

George Shiras III, another celebrated visitor, arrived in New Brunswick in July 1907. Shiras was a former U.S. Congressman and a hunter who became an early advocate for shooting with a camera instead of a gun. The year before, *The National Geographic Magazine* had published seventy-four of his wildlife photographs, an unprecedented spread. Now Shiras wanted to photograph the moose and deer of the Tobique country. After meeting Shiras' train in Plaster Rock, Moore immediately impressed the photographer by poling him several miles up the Tobique, which was running at a spring-like pitch following heavy rains. Against a strong current, it took three days to reach the lakes but Adam, who did all the poling, never wavered. When finally they reach Nictau, Adam commented, "There were plenty of moose in the water today." The remark baffled Shiras, because he'd seen nothing. Then Adam pointed to telltale gray-brown hairs floating on the surface of the water and, sure enough, the next day "it fairly rained moose," said Shiras. From then on, Adam became, in Shiras's mind, "the famous guide, trapper, and philosopher of these woods."

Adam made it clear at the outset that "hunting" with a camera didn't make much sense to him. His conversion came one night when he and Shiras went out on Nictau Lake in a canoe with a jacklight mounted on the bow. Presently, the light fell on the translucent eyes of a moose wallowing along the edges of a bog. Shiras fired his improvised flashgun (a bullet-less .22 calibre rifle with a protective pan on the muzzle) to take a picture. The explosive sound of the flash powder startled the moose, and the animal began thrashing about in the water. Adam's roar of laughter rang long and loud across the lake. After that, he was first in the canoe every night.

An American who had an even greater effect on the Moore family was a young man named Donald Ryder Dickey. He was still a student at Yale University when, in September 1909, he first arrived on the Tobique on a chance hunting excursion. Shiras had left behind his "shining outfit," and Adam Moore, now a full convert, took Dickey out on the lake of an evening to try it. This time, the flashgun didn't bother the moose and they were able to get in close range. Adam also introduced Dickey to the Red Brook Salt Lick, a known congregating area for caribou and moose, where a log blind for photographers had been put up in 1905. We can't say all this was the beginning of Dickey's interest in photography (he brought along two cameras), but it was certainly the start of his fascination with the Tobique. He would make several more trips to the region in the following years, in the course of which he introduced Adam's son Bert to the wondrous possibilities of wildlife filmmaking.

Donald Dickey had been born into a well-off family in Dubuque, Iowa. His grandfather was paymaster and right-hand man to a fellow known as Diamond Joe Reynolds, a shipping operator on the Mississippi and Missouri rivers. When Reynolds died, Grandfather Dickey succeeded him as company president, and he also had interests in mining and railways. Later, in California, Donald's mother Anna introduced her son to the world of nature. She had befriended the noted conservationist John Muir, and when the boy was in his mid-teens, he and his mother had accompanied Muir and others in a climb up 14,495-foot Mount Whitney. Afterward, Muir wrote to Anna; "Altogether a good trip in which everybody was a happy scholar at the foot of nature, and all learned something direct from earth and sky, bird and beast, trees, flowers, and chanting winds and waters:

hints, suggestions, little-great lessons of God's infinite power and glory and goodness. No wonder your youth is renewed and Donald goes to his studies right heartily." He also added; "Next year you and Donald should make collections of at least the most interesting plants. A plant press, tell Donald, is lighter and better than a gun. So is a camera and photographs of trees and shrubs are much to be desired."

Eventually Donald enrolled at the University of California in Berkeley. He was there when the San Francisco earthquake occurred and served on the fire lines. Then he switched to Yale, in New Haven, Connecticut, a member of the Class of 1910. He was serving as captain of the gun team in his senior year, when he suffered a serious heart attack.

Returning to California, he remained bedridden for all but an hour a day. He moved to a friend's ranch in the Ojai Valley, where he rested in a steamer chair placed in an orange grove. Above him, beautifully coloured birds flitted and nested among the branches. He asked for a camera, and got it fitted with a thread that allowed him to operate the shutter from where he sat. This semi-invalided pastime began a life-long passion for photographing birds.

Donald Dickey was still rebuilding his strength when he returned to the Tobique in 1913. Wildlife photography had become his major preoccupation, and by now it also included moving pictures. Approaching the valley on a cool, clear morning in early August, he wrote that "I spent it dreaming of our good times in 1909 and of the love I bear this wilderness country." The Tobique had become part of his recuperative process. Within a day or two, he was at the Red Brook Lick. "It is at this place," he said in his journal, "that the game trails for miles around focus and they [the animals] come in such numbers that the mud looks like a hog wallow so tramped up is it at this time." (It still looked that way on a visit nearly a hundred years later.) Barely had Dickey set up his movie camera on a birch stump, and his still cameras on cracker barrels inside the log blind, "when in walked an (to my eye) immense +15-point buck [deer]. It was now very cloudy but I got 2 pictures before he grew suspicious and walked out." An hour later, a cow deer and her calf wandered into the lick. "I had movie [camera] well-oiled and muffled and they paid little attention while I ran off 40' or 50' of movie...."

More than two months later, he was still on the Tobique, as verified by another surviving artifact from those days, the register for Miller's. The hotel stood near The Forks, where three branches of the Tobique merged into

Fig. 6.3 Deer coming down Rocky Brook to Red Brook Lick.

the main river, and it was the place that people often stopped as they entered or left the river system's upper reaches. The hotel's hipped roof made it look somewhat like a large barn, but it had its own touches of elegance, like linen on the dining tables, and its own social structure in which guides, loggers, and trappers slept in a large, dormitory-style room on the third floor. The hostelry's book sometimes bore the look of a social register. Three days before Dickey's bold signature appeared on November 16, those signing in included Ralph Pulitzer and his wife, son of publisher Joseph Pulitzer.

Between 1913 and 1922, Dickey made five more trips to the Tobique, which was remarkable given the distance he had to travel, but he revelled in its wild ambiance, and he was definitely serious about his picture taking and moviemaking. He had Adam's son Bert rebuild the blind at Red Brook Lick and, arriving in August 1916, was well pleased with the results. "It is a well-built log cabin with chinked walls, water-tight birch bark roof and a funnel or chimney from the peak to carry all scent above the heads of the game." Bert had also piled a deep layer of moss on the floor, making bedding down for the night more inviting.

Fig. 6.4 One of Donald R. Dickey's photographs that constitute a fine study of wildlife habits — capturing such traits as the animal feeding under water, "lopping" or dropping its ears so as to let the water drain from them, their profile as they walk woodland trails, how they sometimes "spraddle" their legs as they stand, etc.

At Red Brook, Dickey experimented with various photographic techniques. These included stretching trip threads, *a la* Eadweard Muybridge, across well-travelled animal paths. When an animal touched a thread, it set off the flash powder and simultaneously opened the camera lens for a one-fiftieth of a second exposure. This was a technique a wildlife photographer named Martin Johnson had used in Africa, and it earned Donald Dickey a salute from a magazine called *The World's Work* as "The Martin Johnson of America." He got pictures of startled moose, deer, black bear, even a frightened fox. Immediately after the picture was taken, he sometimes played his lights on the animal so that he could film its behaviour following the first moment of surprise. Deer, for example, usually bounded away in fright, but some went only a few feet and then, standing perfectly still, flapped their ears to detect where the danger lay.

Dickey's faithful assistant and woodland mentor in all of these adventures, especially in the first years, was of course Adam Moore, and the two became close. Early on, "Dick"—as his friends knew him—took to calling the old guide "Dad," probably as much for his sagacity and commanding presence as for his age, which, in 1913, was sixty-two to Dick's twenty-six. Later, when he showed his film on the American lecture circuit, Dickey would refer to Adam in affectionate terms as he described the Tobique as "a spot in New Brunswick that taught me the ways of canoes, and of moose, and of Scotchmen." Numerous entries in Dickey's logbooks confirm that Adam became a believer in the value of nature photography and film-making, even though he continued to host traditional hunters. In one instance, Dickey recorded that Adam "worked the water ruse to perfection, sloshing feet and hand for all the world like an old cow" in order to attract a bull moose into range of the camera.

Dickey's stays in New Brunswick normally extended over several weeks, during which he also cruised the lakes and rivers with his cameras. By day, the canoes were camouflaged with thickets of cut branches, and by night they were equipped with a jacklight or bullseye lantern. Moose or deer, drinking near a shoreline and apparently thinking the light came from the moon, paid little attention until the flash was fired. Then, sometimes, all hell broke loose.

At the University of California at Los Angeles, where Dickey's photographs, journals and other materials are archived at the Louise M. Darling Biomedical Library, is a collection of out-takes that contains numerous shots of deer and moose, including some of the latter swimming, galumphing ashore, and exhibiting a distinctive trot called "the moose glide." There is also a sequence where Dickey, responding to his inner cowboy soul, leaps from a canoe and tries to ride a moose bronco-style, something he apparently attempted more than once. In other clips, Adam is shown paddling, chopping a tree, carving wood, and doing a moose call.

Also in the UCLA library is a finished Dickey film made on the Tobique called *Game Trails,* running just over ten minutes. It opens with a slow motion sequence of deer at the Red Brook Lick, and then moose, including young calves, are shown drinking the water. There are sequences, too, of Dick and Adam setting out the still cameras and camouflaging them with bog moss, and of Adam stretching out the trip thread.

Adam and one or more of his guides usually attended Dickey on these picture taking adventures. Then, as Adam got older, son Bert assumed a larger role, and he, especially, took an interest in the proceedings. Bert had always been a tinkerer. At fifteen, using wood, tacks, pieces of metal and wire, he'd built a box camera the size of a small Rubik's Cube and made it work, custom-cutting his film in a dark room. After he started going to country-dances, he constructed his own fiddle. Later, he built a kind of snowmobile, combining an outboard motor with an air propeller, and he built a somewhat similar machine for the water. "Went for a spin with Bert in his hydro-canoe-plane," Dickey reported to his journal one day in 1916. "In spite of the infernal noise the contraption makes, the game always seems to wait for a good look at it before running." A more conventional creation was the Moore Guide Special, the canoe he designed with alternating long and short ribs that made it light, and which had a profile that was wide and flat so it skimmed easily over the shallow areas when water was low in the Tobique

But Bert's most outstanding creation was his moving picture camera. As he spent more and more time with Donald Dickey, Bert's fascination with movies as a means of showing nature grew. By the twentieth century's second decade, motion picture cameras were readily available from commercial suppliers. Akeley Camera Inc. of New York City, for example, had a magazine-loaded unit that had been widely used by the American Museum of Natural History, the U.S. Department of the Interior, *Field and Stream* magazine and others. The trouble was, the Akeley camera sold for $1920, plus $115 for a six-and-a-half inch telephoto lens, and $45 each for extra film magazines, and Bert Moore simply didn't have pockets that deep.

So he decided to build his own camera. He actually built two cameras; both with housings made of light wood—one, a smaller, less complicated version of the other. You certainly don't have to look long at these cinematic *objets d'art* to appreciate the depth of Moore's independence and talent as a backcountry innovator. Parts of his cameras were scalped

Backcountry Filmmakers

Fig. 6.5 Burton Stanley ("Bert") Moore, a guide and filmmaker on New Brunswick's Tobique River, using cameras he built himself, made nature films in the early 1920s that rank him as a pioneer in the genre. One of his cameras is shown here, along with the wooden film magazines he used with another camera.

from other machines. They included phonograph gears and an old low-tension marine magneto. Still, it required the skill of a machinist, which he'd been during the First World War, when he worked at a foundry in Fredericton, to achieve, for example, the synchronization that enabled each frame of unexposed film to appear in the camera gate at the precise split-second the shutter flicked open to capture the image. Several screw holes left empty in the frame of the larger camera as he experimented with positioning the gears suggest it didn't come easily.

Loaded with two hundred feet of film, the larger camera weighed just seven pounds. Carrying it and a lightweight tripod, Moore found he could trudge about the forest with relative ease. When he took along a telephoto lens, he resorted to a basket backpack made by local Indigenous craftsmen because the eighteen inch long lens required a heavier tripod, lest it all tip over. He also had a battery driven electric motor and a remote switch that allowed him to set up the camera and then operate it while hidden behind a log or a cluster of trees. Another unique adaptation was his film "magazines," little wooden boxes, black and rectangular, about five centimetres deep. A loaded box fed 35mm film through the camera, and

Discovering the Movies in New Brunswick

an unloaded one gathered it after exposure, making loading and unloading the machine in the bush much easier.

The finished films reveal another side of his creativity. His close-ups of birds and animals, shot in the early twenties, are spectacular, and, what's more, he fit them into the context of a story about nature. In one sequence, a Canada jay, a hairy woodpecker, and two chickadees compete for a piece of venison. Each bird is filmed in striking detail, while written intertitles describe the building drama. Moore uses written intertitles to describe the building drama. Another film tells the tale of "an interesting day on snowshoes," in which a woodlands traveller encounters first a grouse, then a deer stranded up to its belly in snow, then a moose. There's also a pause for lunch in a snowbound cabin. It is all very appealing and evocative of life in the Big Woods, circa 1920.

Fig. 6.6 Bert Moore (left foreground) with Donald R. Dickey of Pasadena, California (to Moore's right) his film-making mentor, in his "Movie Canoe" with camera mounted.

Wildlife fascinated Moore, and he was proud of the rare shots he obtained—a bay lynx (bobcat) taken by surprise, and a pubescent moose, its antlers about to emerge, brought to the camera by imitating the mother's call, and who subsequently followed him two miles back to his cabin door. He took particular pride in his footage of a ruffed grouse (partridge) in the act of "drumming," the first film ever shot of this behaviour. It revealed that the sound, so familiar to hunters, came not from the bird beating its breast but from its "strong, stubby wings" pounding the air.

Nor was the act a mating ritual, as some people thought. Rather it was a territorial imperative, announced to all in hearing range—other partridge in particular—that they had intruded upon another's turf.

Moore made these observations in early May 1919, while spending a fortnight deep in the Tobique woods. He had gone to a spot "where partridges are much like domestic fowl" and thought the job would be easy. He even located an old pine log to which his subject returned regularly to drum. Situating himself behind a blind of balsam fir and poking his camera lens through the boughs, he waited and gradually became educated in the peculiar habits of the partridge, including, to his dismay, its preference to drum when the log was in shade rather than sunlight. It was only at the end of the second week that he finally got his film, and then only after a prolonged period of cranking the camera with no film in it to get the bird accustomed to the sound.

This kind of patience reflected a man "tremendously interested in wildlife," remembered Louisa Morse of Wilmington, Delaware. Mrs. Morse, who first went to the Tobique as a child in 1924, recalled that Bert "knew everything about the country. There wasn't anything you could stump him on—flowers, trees, wildlife. He had a tremendous wealth of knowledge of the area."

Mrs. Morse's family, the Spruances of Wilmington, was typical of the well-off Americans who came to New Brunswick in those days. Her father, Colonel William Spruance, had been in charge of U.S. munitions during the First World War and had then returned to E. I. duPont de Nemours cellulose products division after the war—duPont's Spruance Plant in Richmond, Virginia, is named after him. The Spruances had vacationed at Maine's Belgrade Lakes region early in the century but were looking for a place with good fishing and abundant wildlife, criteria already becoming difficult to meet in the U.S. Colonel Spruance had hunted in the Miramichi watershed in the late teens with another renowned outfitter, Arthur Pringle, who advertised that he had "the best caribou grounds in New Brunswick." But the colonel wanted a camp setup that would also be suitable for his wife and three children, and that's what brought him to the Tobique, probably after meeting Bert Moore at a sportsmen's show in the States.

By the 1920s, Adam Moore had retired, and Bert was running the outfitting business. To the Spruances and others, the Moore home camps at Nictau Lake sounded immensely appealing, with their promise of "good

Fig. 6.7 Promotional brochure for Moore's camps along the Tobique operated by Adam and Bert Moore.

trout fishing, ideal canoeing and bathing, moose seen daily from camp and deer always in sight, a regular mine of interest for the photographer." But it was a long trip to get there—four days from Wilmington. For the penultimate leg, Bert would meet the train at Presque Isle, in northern Maine, and then drive the party eighty miles to Miller's Hotel on the Tobique, from whence guides would pole them upstream to the camps, one adult to each canoe, a long final day's journey.

The rewards were, however, as advertised. "We had a tremendous amount of game up there in the early days," Louisa Morse remembered. At twilight, she and the family would watch as deer and moose came to the lake to drink. Sometimes, they'd go to the photography blind at Red Brook Lick, where it was common to see twenty or thirty deer at a time. In Bert Moore, Bill Spruance found "a real sportsman and companion, keen hunter, and expert fly fisherman, a lover of nature and wildlife, in fact, a naturalist of experience and ability"—phrases he used to introduce Bert and his movies, "some of the best reels I have ever seen."

The films testified to Moore's love of nature, and so did the essays he composed, based on his observations in the wild. For a man whose formal schooling had ended in Grade Two, he wrote remarkably well. "In a little

Backcountry Filmmakers

more than a quarter of a century of matching wits with the elements of the north woods," begins one narrative, "I have found nothing more interesting than the beaver." Then follows a cogent and comprehensive discussion of the animal's character and habits.

But, as with woodsmen who "love" the very trees they harvest, Moore's admiration for the creatures of the wild stopped well short of wanting to preserve them all. He was decidedly not a cinematic counterpart of Charles G. D. Roberts, the New Brunswick born author whose fictional tales of animal life had a popular following. (Adam Moore reportedly once characterized Roberts' stories as "damn lies.") Bert saw the moose as a "noble mammal" to be seen and filmed, yes, but also one to be taken down with a powerful rifle; he found neither offence nor contradiction in "securing a head with wide spreading antlers, as a trophy."

By the early 1930s, the province was sending whole railway baggage cars full of wild creatures on its promotional junkets—moose, deer, black bears, Canada lynx, and various species of game fish. These were part of elaborate exhibits that also included entire log cabins assembled on site and surrounded with freshly cut, fragrant balsam fir trees. Guides and outfitters also dropped by the White House in Washington to deliver a hamper of moose meat for President Herbert Hoover. They visited the mayor of Philadelphia with professional ballplayer Eddie Collins, appeared in Fox Movietone and Paramount newsreels and on radio, and staged a moose-calling contest at New York's Pennsylvania Hotel. On one occasion, Bert Moore played the harmonica in a skit at the Boston City Club.

While the stunts got people's attention, Bert believed that his movies, by focusing on the exalting qualities of nature, were capable of making even the uninitiated believers in the forest mystique. In the films lay "the secret of what lures tired humanity to [its] most restful recreation place." he wrote in a promotional blurb. Moore rarely showed moose, deer or partridge being hunted, although this and sports angling were his primary occupation. His films were about nature rather than the harvesting of it. Even a movie titled *A Year in the Wilds of New Brunswick*, which contains a sequence on trapping, struck an apologetic note. "As long as people choose to wear furs and will pay high prices for them," read one of the intertitles, "many of the small animals will be trapped for their pelts."

A trunk containing some of Bert's movie material was stored for many years in the rafters of a garaged at the Perth-Andover home of his son, Paul Inside were several canisters of film (these turned out to be mostly out-takes from Bert's finished productions). There were also a number of printed intertitle cards from those productions, and, of particular interest, the typewritten scripts for two of his Associated Screen News films, *The Happy Hunting Ground* and *Tobique Secrets*.

As scripts for early Canadian silent films (they contained the text for the intertitles and described where they were to be inserted in the films), these two items, each a few pages long, were automatic artifacts. But, in addition, they offered a surprising illustration of what a small and coincident world the movie business still was a quarter-century or so after its beginnings. At the top left of each page, just below lines that read "B. E. Norrish presents" (Ben Norrish, a noted Canadian film pioneer, was Associated Screen News' first general manager), was another typed line identifying the scriptwriter. His name was Terry Ramsaye.

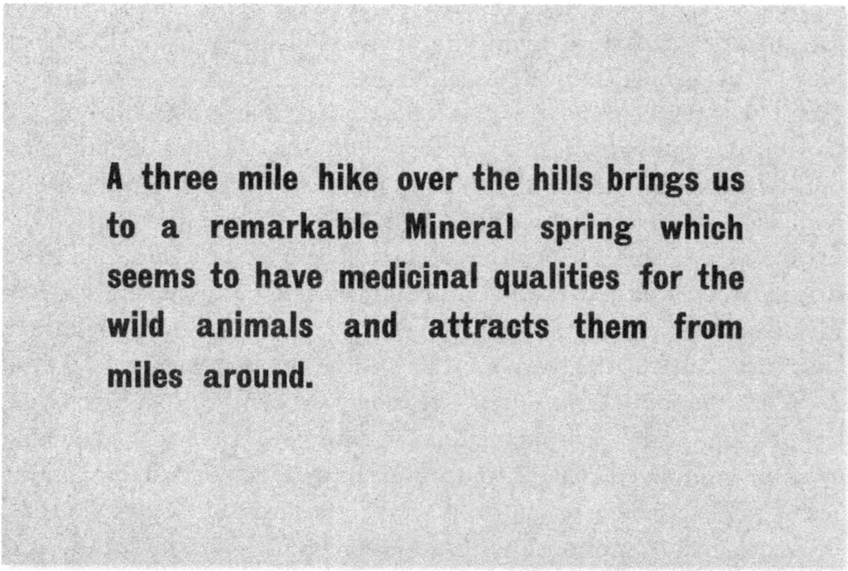

> **A three mile hike over the hills brings us to a remarkable Mineral spring which seems to have medicinal qualities for the wild animals and attracts them from miles around.**

Fig. 6.8 Intertitles that Terry Ramsaye wrote as scripts for films that Bert Moore shot. Ramsaye later wrote the first history of American motion pictures.

Terry Ramsaye's name is part of the larger history of motion pictures. In 1926, he wrote, and Simon and Schuster published, *A Million and One Nights*, a two-volume set that was the first American history of the movies. Colourfully written, Ramsaye's rendition of that history can sometimes be questioned for its accuracy (he dismissed Eadweard Muybridge's developmental work, for example, and his description of the lively events that supposedly surrounded Billy Bitzer's filming of that first artificially lighted prize fight tends to test one's gullibility). But, in its time, *A Million and One Nights* was considered a landmark achievement, and the volumes still fetch a good price for dealers in antique books.

Yet here was Ramsaye, just a few years earlier, writing freelance scripts for films that Bert Moore shot with a homemade camera way off in the forests of New Brunswick. One of Ramsaye's intertitles reads; "When a deer gets started to drinking mineral water, there is no telling when he will be home." Then, as the cervine party at the Red Brook Lick swells to a mob, another reads; "It looked like all the White Tails in Canada were coming in for a drink."

Donald Dickey's cross-continent trips to the Tobique lasted into the early twenties. There is a photograph from one of those trips that speaks eloquently of the romantic adventure that all this was. It is a picture so classic that it looks as though taken from a movie itself. Donald and his wife Florence are tenting somewhere deep in the Tobique forest. It is a night in 1921, and he, a tall man with movie star looks, is standing, pipe in his mouth, shirtsleeves rolled up, peering pensively at a blazing campfire, looking every inch a wilderness explorer. She, equally pensive, is seated on a canoe cushion on the ground beside him, her hands clasped across

Fig. 6.9 Donald R. Dickey of Pasadena, California and his wife, Florence, on their honeymoon on the Tobique River in New Brunswick.

her knees. It is, in fact, their honeymoon, a delayed one at that, and obviously a working trip, for, perched on a tripod behind them and to one side of the carefully framed picture, is a box-like motion picture camera. "Dick," is at it again, filming the animals of the Eastern forest, even as he and Florence get used to married life together.

Dickey's final trip came in 1922, and out of it came *Game Trails of the North Woods*. In January, just before he left for a lecture tour of the East, he previewed the film for several hundred members of the Valley Hunt Club in Pasadena. A story in the Pasadena *Star News* said the National Geographic Society had invited him to show his films in Washington, and other invitations had come from the American Museum of Natural History, the Columbia University Club of New York, and assorted other organizations. A special presentation was scheduled for Cleveland, Ohio, where, with the help of a mutual friend, he arranged for Adam Moore to attend so that he might introduce the old guide, now seventy-two, as the man "whose loyal help and dexterous paddle have contributed so largely to the joy and success of my North Woods work."

Despite all of this, Dickey was frustrated to the point of embitterment about one aspect of his work—his inability to get his films shown in mainstream theatres. In letters to friends, he unburdened himself explicitly, blaming those who controlled the motion picture industry and their preference for "the salacious tommy-rot that they think gets by best with the public." Still, he continued shooting movies, photographing birds, and collecting animal specimens for another dream—establishing a natural history museum in California. His collection eventually topped fifty thousand specimens, one of the last great private collections. He also kept up a correspondence with Adam Moore, typing out his letters at a desk in the comfortable study of the Dickeys' Spanish-style home in Pasadena, a study with a fireplace and a trophy moose head mounted on one wall and a caribou head on another. For his part, Moore kept him informed about Tobique happenings, including a huge forest fire that destroyed much of the area around the Nepisiguit lakes just a year after Dickey had chosen it for his final filming.

Donald Dickey often mentioned going back "up Tobique," but he never made it. In 1932, his heart finally gave out, and he died at the age of forty-five. Today, at the Los Angeles Natural History Museum, his memory is honoured with a glass-enclosed display of some of his guns, field equipment and one of his still cameras. Several tall, spectacularly plumed, and preserved birds are part of the display. On a wall opposite is a mounted *bas relief* bust of Donald Dickey.

Bert Moore's story, on the other hand, has remained largely untold. The fact that he himself was making a little movie history seems never to have occurred to him before he died in 1972, at the age of eighty-nine. Nor, apparently, did he fully appreciate the intrinsic value of his films. Years later, his son, Paul Moore, told the story of an American sport who had once offered his father forty thousand dollars for his films. Bert turned him down. "You're just trying to make a gift to me," he said.

Not long ago, the Provincial Archives of New Brunswick received a collection of the records of Bert Moore's years as a guide, outfitter, sporting camp manager, and wildlife film-maker—a gift from a great-grand-daughter, who rescued them as they were about to be carted off to a landfill. One of his homemade motion picture cameras was entrusted a few years ago to the New Brunswick Museum. Copies of his films, for which the American sport once offered him forty thousand dollars, are kept at the New Brunswick Archives and at the Library and Archives Canada in Ottawa. Other bits and pieces pop up from time to time: the rudder from a canoe on which Bert mounted a sail to use on the Tobique lakes and a collection of vintage movie promotional slides from the Specialty/Capitol Theatre in Andover where Bert sometimes showed his wildlife films. The new owners of a house that was once the home of Bert and his family found this collection in the attic.

You can also find, on a street corner down the hill and close to the river, what is left of a log cabin Bert built for one of the U.S. sportsmen's shows in the 1930s. It's a squat-looking take-out place today, and the last time I stopped there, you could get fresh-cut French fries and a good hot dog—but no hint of either the man who built it or of the remarkable things he did in the wilds of New Brunswick.

Chapter Seven

End of a Dream

The dapper young man who stepped off the train in Saint John one midsummer day in 1922 had quite a story to tell. He was an advance man, he said, for the "well-known Canadian producer" Ernest Shipman, maker of fictional "photo-plays." With several successes to his credit already, Shipman had just organized a production company in the young man's hometown of St. John's, Newfoundland. Now he was preparing to do the same in Saint John, New Brunswick.

The city's leaders listened carefully. Through the theatres and distribution centres, the movies were having some impact on Saint John, but nobody had yet made a full-fledged feature film in the city or, for that matter, in the rest of the province. So, the young Newfoundlander got the civic leaders' attention. And they, in turn, made sure they got his name. "Smallwood," he said, "J. R. Smallwood."

Thus began one of the most meaningful episodes in Canadian cinematic history. By the time it was over, Shipman's movie career was finished, and so was a bold and colourful attempt to create a home-grown film industry. Almost ninety years later, the events surrounding this attempt to make a feature motion picture down by the sea in Saint John, in 1922, still stand out as a dramatic example of why American movies have always dominated Canadian screens.

Joey Smallwood met Ernie Shipman in New York at a time when Joey was down on his luck. Not yet twenty-two and broke, he was sleeping on the marble park benches outside the New York Public Library, awaiting a promised job with *The New York Times*. A theatre operator back in St. John's had suggested he look up Shipman and try to persuade him to make a movie about Newfoundland.

Meeting him for the first time, Joey was struck by how much Shipman physically resembled the new Canadian prime minister, MacKenzie King.

Fig. 7.1 Ernie Shipman, the hustler who tried to build a Canadian movie industry.

They were roughly of the same height and build, and both had round faces with high foreheads. But that's where the similarity ended. While King was colourless and very proper, Shipman was as flamboyant as they come, a captivating dream-spinner and an ardent salesman who seemed capable of making even the most unlikely of schemes sound feasible.

Smallwood listened as Ernie outlined his approach to movie making. It cost about one hundred thousand dollars to produce a motion picture, he said, with local investors asked to put up sixty per cent of that sum and Ernie to supply the balance. Profits were divided equally.

"Do you think the people of St. John's would go for a scheme like that"?

Joey thought they would.

"Would you go down and organize them for me"?

Smallwood caught the next boat for Newfoundland, where he proceeded to line up potential backers. Later, he moved on to Saint John, Halifax, and Charlottetown and did preliminary groundwork for similar film ventures in those centres.

To the businessmen who gave him a hearing in Saint John, Smallwood's enthusiasm, destined to become so familiar to a later generation of Canadians, was evident as he rhymed off Shipman's previous photo-plays. They included *Tarzan of the Apes*, *The Romance of Tarzan*, *Lavender and Old Lace* and, filmed in various Canadian locations, *Back to God's Country*, *The Sky Pilot*, *Nomads of the North*, *Cameron of the Royal Mounted*, and *The Man from Glengarry*. He currently had film companies in Calgary, Winnipeg, Ottawa, and Sault Ste. Marie, said Joey, and Shipman's whirlwind impact on St. John's had been such that, in only a week, he'd attracted support from the city's best citizens, including the Goslings, Bowerings and Bairds.

"Mr. Shipman is a hustler, if ever there was one," declared Smallwood, meaning this as a compliment. The Newfoundland production was all set, the director, cameraman and actors would arrive in a fortnight, and, by October, a genuine Newfoundland photo-play would be in theatres, starting on an exhibition circuit that would eventually take it round the world. "So once things get started here," Smallwood told his Saint John listeners, "quick action may be looked for."

As it turned out, no Shipman movie was made in St. John's, Halifax or Charlottetown. Long afterward, Joey Smallwood said the only good "all my work in the four capitals" ever produced was that he got to know them better. But his memory was faulty. Shipman did make an East Coast movie in Saint John, and it became both his personal Waterloo and a landmark in the melancholy saga of Canadian attempts at fostering a domestic film industry.

The movie was *Blue Water*, based on a novel by Frederick Williams Wallace, who'd dashed it off several years earlier after a stormy, winter fishing trip aboard a schooner out of Portland, Maine. The tale, based on the lives of "Bay of Fundy fisherfolk," was highly moralistic and loaded with dramatic adventure, storms at sea, barroom brawls, and young love, all the essential ingredients of a successful contemporary potboiler (and indeed Wallace's book did go through several printings).

It is to Shipman's credit that he chose to base his movies on novels—and actually paid authors for the right to do so. That had not always been the practice in the rough and tumble early days of motion picture production, when film men often simply appropriated writers' work, with no thought given to compensation.

This didn't mean, though, that Ernie necessarily qualified for sainthood. Perhaps the best characterization of him came from Nell Shipman, his wife for several years in the teens, who wrote many years later; "Men like Ernie Shipman made the '90s gay—a vanished breed. He had the bounce of a rubber ball, the buoyancy of a balloon, though the first can wear out under hard usage and the last suffer ill winds and the prick of evil fortune."

Ernest Shipman was born in Hull, Quebec, in 1871, and by age 26 was running something called the Amalgamated Amusement Company, managing touring companies and honing his survival skills in the hard world of turn of the century show business. Nearly forty when he met Nell, he'd already been married three times, while she, a nervous teenager just turning eighteen, was looking for a theatre job in Seattle. In one of his better career moves, he gave her one, and she, succumbing to his blue eyes and impish grin, soon became Wife No. 4.

Life with Ernie was an adventure. After Nell became pregnant, she fretted as her delivery date approached and Ernie procrastinated in providing the nursery furniture he'd promised. Almost literally at the last moment—in the middle of a fierce storm just hours before the child was born—a truck rolled up with all the necessary child-care paraphernalia: crib, pram, high chair and bassinette. Ernie had won them in a poker game.

Another episode with an unhappier ending occurred when Ernie couldn't pay a railway bill and was thrown into jail, from which Nell had to extricate him with borrowed bail money. Even then, Ernie chastised his wife for springing him loose before he'd had a chance to clean out his cellmates, who were all rich guys behind on their alimony payments.

But if Ernie was an old fashioned trouper, Nell, too, possessed a gritty resilience, and they made a successful team. A woman of compelling, if not beautiful, looks, she developed as both an actress and a writer, just at the time Ernie began dabbling in motion picture production.

They were then living in South Pasadena, California, and only recently had the movies begun moving west. A few years earlier, almost all American films had been made in the East; Hollywood was just a rural tract of barley fields and orange groves. But in 1907, wintry weather chased a crew out of Chicago to finish filming *The Count of Monte Cristo* at Laguna Beach, south of Los Angeles, and so began the movie-makers' migration to California's year-round warmth, guaranteed sunshine, wonderfully varied landscape, and, some said, its distance from Thomas Edison in New Jersey, who was trying to stop infringements on his motion picture patents. By 1915, more than half of American movies were being produced in Hollywood.

That was the year the Shipmans caught a break when Nell, who'd been cranking out film scripts at twenty-five dollars a reel, landed a starring role in a wildlife adventure film, *God's Country and the Woman*, while also utterly captivating the story's author, James Oliver Curwood. Her charming performance on the screen led, three years later, to another Shipman-Curwood production, at the beginning of Ernie's grand attempt to start a moving picture industry in Canada.

In November 1918, the Shipmans and Curwood signed a contract giving Nell exclusive rights to the author's stories for the next two years—quite a coup since Curwood was one of the most popular writers of the day. (His output over a thirty-year period would eventually total twenty-six novels and one hundred and twenty-two movies.) The first film under the new arrangement was *Back to God's Country*, and it was to be filmed in northern Alberta.

Before Curwood met the Shipmans in Calgary to start production, Nell took Curwood's story and worked up a script that was not exactly faithful to the original. When the author read the script, he was furious. In the margins, he scribbled his comments. They included the words "Rotten!" "Crazy!" "Bunk!"

Ernie, terrified the prized author might cancel their deal when they got together, urged Nell to give in. "Agree to anything," he told her. And she, still suffering the after-effects of a bout with 1918's virulent influenza, and hardly resembling the wilderness dream girl of the movies, was ready to do just that. Then, right at the outset of their meeting, the famous author committed a terrible gaff. Pointing to the words "Iris in" on the script, he angrily declared, "There is no character in my story named Iris!"

Nell could barely stifle her laughter as she patiently explained to Curwood that "Iris in" was merely a technical term. It meant the iris on the camera lens should open slowly, like a flower, to begin a scene.

Curwood was so embarrassed by his mistake that he was as docile as a puppy for the rest of the discussion. When he and Nell finally emerged from the meeting, they were arm-in-arm. "We've added a million dollars to the picture," he proclaimed loudly.

It was shot, with great difficulty, the following March in Alberta's Peace River country. The leading man caught pneumonia and died in an Edmonton hospital. The company manager froze his feet and walked with a limp for the rest of his life. The studio carpenters quit when the temperature sank to forty-five degrees below zero. Nell, meanwhile, had to endure assorted trials, including frigid log cabins, a viciously cold night before the cameras on Lesser Slave Lake, and then, just before Mrs. C. summoned him for the train to go home, an awkward romantic advance by James Oliver Curwood.

One thing audiences certainly remembered about *Back to God's Country* was a scene in which Nell appeared *au natural*. The script had called for her to take a swim in a woodland pool, and she had intended to do the scene wearing a skin-coloured leotard. But the fabric wrinkled when it became wet, so Nell, trouper that she was, doffed the leotard. Ernie, of course, exploited the scene in his advertising, and *Back to God's Country* made half a million dollars in its first year, giving its Calgary backers a substantial return on their investment.

It was a great start, and Ernie now concocted a plan to make a series of movies right across the country. He would repeat his Calgary approach in various Canadian locations, establishing local production companies, attracting local investors, and, he hoped, realizing big returns on his films.

He would have to do it, however, without Nell. The pair split after completing *Back to God's Country*, and she eventually moved to Idaho to make wildlife films. But nothing deterred Ernie, neither Nell's departure, nor the end of the agreement with Curwood. He simply moved on to Winnipeg, where he reached agreement with Canadian author Ralph Connor to put twelve of his stories on the screen, starting with *The Foreigner*, whose title was changed to *God's Crucible*. (Getting God into the title was a good idea, and, besides, Connor was a man of the cloth.)

In a sense, Shipman's timing for making Canadian movies couldn't have been better. Ever since D. W. Griffith's great success with *The Birth of a Nation*, a clamour had been rising among Canadians for an historical epic about their country. They wanted to see their own stories on the screen, too, and the cry got louder when, during the First World War, newsreels began featuring American doughboys, who'd only entered the war in 1917, while rarely showing Canadian soldiers, who'd been fighting since 1914.

In another, crucial sense, though, Shipman's timing was terrible. Starting with *God's Crucible*, he began to have trouble getting distributors for his movies, which meant he couldn't get them into theatres. For *Back to God's Country*, a company called First National had been his distributor, but First National apparently declined his next film. So Ernie was forced to turn, under less favourable terms, to the smaller W. W. Hodkinson Corporation.

In 1914, W. W. Hodkinson, a one-time salesman for a correspondence school, had teamed with four others to form Paramount Pictures, taking as their logo a snow capped mountain in the Wasatch Range of Hodkinson's native Utah. Paramount was originally created as a distribution company, Hodkinson and his partners having correctly concluded that in this middleman's role lay the real power and profit of the moving picture business. They did very well—better, in fact, than one of their suppliers of films could tolerate.

This was a former furrier named Adolph Zukor, one of several immigrants who were drawn early to the American moving picture business by its excitement and potential for huge profit. Legend held (and there was perhaps more legend than pristine truth in early cinematic history) that Zukor's interest in the movies had initially been sparked by the first screen kiss in 1896, but in time his fascination became less prurient and more decorous. He decided that the real future of movies was in making them a respectable form of entertainment. Thus was born Zukor's Famous Players Company and its defining slogan, "Famous Players in Famous Plays." By the beginning of the First World War, Famous Players was making about fifty pictures a year, and William Hodkinson's Paramount Pictures was distributing all of them—for a very handsome percentage.

Adolph Zukor, who had worked his way up from humble beginnings, was not one to let somebody else make most of the money. Soon he bought out three of Paramount's shareholders, and then he ousted Hodkinson as president. Hodkinson tried to survive by forming the W. W. Hodkinson Corporation, but, by 1924, he was gone from the business. Beyond Zukor's voraciousness, he was victim of a trend that was changing the moving picture business. It was becoming vertically integrated, with the same companies handling all three of the previously autonomous functions of production, distribution and exhibition. Inevitably, the change was affecting Canada, too, and presently it would impact Shipman's bold plan for making Canadian films.

But if Ernie intuited impending doom, he didn't show it in Winnipeg. He completed *God's Crucible* and began filming *Cameron of the Royal Mounted*, retitled from Ralph Connor's prosaic *Corporal Cameron*. Typically sentimental, it told the story of a Scottish immigrant who runs afoul of the law, joins the Royal North West Mounted Police, fights crime, clears his name, rescues his girl. There were even real Mounties in the movie.

Next, Shipman moved on to Ottawa where, in early 1922, at the Canadian premiere of *Cameron of the Royal Mounted* before one thousand invited guests, he announced plans to film two Connor stories in the capital, *The Man from Glengarry* and *Glengarry School Days*. Both pictures were made later that year, as was another film, *The Rapids*, shot at Sault Ste. Marie. Even as his distribution problems mounted, Ernie was turning 1922 into his most productive year—and still to come was *Blue Water* in Saint John.

It is easy to imagine the excitement in the city when the news broke in the Saint John *Globe* on August 1, 1922. "Things look optimistic for the making of the first New Brunswick photo-play," read the lead to the story. "News-reels, scenics and travelogues there have been, of course, but never a connected story of the screen. Ernest Shipman, the well-known Canadian producer, is due here in a week or so to arrange for the production of the photo-play."

The story listed Shipman's previous films and described his current ventures, including a plan to make four pictures a year in Italy, and one that was said to be already in production in Mexico. As for his Canadian movie making, the story was Shipmanesque in its optimism. "There is an unfailing and ever-widening market for big, red-blooded, out-door pictures such as this producer is making, and First National [the distribution company] has asked for as many as he can produce."

This wasn't quite true, of course, but overstatement was nothing new in the movie business. Besides, parts of it *were* true. Ernie had indeed signed a contract with a company in Rome to produce four pictures a year.

Perhaps the most charitable retrospective view of Shipman in that summer of 1922 is to say that, even amid signs of the coming American squeeze on the business, he clung to the belief that, by dint of his promotional flair, he could soar above all obstacles. So, within a fortnight of Joey Smallwood's visit to Saint John, a provisional board of directors for

End of a Dream

New Brunswick Films Ltd. was formed. It included Shipman, theatre man F. G. Spencer, the clergyman-author Hiram Cody, and various prominent businessmen. "It is altogether probable that one of the Rev. H. A. Cody's stories, or possibly one of the animal or nature stories of Charles G. D. Roberts, will be next to be produced," speculated the Saint John *Globe*, again echoing Shipman. Meantime, *Blue Water* would be completed in October and be "ready for the markets of the world in November."

Heady stuff—and so was the news that Faith Green would adapt *Blue Water* for the screen. She'd worked for Shipman before and knew how to write movie scripts. She'd soon arrive in Saint John "to assemble the local incidents and atmosphere."

By the end of the second week in August, forty-five thousand dollars had been subscribed to make the movie, presumably including the thirty-five thousand Shipman said he always put in. Now a campaign began to recruit more investors. On August 23, a large advertisement appeared in the *Saint John Globe* announcing "St. John's Opportunity to Share Fortunes of Motion Picture Magnate." Shipman was described as a man whose productions had "electrified the Picture World" and were "fast earning millions." Also included were enthusiastic endorsements of him from the boards of trade of Ottawa and Sault Ste. Marie.

The ad listed the thirteen directors of New Brunswick Films Ltd., now expanded to include Lieutenant Governor William Pugsley, Premier Walter Foster, and additional merchants and businessmen. The motivation common to all of these backers—"First Citizens of the Province," Shipman called them—was boosterism; they believed the film would be good for the city and province. Hiram Cody, though, was also interested in having one of his books made into a movie, and others were drawn by Shipman's promise that "advance royalties should permit substantial dividend returns soon after mid-November."

The possibility of personal profit was a major selling point. Movies were generating fortunes, Shipman said, and it was time for Canadians, who were spending four million dollars a year on American films, to share in the largesse. Citing his own track record as a virtual guarantee of success, he declared, "There is a minimum profit of one hundred thousand dollars in each carefully made Canadian picture and considerably more than this amount has already been received from some of the more successful ones." His *Tarzan of the Apes* had grossed more than eight hundred thousand dollars, he claimed, and *Back to God's Country* had pulled in half a million.

Cameron of the Royal Mounted and *God's Crucible*, just released, had already climbed above one hundred thousand dollars. *Blue Water*, he said, was a rare opportunity that would benefit not only local investors but also merchants, hoteliers, transporters and other service providers because eighty per cent of production costs could be spent right in the city.

These claims, made in Ernie's routinely unrestrained style, contribute to one's retrospective ambivalence about him. Yes, he was a sharp operator, but his statements about the economic benefits that could accrue to a region from a motion picture have been echoed by provincial and state film promotion agencies ever since. Did that make him a visionary, too? In Saint John, he saw cinematic potential in the river's beauties, the Bay of Fundy's enormous tides, and "the picturesque buildings and places about the city." Put these attractions on the screen, he said, and the tourists will come.

This was music to the ears of the local boomers. Tourism was still a fledgling in New Brunswick in 1922. Although the railways vigorously promoted provincial travel, and a New Brunswick Summer Tourism Association had existed since before the turn of the century, the province thus far had mainly staked its reputation on the abundant hunting and fishing found in its wooded interior.

In mid-August, Faith Green arrived and, moving into rooms at the Hotel Dufferin, announced that she'd like to hear about local incidents and legends that might be worked into the script. In fact, she already had plenty to work with in Fredrick William Wallace's tale about East Coast folk whose seafaring bent was succinctly described by one of the characters; "It's in our blood, an 'tis salt water that runs in our veins."

The story revolved around young Frank "Shorty" Westhaver, a rascal of a lad left fatherless after a calamity at sea near Sable Island. Accepting the advice of his wise, old Uncle Jerry, Shorty gets a modest grade school education, even develops a taste for Longfellow's poems, then goes to sea. By his early twenties, he's a full-fledged fishing skipper, sailing out of Gloucester, Massachusetts. When his pretentious childhood sweetheart, Carrie Dexter, a nurse-in-training in Boston, dumps him for another fisherman from back home, Shorty, who normally avoids liquor, gets roaring drunk and starts sailing toward another catastrophe at Sable Island—until the ghost of his long-dead father intervenes and keeps him from striking the shoal. Winding up in hospital, Shorty has a visitor. Why, it's Miss Lily Denton, whom he'd earlier rescued from yet another storm at sea. Sure enough, love is soon a-bloomin', and this time it's real. Thus do Shorty and Lily, on a glorious August day, marry and sail into the sunset. Iris out. The End.

Beginning in mid-August, excitement fairly bubbled in Saint John's newspapers as Shipman and his associates planted story after story. Especially compelling were the testimonials from people like former Mayor Schofield, who said he'd become a large shareholder and president of New Brunswick Films because, yes, he wanted to make some money, but mainly because he felt a responsibility as a citizen. "It is up to all of us, not only in the city but the province as well, to put our attractions on the screen." Because movies were "the main thing today with people," a picture like *Blue Water* could do more to advertise New Brunswick than any other means.

"Personally," declared Premier Walter Foster, "I feel that here is our opportunity at last to have something big done for our province and incidentally our pocketbooks, an opportunity that should be made good on by every businessman with a sense of citizenship and enterprise."

To these earnest civic leaders, the making of *Blue Water* was New Brunswick's long-awaited Big Break. After the brief bloom of the immediate post-Confederation period, the province had lapsed into being a largely overlooked backwater. It was like the young beauty behind the soda bar, longing to be "discovered." It had been a long wait. But now here came the movie man, promising to make her a star.

The businessmen and politicians pledged their honour to Shipman. Foster; "Very obviously I could not lend my support unless the undertaking showed itself certain in every way of fulfilling its purpose." Schofield; "A notable thing about this company is its clean financing." And Foster again; "The best is none too good for us, and we have it. Mr. Shipman's producing organization and record stands out by itself. No other has done what he has done, coming back to Canada and putting over one success after another right across Canada without a break."

The testimonials were intended to draw investors to *Blue Water*. Shipman estimated a sum of ninety-nine thousand dollars was needed. With J. M. Robinson and Sons and Eastern Securities handling the stock issue, shares were sold at one hundred dollars each, payable in three installments, the last due on October 1. By the end of August, half of the financing had been arranged. Three weeks later, another advertisement urged procrastinators to hurry "because a sudden closing of the [share]

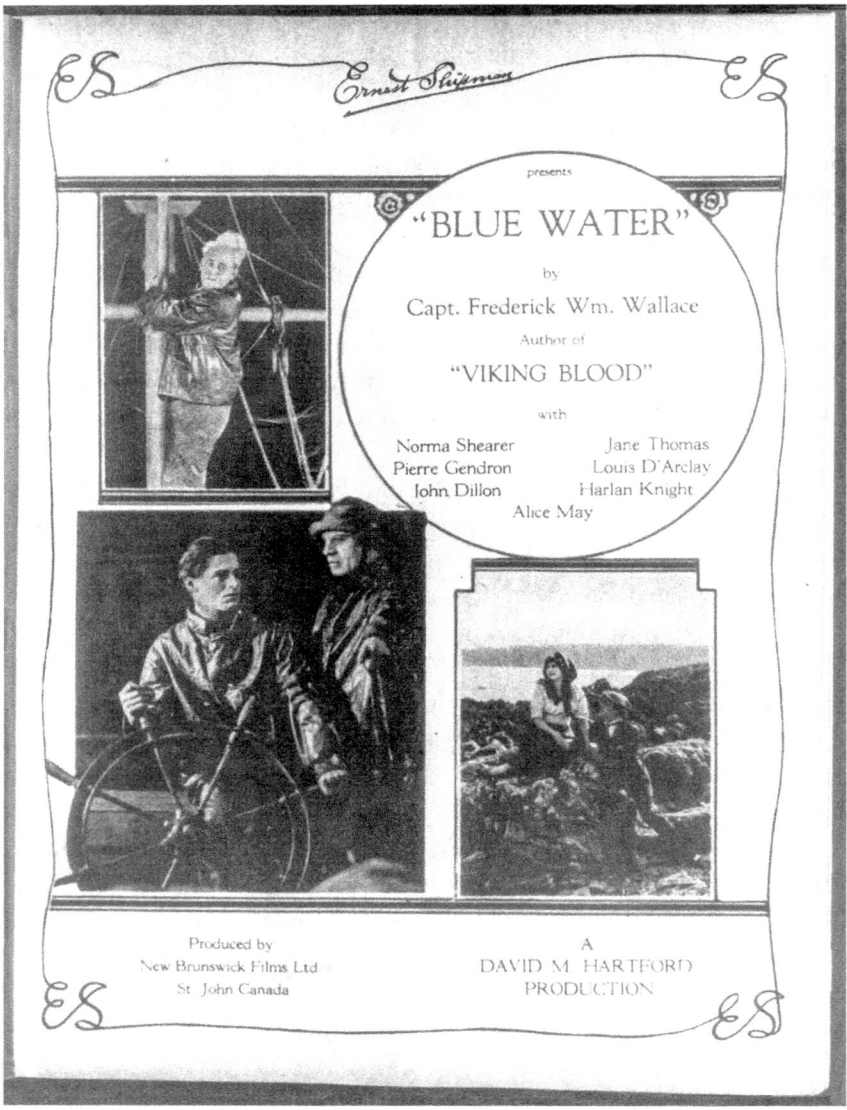

Fig. 7.2 Advertisement for Blue Water *shown in Saint John in mid-April, 1924. It was not commercially successful and marked the end of Shipman's bold attempt to establish a Canadian film industry. The ad is one of the few remaining traces of Ernie Shipman's last Canadian movie that was screened only a few times in Saint John and no longer exists.*

End of a Dream

list is seriously contemplated"—probably a prod intended to stimulate lagging sales.

Meanwhile, the production crew arrived, led by David M. Hartford, a veteran actor and stage and film director who had directed *Back to God's Country* and two other Curwood stories. He'd also directed *The Rapids* at Sault Ste. Marie. A tall, handsome man with curly, silvered hair, Hartford had previously worked with two of the largest American moving picture companies, the Thomas Ince organization and the Essanay company of Chicago. Like Shipman, Hartford claimed his films had never lost money. If a picture was good enough to be released, he said, it was bound to make money. "The release of *Blue Water*," he declared, "is an assured thing in three months, and there is just the question of which is the best [place], where the least competition lies…"

James MacMurray, one of the local brokers, took screenwriter Faith Green on a motor tour of the countryside around Saint John, seeking a typical fishing village as a setting for the film; she especially liked Lorneville, just down the coast, where a gleaming white church stood atop a hill overlooking the Bay of Fundy. It provided a wonderfully romantic setting, and the writer imagined the film opening with humble fisherfolk emerging from the church after Sunday services.

"You know," said Hartford, "we could have faked this picture down off either the coast of Florida or California, but we could never have caught the atmosphere or quaintness of the life as it really is round these parts." Authenticity was desirable because, "Your fishermen are soldiers in every day life and the hardiest, bravest of men, living the high life and humble." To help the movie-makers get it right, Frederick William Wallace even provided two reels he had shot of the fishing fleet on the high seas.

From the crew's headquarters at the Hotel Dufferin, on King's Square in the centre of the city, Hartford's long-time assistant Gavin Young put out the word that the picture required extras to fill minor roles. Aspiring Mary Pickfords and Douglas Fairbanks were advised to contact him immediately.

Blue Water's cast included actors Hartford had worked with before as well as newcomers. Among the last group was an aspiring young actress whom he probably interviewed in early September when he and Young reviewed the script with Wallace in New York. This young woman, who had just turned twenty-two, had previously had bit parts in several movies, including D.W. Griffith's *Way Down East*. But Griffith had offered no

encouragement for her career, and Florenz Ziegfeld also had rejected her for his Follies. So her main renown to date was as the Springfield Tire and Rubber Company's billboard girl, Miss Lotta Miles.

But the actress, whose name was Norma Shearer, was a determined young woman, and it is a lesson in life's improbabilities that, of all the people involved with *Blue Water*, she would be the one to become famous. She may have got the job because she was a Canadian, born in Montreal, and because she had a sharp agent, Edward Small, who also launched the careers of actresses Clara Bow and Corinne Griffith. For *Blue Water*, she was chosen to play Lily Denton, Shorty Westhaver's true-blue sweetheart.

Shooting on the film began around the end of September. Walter Golding, who never missed a promotional opportunity, scheduled a screening of Shipman's *Cameron of the Royal Mounted*, and took out newspaper ads connecting that movie to *Blue Water*.

Had nothing more than boosterism been required, *Blue Water* would have been a great success. But another thing needed was decent weather, a definite uncertainty at that time of year on the Bay of Fundy, and, sure enough, the weather turned wet and miserable soon after the film-making began. In early October, half an inch of snow fell just one hundred miles up the coast, a portent of things to come. A month later, the entire province was blanketed. By then, many days had already been lost to the weather, and the crew had slowly come to the realization that they couldn't finish the picture in Saint John. Mention of the film also disappeared from the local press, probably a sign that things weren't going well generally.

Meanwhile, Ernie Shipman, on the night before Halloween, showed up in Sault Ste. Marie for the premiere of *The Rapids*. Ten thousand people reportedly lined up to see the film. Their enthusiasm, however, apparently did not impress Hodkinson, the distributor, who took another six months to release the film commercially.

In late November, Shipman was in London, Ontario, telling the local Canadian Club about the Bluenose tales he was expecting to put on the screen. The speech was instructive about what Ernie perceived as the Canadian opportunity in films. The United States, he told his audience,

Fig. 7.3 (facing page) Canadian film star Norma Shearer, lead actress in Blue Water, *who went on to an illustrious film career in the U.S., nominated six times for academy awards, wining an Oscar in 1930 for best actress in* The Divorcee.

had gone through a period at the outset when motion pictures were in the hands of tasteless and unintelligent exploiters. But Canada had been spared this unsavoury beginning. This country was poised to jump into the business at a more sophisticated stage. There were no censorship problems to overcome, no undesirable traditions to live down. We could simply put our ideals and achievements on the screen for the world to see. Moviegoers in many nations would come to appreciate Canada as a place not just of ice and snow, but of bountiful harvests and wonderful living conditions.

In a supreme bit of irony brought on by the weather, *Blue Water* had to be completed in Tampa, Florida. Sometime in early 1923, a print, possibly a rough cut, came back to Saint John. Reverend Hiram Cody joined the other shareholders for a private screening at the Imperial. Afterward, he wrote in his diary, "It is very good." But a month later, following a meeting of New Brunswick's Film's directors, he recorded a more somber entry; "It looks as if we are to lose everything."

In late February, there was another screening, after which the shareholders dispatched Fred Spencer and another envoy to New York to have new film subtitles made for their silent film. A fortnight later, they opted to put up more money, and Cody, for one, "went bond for $500 extra."

Apart from any technical or artistic weaknesses in *Blue Water*, the biggest problem Shipman and his entire Canadian movie venture faced was the squeeze imposed by the Americans. Borrowing the techniques of chain stores (centralize functions, spread costs over more operations), the American leaders of the industry were, step by step, seizing control of it. This process, which had begun about 1914, was nearing completion in 1923. When the dust settled, these new-bloom moguls would control not only the making of movies but also the exchanges that distributed them and the theatres that showed them. For outside, independent producers like Ernie Shipman, the practical effect was to cut them out of the loop, or at least prevent them from getting adequate returns for their films.

In March, 1923, Ernie took out a sixteen-page advertising section in *The Moving Picture World*. Designed to promote his films, including *Blue Water*, the section began with a picture of Shipman in a defiant, bulldog-like pose and boldly proclaimed his plans to defy the "trusts" and "booking combines" and market the pictures at home and abroad. Under the heading "TELLING THE TRUTH IN PICTURES," he called on Canadians "to get behind the local exhibitors in boosting those dramas of

End of a Dream

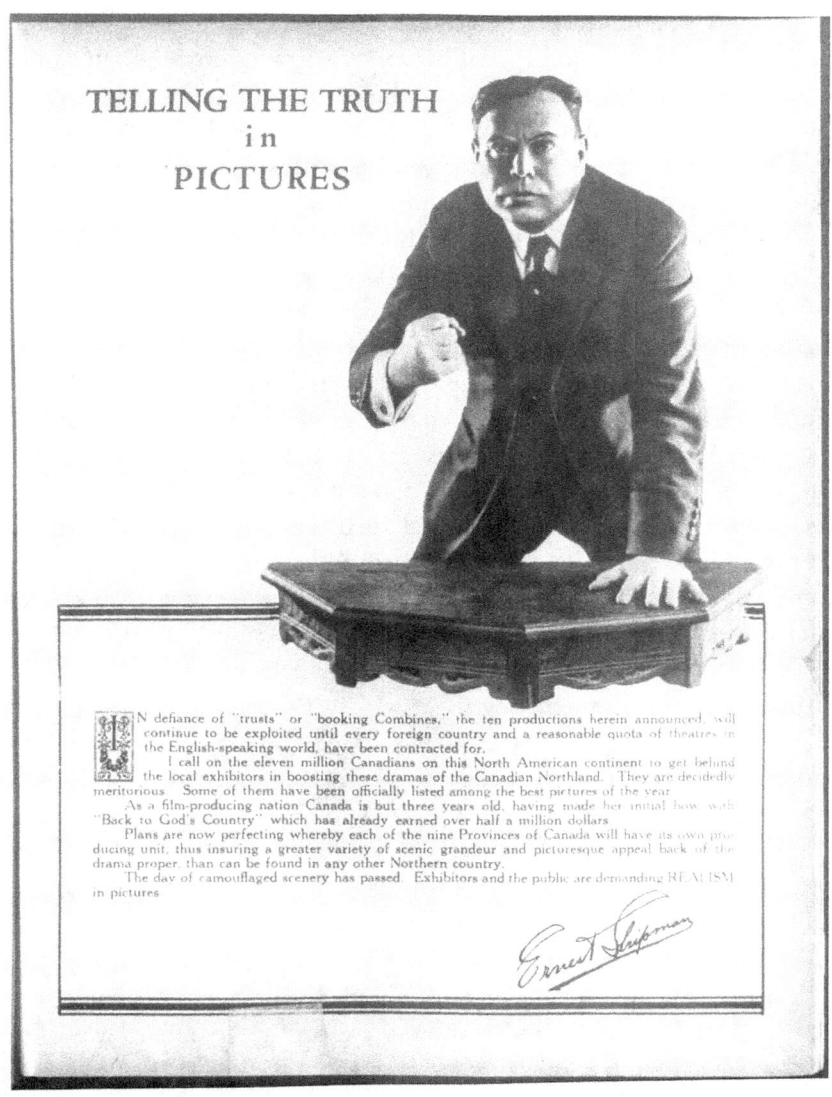

Fig. 7.4 "Telling the Truth," the first of sixteen pages of advertising taken by Ernie Shipman in the Moving Picture World. *It was followed by ads on all of Shipman's movies and was intended to get bookings of the movies in theatres.*

the Canadian Northland. They are decidedly meritorious. Some of them have been officially listed among the best pictures of the year."

Stretching the truth (or perhaps hoping against hope), he also declared. "Plans are now perfecting whereby each of the nine Provinces of Canada will have its own producing unit, thus insuring a greater variety of scenic grandeur and picturesque appeal back of the drama proper, than can be found in any other northern country. The day of camouflaged scenery has passed. Exhibitors and the public are demanding REALISM in pictures."

What stood in his way, though, were those trusts and booking combines, run by men whose mild appearances belied their monopolistic movie business ambitions. In a 1975 book, *Movie-Made America*, culture historian and critic Robert Sklar described them as "balding little men in dark double-breasted suits" who peer out benignly from black and white 1920s photographs. "No one who feared or contested their power, however, would have been fooled by such diffident poses," said Sklar. "Behind those affable masks, they were convinced, lurked ruthless calculating minds, vast ambitions and imperial lifestyles: palatial mansions, chauffeured limousines, private tennis courts, million dollar incomes. These men were the moguls whose daily commands shaped the national consciousness." Sklar could have broadened this to *international* consciousness, because, from the very beginning, the movie men regarded Canada as merely an extension of their American fiefdom.

This attitude was never more egregiously demonstrated than it was during a visit to Toronto by Lewis Selznick in 1922. A one-time colleague of Louis B. Mayer, who in time came to despise him, Selznick apparently saw himself as a kind of movieland plenipotentiary, ready to dispense at will advice to a country not his own. Canadians should forget about making feature films, he said, and concentrate instead on "government scenic releases," taking care to inject more humour and human interest, so lacking in previous efforts. This done, and with a "generous immigration policy, the country will forge ahead fast."

Canada didn't have a big enough population to support homegrown feature films, he advised, and it shouldn't expect to be able to export its movies; "You cannot hope for business success if you look for profits outside your own land." And then came this; "If Canadian stories are worthwhile for making into pictures, companies will be sent to Canada to make them."

Nearly ninety years after these words were uttered, they still flame off the page. If said today, they would, one hopes and expects, provoke a great outcry in Canada and an international *contretemps*. Yet things haven't changed that much. Canadian films, with rare exception, are still a hard sell at home and abroad. Our obsequious rapture with Hollywood continues.

What Selznick didn't explain in 1922 is that Canadian filmmakers couldn't "hope for business success" beyond their borders because the American system wouldn't permit it. Even within Canada, the production-distribution-exhibition loop was closing. Soon after Selznick's visit, *The Moving Picture World* reported that Famous Players Canadian Corporation, which was, in effect, the northern arm of Adolph Zukor's U.S. conglomerate, was about to buy Canada's largest theatre chain.

Zukor had already, between 1919 and 1921, brought six hundred U.S. theatres into his vertically integrated Famous Players-Paramount orbit. Now the fifty-house chain owned by brothers Jule and Jay Allen, driven to bankruptcy by the American-financed competition, was ripe for the picking. Three years earlier, none other than Lord Beaverbrook, the former Max Aitken of New Brunswick, had tried to rescue the Allens with an infusion of British money, but the offer was declined. Now, with completion of the Allen sale to Famous Players, the Americans made a giant leap into the Canadian market.

Ernie Shipman fought on. An article highly sympathetic to him appeared in, of all places, Henry Ford's newspaper, *The Dearborn Independent*. It disparaged those controlling the film industry as "recent graduates from the cloak and suit trade [who] seem to consider themselves peculiarly qualified to set the standards." The story also enlarged upon what had become the standard Shipman litany—that, in 1923, he had "already arranged to make pictures in Halifax, Vancouver, Charlottetown, and St. John's, Newfoundland" and had "tentative plans" to make others in Montreal, Toronto, Hamilton, London and Windsor.

It was just puffery; the films were never made. Even *Blue Water* languished for another year before finally having a premiere in Saint John. That event, in mid-April, 1924, was decidedly low-key, suggesting lost money and dashed dreams. Even the formerly sycophantic Saint John *Globe* sank its four-paragraph "review" to the bottom of an inside page and damned the film with faint praise. "For a first attempt at putting on a St. John picture," said the paper, "*Blue Water* is by no means unsatisfactory. On the contrary, it is well done and should be especially interesting to inland communities where the billowy salty air is not so commonplace as it is with us." There was no mention of Ernie Shipman being at the premiere; he probably wasn't there.

Blue Water was his last movie, the end of his great pan-Canadian cinematic adventure. Never again would a Canadian filmmaker attempt such an audacious and grandiose scheme. He was something of a rogue, to be sure, but it obviously took someone like him to try and compete with the voracious likes of Adolph Zukor, Lewis Selznick, Louis B. Mayer and the others, who, backed by enormous resources, were determined to absorb Canada into their film empires—and who, of course, ultimately succeeded. Shipman had courage; he is, on balance, a sympathetic character in Canadian cinematic history.

Blue Water, the movie, disappeared, possibly disintegrating into dust in some forgotten corner between Saint John and Florida, where Barry Shipman, Ernie's son, long afterward remembered once having seen it. Its making, though, was a milestone, the moment when it became obvious that creating a truly Canadian film industry had become impossible. By 1924, ninety-five per cent of moving pictures shown in Canada were American, and it's been that way, more or less, ever since. The failure of *Blue Water* and the circumstances surrounding it are themselves the stuff of a feature film—which, of course, has never been made.

More than three-quarters of a century later, all that remains of this little drama-within-a-drama are a few arresting frames which, summoned to the mind's eye and imagined as the closing sequences of a moving picture as the credits roll, reveal to us snippets of the principal characters' future lives....

Here, for instance, is Joey Smallwood, somehow looking right in black and white. Leaving the movies behind, he soon resumes his career as a journalist and aspiring socialist in New York. Then, drawn back home by the magnetic Rock, he becomes a bit of everything: publisher, union organizer, broadcaster, farmer, and, finally, a politician who sees joining Canada as Newfoundland's last, best hope....

Here is Walter Foster, the boyish premier of New Brunswick who, in 1922, enthusiastically urged all businessmen "with a sense of citizenship and enterprise" to back *Blue Water*. By early 1923, he is in such personal financial difficulty that he has to give up the premier's job....

An image looming up from Saint John's Union Club is of a goodbye party for the *Blue Water* director, David Hartford, in late October 1922. As Hartford is saying his farewells, the Reverend Hiram A. Cody, hoping one of his stories can become a moving picture, approaches and gives Hartford four of his books. It is a poignant moment. Cody lost a good deal of money on *Blue Water*, and no story of his ever became a film. Hartford himself didn't direct again for four years....

End of a Dream

A career moving in the opposite direction is that of Norma Shearer. Even as the *Blue Water* venture is unravelling in the spring of 1923, she is on a transcontinental train bound for California. In Hollywood, Louis Mayer arranges a screen test for her. Then, she meets Mayer's protégé, Irving Thalberg, marries him, and by the 1930s is the reigning queen of Metro-Goldwyn-Mayer Studios. Among the millions who thrill to her screen performances is a poor, illegitimate fifteen-year-old Argentine village girl, the future Eva Peron, who sees Shearer's *Marie Antoinette* six times, and dreams that someday she might become an actress, too....

Finally, there is the fading image of Ernie Shipman. Still irrepressible and resolute even after his Canadian dream ends, he tries other filmmaking ventures in Morocco, on Long Island, New York, in Florida and England. None work. By the late twenties, he is living in New York City with his fifth wife and is an agent for a prizefighter, William (Young) Stribling. There, in Jackson Heights, Queens, he dies in August 1931, on the eve of his tenth wedding anniversary. Death is attributed to cirrhosis of the liver. He gets a five-paragraph obituary in *The New York Times*, and, in an irony nobody could have appreciated better than he, no mention at all in major papers north of the border.

Chapter Eight

A Movie Mogul Comes Home

The villagers weren't much interested that a Hollywood movie mogul would shortly be arriving in their midst. The big news in Harvey Station on this May morning in 1939 was that, at the previous day's competition in the village's annual cattle show, a cow named Puppy's Idella had been crowned Grand Champion Female, and this only a few hours after she'd given birth to a fine calf. Now *that* was really something. Come to think of it, it was like something out of the movies.

What a few people did notice was that, not long before an Eastbound train was due in that morning, two leading politicians from Fredericton had arrived at the station by automobile. They were John B. McNair, New Brunswick's attorney general, and Fred W. Pirie, the minister of lands and mines. They had come to welcome the prominent visitor to the province and escort him back to the capital.

Presently, the whistle of the steam locomotive sounded, and the train came winding along the edge of Harvey Lake and into the village. The politicians watched for their man as the passenger coaches slowed to a stop in front of the depot, and then spotted him as he descended from his car. He had a few pals with him, but it was easy to single out Louis B. Mayer. He had the kind of face and portly physique that one remembered from newspaper and magazine photos.

Mayer ran Hollywood's most successful studio, Metro-Goldwyn-Mayer, and his arrival in New Brunswick hadn't happened by chance. The provincial government and the University of New Brunswick had been working on it for months, especially the university. The genesis of the trip went back even further, to three years earlier, perhaps, when Mayer had paid a brief, nostalgic visit to Saint John, where he had lived as a boy.

Newspapers reported on how pleased he was to revisit his old haunts and the joy it brought him to be "back home." It was something a few people in the province didn't forget.

At the University of New Brunswick, in Fredericton, things had not been going well. The Great Depression had taken its toll. Campus buildings were showing their age, but the administration had decreed that only the most critical repairs could be made. Deficits were rising, and things were so tight that, during spring examinations, University President C. C. ("C-squared") Jones, normally the most genial of men, had taken to touring the aisles of the room where seniors sat writing their exams. At certain desks, he would stop, lean in, and whisper a terse message into the occupant's ear; unless arrangements were made immediately to pay the balance owing on his or her tuition, the student would not be allowed to graduate. That's how bad the situation was for the university. What could be done? Then, somebody had an idea. Out in Hollywood was Louis B. Mayer, the former New Brunswicker recently described in the press as the highest paid executive in the United States. Why not award him an honorary degree? Who knows what good fortune might flow from that simple deed?

So it was duly arranged. There had been an exchange of letters in which Jones had invited Mayer to come to Fredericton to receive his degree at the spring graduation, and Mayer, after some delay, for which he apologized, had accepted with gushing enthusiasm. Now here he was, a few months later, being greeted by two important politicians who'd driven out from the city to show just how warm and welcoming New Brunswick could be to one of its own.

Louis Mayer never knew his precise date of birth, although he did understand that it occurred in the Russian Ukraine, about 1885. His birth name was Meir, Lazar Meir, and he had emigrated as a child, with his mother Sarah and father Jacob, first to London, then to New York, and finally up the coast to Saint John, New Brunswick, where there was an established Jewish community. In Saint John, Louis went to elementary school, the only formal education he ever received. He also got instruction in Judaism. A photograph from those years shows him as a sweet young boy draped in a prayer shawl and wearing a fedora and a white bow tie; the occasion was his bar mitzvah, at age thirteen.

He may also have seen his first motion picture in Saint John, at the Opera House, but in truth he had little time for frivolity. As soon as he was old enough, he joined his father in the junk and salvage business that had given Jacob a toehold on the city's stony headlands. A document that found its way to the university archives hints at the possibility that they did rather well. It is a contract letter, dated January 10, 1903, and signed by J. and L.B. Mayer, with which they hired one G. W. Stevens of Saint John to work for them as an engineer and "all-round superintendent" at a wage of $6.50 for a six-day week. Stevens would also be able to live fuel- and-rent free "in one of the houses on the land at Coldbrook, NB [east of Saint John] owned by us..."

The work also contributed, in its own way, to Louis' further education. He learned about being tough, about wheeling and dealing, and at least a few things about construction. Years later, when he was building on the beach in California, he insisted that pilings be placed under both the house and the swimming pool, lest it all tumble into the sea. "My father knew all about pilings from New Brunswick," his daughter Irene recalled.

Returning to Fredericton from Harvey Station, the two politicians found it easy to converse with their guest. Both were steeped in the lore of New Brunswick. The driver, John B. McNair, was a lawyer, current attorney general of the province, and a future premier. His colleague, Fred W. Pirie, was an up-country potato man, the current minister of lands and mines, a future Canadian senator. As McNair drove his car into the low hills that framed the village, they pointed out the rolling pastureland, nascent with fresh green, that helped make Harvey a dairy centre and nurtured the likes of Puppy's Idella. Later, descending a long hill into the St. John Valley, they took in the spectacle of the mighty river, still running near full springtime spate.

There were larger events to talk about, too. The news from Europe was not good. Adolph Hitler had just toured Germany's defensive Siegfred Line, and *Der Angriff*, Joseph Goebbel's propaganda organ, had taunted, "Anyone who believes he can overrun the Siegfred wall will bleed to death." Great Britain announced it would call up forty to fifty thousand conscripts on July 1. For the moment, though, the world was still at peace, and a few hundred miles to the west, the King and Queen of England arrived on this very day in Quebec City to begin the most famous Royal Tour in Canadian history.

In Fredericton, the population of the old Loyalist capital was being exhorted to get ready for the royal couple, who were due to stop there the following month. "Be Prepared for Royal Visit," said a sign in the window of McMurray's stationery store, amid a display of banners, bunting, crepe streamers, and photographs of the royal family that would have done proud a shop in London. Arriving in the city, Mayer, along with three friends who accompanied him from the States, were taken to its best hotel, an old-fashioned country hostelry called the Queen. Over the years, everyone from big-league baseball players to members of America's leading financial families had stayed there, but Mayer was its first movie mogul guest, and he was treated with appropriate deference.

The first formal event of the visit was a noon luncheon, which allowed time for Mayer to stroll through Fredericton's compact downtown with his three old pals and comrades-in-arms. David Stoneham was a Boston lawyer who, a quarter-century earlier, had helped Louis acquire regional distribution rights in New England for D.W. Griffith's *Birth of a Nation*, which effectively launched him on the road to riches. Another was J. F. T. O'Connor, a former comptroller of currency for the United States Government and a good political friend. Three years earlier, he'd persuaded Republican Mayer not to lead the Hollywood movie colony in opposing Democratic President Franklin Delano Roosevelt's bid for re-election; Mayer's reward was an invitation to the White House. The third member of the party was the legendary publicity man and Mayer loyalist, Howard Strickling, who probably had shared more of Louis' best and worst moments than anybody else.

Since all of these men had a connection to the movies, it seems reasonable that they should check out what was playing at Fredericton's two theatres, both close at hand. At the Capitol, which Fred Spencer had built a couple of decades earlier, the feature was *Son of Frankenstein*, a Universal Studios picture starring Bela Lugosi and Boris Karloff. On adjacent Queen Street, the larger Gaiety Theatre was showing *Dramatic School*, starring Paulette Goddard and Luise Rainer.

Seeing a poster for a Luise Rainer film was sure to stir mixed emotions in Mayer. She had been celebrated as one his many "discoveries" in the early thirties, although she was already a leading actress in the German cinema before he brought her to the U.S., where, he insisted, she change her birthplace to Vienna (from Dusseldorf) and her nationality to Austrian. Beautiful, smart, opinionated, she had been an instant success, winning Academy Awards in her second and third films. Just as quickly, she began to irritate Mayer with her opinions on everything from fascism to set designs. Most galling of all was the relationship she began with the socialist playwright Clifford Odets. On Oscar Night, 1937, when she was chosen best actress for her performance in *The Great Ziegfeld*, she was a no-show on Odets' advice that the Academy Awards (which had been started by Mayer) represented capitalism at its most unseemly. Then she and Odets raised quite a fuss when Mayer dispatched Strickling to drag her to the ceremony. The scene was repeated, more or less, the following year when she won again (for *The Good Earth*). She also accused Mayer of being soft on Nazism, and she was difficult on the set of *Dramatic School*. So he fired her. She would make only one more picture in America and later offered a caustic summary of her life in Hollywood; "For my second and third pictures, I won Academy Awards. Nothing worse could have happened to me."

Mayer got into the motion picture business in Haverhill, Massachusetts, a gloomy textile town north of Boston, where he arrived in 1907. There, using borrowed money, he bought or leased an old burlesque house that was named The Gem but was in such decrepit condition that locals had taken to calling it The Germ. Mayer refurbished it, did well enough to be able to persuade two local businessmen to help him build a new and larger theatre, and ultimately gained control of all of Haverhill's theatre business. After a failed attempt to become a theatrical producer in New York, he came back to Massachusetts and branched into motion picture distribution and production, getting an early taste of the benefits of controlling the picture process from start to finish.

In 1915, D.W. Griffith and Billy Bitzer completed *The Birth of a Nation*. Griffith was at a pre-release reception in New York when he was interrupted by a telephone call. It was Louis Mayer offering him fifty thousand dollars and a fifty-fifty split after expenses for New England distribution rights to the picture. *The Birth of a Nation* became the industry's first blockbuster, and Mayer made half a million dollars. Some people said he had fudged the books to turn that kind of profit.

After that, Mayer started producing his own pictures. His first effort was an eighteen-episode serial, *The Great Secret,* with Francis X. Bushman and Beverly Bayne. Unknown today, except by cinephiles, they were the period's most romantic couple, on the screen and off, and Miss Bayne's comely image—to add a New Brunswick twist—once graced a chocolate box put out by Ganong Bros., the venerable candy making company of St. Stephen, NB. *The Great Secret*, though, was a box office failure and marked the beginning of the actors' descent into obscurity.

Undeterred, Mayer next raided the successful Vitagraph studio and stole one of its biggest stars, Anita Stewart. Lawsuits ensued, but again Mayer was unfazed. He joined the Select Pictures Corporation, which introduced him to the ways of the infamous Lewis Selznick, who later would offer unsolicited advice to Canadians about who should make their movies. In time, Mayer came to detest Selznick, not for that reason, but simply on general principles. Selznick's son David eventually married Louis' daughter Irene, but the breach never really healed; a grudge is a grudge.

Following the lead of other moviemakers, Mayer, in 1918, moved to California. He made his first films at the so-called Selig Zoo, where producer William Selig kept a menagerie of animals. Half a dozen years later, Louis caught a break when Marcus Loew, who owned a chain of theatres, decided he needed a better source of pictures to compete with Adoph Zukor's Paramount operation. So he bought Metro, one of Mayer's former companies, and began negotiations to acquire another outfit, Goldwyn Pictures. He asked his lawyer, Robert Rubin, whom he should get to run the studio. The tall, refined Rubin recommended short, unrefined Louis. The new enterprise was called Metro-Goldwyn-Mayer.

There was a period of crisis in 1927 when Marcus Loew died suddenly, and the new boss of the controlling company, Nicholas Schenk, tried to sell the studio. (All he knows about movies you could stick in a cat's ass, Mayer once said of Schenk.) No deal was made, and in the Great Depression year of 1931, MGM made twelve million dollars. Soon it would be the best motion picture studio in Hollywood.

Louis Mayer was tough and pugnacious. Biographies and articles are peppered with instances where he resorted to his fists in arguments. At the same time, he was sentimental, even to the point of being maudlin, a contradiction in his make up that was abundantly on display during his 1939 visit to New Brunswick. He had already shown it some months earlier, after University president, Dr. Jones, wrote to him with the offer of an honorary degree. Replying "with a deep sense of gratitude," Mayer couldn't resist adding a line that sounded like it came from a cornball movie script; "The mere mention of the name of the Province," he told Dr. Jones, "brings to my heart the strains of my favourite melody, 'Home Sweet Home'."

This hardly accords with accounts of his early life authored long afterward and in distant places. In his 1988 book, *An Empire of Their*

Own, American writer and film critic, Neal Gabler, says Louis lived on Main Street in Saint John under conditions so deplorable that "Mayer himself preferred to forget these years, and he was vague about them even to his wife and children." Although regularly taunted by anti-Semite louts, he was said finally to have left New Brunswick, with the support of his mother, mainly to escape the tyranny and exploitation of his father.

Within the province, the portrayal has usually been more benign. The family had been "humble," to be sure, but well respected. A former banker turned prominent businessman remembered the firm of Jacob Mayer and Son as a well-regarded account. Sarah Mayer was described in her 1913 obituary as "an extremely charitable and beloved lady." Popular stories also emerged about Louis' days in elementary school and teachers he fondly recalled for their kindness. One teacher remembered the day she asked her pupils what they'd do if they had twenty dollars, and while other kids said they'd buy bicycles and ponies, little Louis Mayer said he'd go into business. Perhaps that was why he acquired a little red wagon that became part of the Mayer mythology. He used it in the salvage

Fig. 8.1 Louis B. Mayer (left), motion picture magnate, who grew up in Saint John, receives a complimentary angling license from Hon A.A. Dysart (right), Premier of New Brunswick, in the Assembly Chamber of the Legislative Building at Fredericton, May 1938.

business, and, lo and behold, before long he had two hundred men working for him—another tale difficult to reconcile with the family's supposed impoverished state and the fact that he was still a teenager when he supposedly had all these people in his employ.

One has to be careful with the folklore that springs up around the rich and famous. From the beginning, Hollywood was a make-believe place, not all of it on the screen—the story of the red wagon appeared in an MGM press release. Success in the movie business depended on marketing, and Louis Mayer was the ultimate marketeer. He gave the people what they wanted, whether it was an anecdote about a wagon, or, in New Brunswick, in 1939, a discourse on the joys of being "home" again.

At the noontime luncheon at the Queen Hotel in Fredericton, he reminded his audience that he had a "great investment" in New Brunswick. That investment was his mother, in her grave in Saint John. "I'm coming home to mother," he said. "I am sentimental enough to feel she knows I am being honoured by my home folks. I believe she knows and is smiling. My heart is overflowing. Money comes, and money goes, but I'm the richest man in the world because I have more truly sincere friends all over the world than any man I know. I am thankful to you, thankful I came from you, and thankful I have come back to you." Later, before another audience in Saint John, he went further; "I talked with [my mother] this morning, and I believe she heard me."

If Mackenzie King, the Canadian prime minister, could converse with his dead dog, I suppose Louis Mayer could talk to his deceased mother. One thing undeniable is that her son had a strong attachment to Sarah. In life, she was a comforting counterpoint to harsh and uncompromising Jacob, and, in death, she became Louis' celestial moral compass.

In October 1913, he had dashed home from Boston to join his siblings and Jacob at her bedside as she lay dying, aged sixty-two, in the Saint John General Hospital. Her death, which was attributed to complications following an operation, stung the family, none more than Louis, whose worship of her in the afterlife was part of a reverence that he came to accord all mothers. He supposedly once decked the actor John Gilbert after the latter referred to his own mother as a whore.

After the sad 1913 trip, Mayer did not return to New Brunswick, so far as anybody knows, for another twenty-three years. Then, in 1936, he came to Saint John for a brief stay during which he walked the familiar streets of his boyhood, visited his mother's grave, and was honoured at a dinner where the head table guests included the city's mayor, the province's chief justice, as well as Fred Spencer, Alice Fairweather, and Walter Golding. It was this trip that seemed to rekindle the notion of Saint John as Mayer's home. In a fawning piece written for a local newspaper, Golding told how, in advance of the "homecoming," Mayer's voice had "almost cracked with emotion at the prospect of once again treading the streets he plodded to school and viewing with the eyes of a grandfather the humble scenes

Fig. 8.2 Walter H. Golding and his wife, Lillian (neé Whelpley) – probably taken during their visit to Hollywood in 1937 where Mayer ensured they saw the highlights and invited them to his fourth of July birthday party. Golding, impresario, publicist, theatre manager, and Saint John booster and activist, promoted theatre and movies in Saint John for nearly 40 years.

of his happy childhood and the genesis of his youthful business career." Golding, who obviously didn't blush easily, also wrote about the "reactions of possessiveness" Saint John moviegoers had whenever the trademark roaring lion announced the start of another MGM feature in their theatres.

The following year, Golding, still managing the Imperial Theatre, got his reward—a trip to Hollywood as Mayer's guest. There he met movie stars, toured the studio lot, watched film scenes being shot, even got a peek into Mayer's office and a chance to sit in the emperor's chair, which he said was "like a private in the army climbing into the king's throne." He also looked up a few former Saint John residents, including Donald Gunn, who worked as a cartoonist for Walt Disney and gave Golding a late-night tour and an introduction to the fledgling world of film animation.

But his biggest thrill came on July 4, when he got invited to the birthday party for Mayer given by the director Clarence Brown and his wife on the grounds of their Spanish castle-style home in the San Fernando Valley. It was chock-a-block with Hollywood people, from old troupers like Wallace Beery and Sophie Tucker, to relative newcomers like the English lad, Freddie Bartholomew (who, Golding was relieved to see, was not the "sissy" he seemed to be on the screen,) and the teen-aged Judy Garland, still a couple of years away from *The Wizard of Oz* and lasting fame. Meanwhile, the guest of honour, wearing a tropical pith helmet, wandered among the dozens of well-wishers "in a daze of happiness." Following a poolside meal, there were tributes to Mayer, including one from Golding, whom the toastmaster, theatre owner Sidney Grauman, surprised with an invitation to speak.

The date for all this—July 4, American Independence Day—was not an accident. Mayer had chosen it for his birth date, just as he had arbitrarily chosen "B," for Burton, as his middle initial. So enamoured was he of his American experience, and so grateful to the country for furnishing his great success, he determined he would celebrate his birthday coincident with the nation's. In his mind, they were part of the same dream, a country whose greatness made it possible for an individual to achieve his.

The reality was a lot more complicated, of course. In *An Empire of Their Own*, Neal Gabler posits a theory based on the fact that America presented a rude awakening to Jewish immigrants like Mayer. They came expecting a land of milk and honey, only to discover that, as Jews, they were discriminated against and denied access to many of the best things the country had to offer. Finding their niche in the moving picture business, which other early entrepreneurs avoided because of its perceived sleaziness, they turned it into a golden escape from their relegated roles as furriers, clothiers, junk and salvage dealers. And yet, even as they enjoyed riches beyond their wildest dreams, they remained excluded from the American Dream. So, contends Gabler, they simply transferred the dream to the screen, where they created an idealized, imagined America, an empire that was patently their own.

This contention itself requires quite a leap of the imagination. It ascribes a common purpose to a rather disparate group of individuals, the studio bosses, about whom it can just as easily be argued that their principal motivation was to make money and achieve success with whatever formula that worked. In the case of Mayer and MGM, one very successful formula was a series of warm and light-hearted comedies about a small-town judge and his mischievous son, played by Mickey Rooney. Although the Rooney character, Andy Hardy, got into all sorts of predicaments, what ultimately triumphed in the stories were family values and the virtues of small-town life, which naturally led to happy endings. It was an idealized world, all right, and Mayer loved the Andy Hardy movies—but mostly because, for all his toughness in business, he was also a romantic.

This being the case, he must have loved Fredericton, too, for it was the *perfect* small town. A couple of years later, a visiting Canadian journalist called it "the last surviving Home Town of America." Bruce Hutchison was gathering material for his book, *The Unknown Country*, a bestseller when it was published in 1942, and he was utterly charmed by Fredericton. Surveying a residential area on the wide flat by the river, he described the down-home feel of its "old rambling wooden houses, obese and expansive, with vests unbuttoned for comfort, basking in the shade—the kind of houses where America used to swing on the porch hammock and kiss its girl in the darkness, where dinner was at noon, with pot roast, and father stoked the furnace and split the wood, and a house was a home, not a camp on the route of a march." The description could have been the set instructions for an Andy Hardy movie.

Getting Louis Mayer to come to Fredericton and receive a university honorary degree was, as much as anything, a triumph of Walter Golding's abilities as a promoter. It was he who'd seized on the idea of New Brunswick as Mayer's "home," and had publicized it widely. So when, in the fall of 1938, the University of New Brunswick Senate approved a motion, put forward by Percy Burchill, a lumberman from the Miramichi district, to award the degree, the language sounded like Golding could have provided it. It spoke of Mayer's "outstanding contribution to the cause of education in the production of motion pictures, improving the standard of that industry," and it noted "his intense interest in the province." This last part,

Fig. 8.3 Cartoon by Ed Sotto, a scenic artist at MGM and a portrait artist, that summarizes the life and career of film magnate, Louis B. Mayer's life. Citizen and Cheriot Chatter, *Culver City, California April 9, 1948.*

at least, was debatable; he had visited New Brunswick just once since his mother's death, and the only other thing he'd done was to commission an MGM subsidiary to prepare a short travelogue about the province. These were, however, desperate times, and the university was making its best pitch.

The university strove earnestly to welcome him into its fold. Mayer himself was very big on "family"—that was how he ran MGM, treating his stars as though they were part of a vast family and taking great personal offence when they behaved badly. He insisted, too, that chicken soup made with his dear, departed mother's recipe was always available at the studio commissary. Now, the University of New Brunswick was inviting him into *its* family. After the luncheon at the Queen, where he stressed his strong pro-British feelings, he went to a student "at home" in Lady Beaverbrook Hall on the campus. And he was back that evening for an alumni dinner to which all seniors and honorary degree recipients were invited, and where Mayer spoke again, mainly about recent Hollywood motion pictures.

Among the graduates in attendance was a young woman from Moncton, New Brunswick, Althea Adair Warren, who, years later, remembered fondly that wonderful graduation week in May 1939, when the weather turned warm, and there was a whole round of activities for the students. At the alumni dinner, she took only passing notice of short and rather unimposing Louis Mayer; she was more interested in the plans of her fellow graduates seated nearby at a long table. But her ears perked up when he mentioned *How Green Was My Valley*, the bittersweet tale of a turn of the century Welsh coal mining family that became a best-selling novel in 1939. A rival studio, 20th Century Fox, had plans to turn it into a motion picture, and Mayer probably used it as an example of the better-quality films Hollywood was then making, another favourite theme of his. Miss Warren was intrigued because Wales, a beautiful country, interested her. That might have been all she remembered of him, except for a little episode the next day that, in its own way, illustrated the romance of film and the persistence of rumour.

Although the University of New Brunswick was tiny (just shy of four hundred students in the 1938-39 year), it had a long history and a full set of durable traditions. They included, on graduation day, a short academic procession that went from the stone Arts Building, the oldest university building in Canada, down a slight slope to Memorial Hall, built in 1923 to honour the university graduates who died in the First World War. On this day, the press interest was naturally focused on the visiting Hollywood mogul. The campus was even treated to a rare sight—a bona fide newsreel cameraman ready to film Mayer's moment of glory.

And now here he came, walking beside Attorney General McNair at the front of the parade and "clothed in academic scarlet, like some historic ecclesiastic in one of his own moving pictures." This description appeared in the next day's Montreal *Star*, which went on for several paragraphs celebrating Mayer's formative New Brunswick roots and his "fairytale" rise to the top. It all had a familiar ring, and, yes, it did turn out to be authored by Walter Golding, who'd written the story as an advance; all *The Star* bothered to do was change the tense.

Walking immediately behind Mayer was another honorary degree recipient, Mary Kingsley Tibbitts of Boston. Half a century earlier, in 1889, Miss Tibbitts had been the first woman to graduate from the University. Later, she became the first female principal of a New Brunswick high school. Now, at Memorial Hall, Louis Mayer and assorted male dignitaries shared the stage with her and with another woman, Mabel Sterling, who was about to achieve a breakthrough of her own, by becoming the first female to deliver the alumni oration. And, in the front rows of the auditorium, sat a graduating class of ninety-six that included twenty-five women.

One wonders what effect, if any, this had on Mayer. One of the ironies of the moment was that he had strictly forbidden his own daughters, Irene and Edie, to attend college, although both apparently wished to do so. It would make them too worldly, he thought. The proper role for a woman was to be a supportive wife and mother, as his mother had been. He felt the same about show business, especially disappointing Edie, who aspired to a Broadway career. His reasons were vague, but he likely feared their being exposed to some of the predatory carousers who haunted the business.

Of this, he had intimate knowledge. Beginning about 1932, Mayer, who was still married to Margaret, a rabbi's daughter whom he had wed years before in Boston, conducted, or attempted, a series of affairs. Not always was he successful, because he was a little gnome of a man hardly attractive to women, he never stopped trying and, ever the hopeless romantic regularly fell in love with beautiful actresses. In one instance, he supposedly tried to jump out the window of a Paris hotel (while Margaret was in France undergoing medical treatment) when actress Jean Howard, a former Ziegfeld Follies girl, spurned his offer of five million dollars to marry him. Only the intervention of faithful and ever-present Howard Strickling prevented him from leaping.

So Mayer's relationships with women, even those of his own family, were complex. None of this, however, diminished his enjoyment of the moment at the University of New Brunswick. It was, in a very real way, a vindication for him. Years before, he had taken into his MGM "family" a young chap, Irving Thalberg. In photos from that time, where Thalberg appears with a group of Hollywood titans, he looks decidedly out of place, as though he were a neatly tailored college professor who has somehow stumbled into a gathering of hard-bitten millionaires. The others are mostly stolid and beefy, while Thalberg, who had near movie star looks, is frail enough to suggest that he could be swept away by the next dry wind blowing in from the desert. But his appearance belied the soul of an earnest striver. As MGM's production head and resident intellectual (he had only a high school education but had begun prodigious reading as a sickly child), he received much of the credit for the studio's leadership in producing quality motion pictures. In time, Mayer became resentful of this (it was, after all, he who had built MGM into an industry powerhouse) and of Thalberg's demands for more money. So the two had a falling out, which never fully healed.

But now Thalberg was gone, dead for three years, his childhood afflictions having finally caught up with him at age thirty-seven, and here was Mayer, whom nobody would ever accuse of being an intellectual, receiving an honorary degree from an institution of higher learning. It was the American Dream come to life, albeit in Canada.

One of the surviving bits of folklore about Mayer is that he never read any of the stories MGM was considering for movies. In a typical year, the studio claimed it sifted through forty-five hundred books, more than three thousand plays, and hundreds of short stories searching for material. After a severe winnowing, those selected reached Mayer. He then had a favourite storyteller repeat the gist of a tale to him, and it was on that basis that he decided to approve it or not. It was a grown-up version of his childhood days, back in Saint John, when he loved to have his mother read to him.

One thing he did have was an eye for talent, even when that talent seemed invisible to others. There was, for example, the case of Norma Shearer. Raised in Montreal, and determined to become a star in moving pictures, she had not gotten off to an auspicious start. There had been the debacle of *Blue Water* in Saint John, and she'd also received a frosty response when she approached D.W. Griffith one winter's night in Vermont, where he and Billy Bitzer were making a movie of the popular stage play, *Way Down East*, and told him of her movie ambitions. Looking down his aquiline nose, Griffith dismissed her with a shake of his head and told her that it just couldn't happen.

But Shearer had spunk, and a strong-willed mother, and together they made their way to California, where Mayer, partly motivated by her Canadian roots, gave Norma a screen test. She failed it. She also flunked another, and then a third, but still got a bit part in a movie, and it was there that her appealingly cool demeanour on the screen finally showed through. Soon she began getting bigger roles, and Mayer put his full resources into promoting her. In 1930, Norma Shearer won the Oscar for Best Actress for *The Divorcee*, and presently she became the reigning queen of MGM and remained so all through the 1930s. Of course, it hadn't hurt that, in 1927, she married Irving Thalberg, having overcome the *faux-pas* of initially mistaking him for a male secretary at the studio.

Althea Adair Warren did very well at her graduation. Not only did she receive her degree, a bachelor of arts with honours in Latin and biology, she also captured three prizes, including the Governor General's Gold Medal for highest standing in the class and the Alumni Gold Medal for Latin Prose. Then she adjourned, with her fellow graduates, their families and friends, back to the Arts Building for the traditional tea in the Great Hall, where she stood chatting when a member of Louis Mayer's party, probably Howard Strickling, approached her.

"Mr. Mayer would like to speak with you."

"Fine. Tell him to come over."

So, thus bidden, the highest paid executive in the United States and a Hollywood moving picture mogul to boot, made his way across the room to speak with a new, twenty-year-old, university graduate.

They spoke for several moments. Mayer was amiable and friendly and seemed interested in her plans, although it was obvious that he didn't have much knowledge of academic matters. She thought he might have singled her out because the third prize she collected at the graduation was one donated by the local Hebrew society. Finally, the conversation wound up with Mayer telling her, "If you ever want anything, let me know."

It was from this brief encounter that a campus rumour arose; that Mayer of MGM had offered the tall and attractive Miss Warren a chance to be in pictures. It was, after all, a plausible story, and it proved to have a long life. Even many years later, friends and colleagues at the university, where she eventually became a professor and wife of a university vice-president, would ask, was it true that Louis B. Mayer had once offered her a screen test?

What Miss Warren actually did, after her graduation from the University of New Brunswick, was go to graduate school. She went to Clark University in Worcester, Massachusetts, where, late in the second term of the following year, she found herself strapped for cash and down to figuring out whether she had enough meal money to last out the term. Remembering Mayer's offer of help, she wrote to him. She did not get a reply. She thought that perhaps her letter had never reached his desk.

Mayer and his party didn't linger long in Fredericton after the graduation. They moved on to Saint John, where, the next day, there was a public luncheon at the Admiral Beatty Hotel and a private dinner at the Union Club. Louis also began planning for a chapel that he and his cousin Nathan Cummings, founder of Birdseye Foods, proposed to build in the local Jewish cemetery to honour the memory of their mothers. Then, somewhere around midnight, he, Strickling, Stoneman, and O'Connor took a taxi to Bangor, Maine, from where they flew to Boston, New York and California.

Fig. 8.4 Memorial Chapel in the Shaarei Zedek Cemetery, Saint John funded by Nathan Cummings and Louis B. Mayer and dedicated to their mothers.

Fig. 8.5 Detail of Mayer Memorial Chapel.

A few days later, Mayer wrote to Dr. Jones, the University President and his wife, graciously thanking them for their hospitality. The excitement of his two days in Fredericton was still with him, he said, the occasion had been one of the highlights of his life, and he would forever look back at it with great fondness. "I shall always cherish the brief hours spent with you, and hope that someday I may have the opportunity of doing something which will in some slight way express my gratitude for your kindness." He was looking forward to seeing them again next year, and, repeating something he had said in Fredericton, wrote that he hoped to return each year for the graduation ceremonies.

The Jewish congregation in Saint John waited a long time for the Mayer-Cummings donation, but, eventually, in 1950 the memorial chapel was built at the Shaarie Zedek Cemetery on Westmoreland Road in East Saint John. Louis B. Mayer did not attend the dedication. He never made it back "home." Nor did the University of New Brunswick ever receive the endowment it had supposedly hoped for.

Chapter Nine

Technicolor Woman

One day in the early nineteenth fifties, word of a spicy California lawsuit found its way onto the newswires of North America. It involved a man named Herbert T. Kalmus and his former wife who, years after their divorce, had decided to sue him for a better settlement. As Hollywood scandals went, this one was relatively minor, but it caught the attention of an editor at a newspaper in Fredericton who, tapping into his storehouse of local knowledge, managed to impart a hometown twist to the story; the wife in the case had grown up in the nearby community of Douglas. Many years later, a woman named Margaret Marceau remembered the story and wrote to tell me about it. Her letter began my pursuit of the strange tale of Natalie Dunphy Kalmus.

They met at a school dance in Boston. Herbert Kalmus was a tall, studious fellow raised in South Boston by music-loving parents who thought he should become a musician. An injury to a finger while playing baseball had ended that hope, and then, after his parents died prematurely, he went to live with his stepmother's family. In 1900, he enrolled in a local technical school that would soon become known as the Massachusetts Institute of Technology.

The girl at the dance called herself Nettie. She was petite and lively, with vivid blue eyes, reddish-gold curls, and a captivating way of tossing back her head when she laughed. Herbert was instantly smitten. They were married in July 1902, in a Baptist Church at the small community of Baldwinville, near the New Hampshire border. Their marriage record shows them as residents of the village, while, under "Occupations," they were said to be "travelling."

After his graduation in 1904, Herbert and Nettie moved to California, where he had landed a job with a private preparatory school in San Francisco. In what seems to have been an idyllic time, they spent Herbert's leisure moments sampling the city's fine restaurants and exploring the small towns and countryside round San Francisco Bay. Then word arrived from an MIT classmate, Dan Comstock, that he and Herbert had won fellowships for study abroad.

While her husband earned his doctorate in Germany and Switzerland, Nettie explored art galleries. Upon their return to the States, she enrolled as a voice major at Florida's Stetson University while Herbert took up a teaching position at MIT. In 1910, he got a job as an assistant professor of physics at Queens University, and Nettie, accompanying him to Kingston, Ontario, did something quite unusual—she signed on as a student in Arts. Faculty wives normally didn't do that in those prim and proper days, but Nettie, now calling herself Natalie, sat for courses in European History and in Mental and Moral Philosophy, the last covering such topics as metaphysics, aesthetics, and ethics.

They moved back to Boston in the spring of 1915, where Herbert, his friend Comstock, and another gifted chap, Burton Wescott, formed a scientific consulting business. One day, a man named Coolidge came to their basement offices and asked them to evaluate a new projector that was supposed to eliminate the annoying flutter that had long plagued moving pictures. After examining the machine, they advised against investing in it, but then gave Coolidge a proposal of their own—to build a system that would make motion pictures in colour.

It wasn't a new idea, and people elsewhere, notably in England, were conducting experiments toward the same end. But Coolidge liked their proposal, and with his backing, they proceeded to develop a basic two-colour process. Coolidge told Kalmus to find a name for it. He did, calling it "Technicolor."

Natalie Kalmus was involved in the Technicolor experiments from the beginning. When the researchers wanted to find out how people photographed in colour, they turned the camera on her. She was the perfect model, with her red hair and blue eyes. They could shoot footage of Natalie and then compare the results with the real thing. So she became the first woman ever photographed in Technicolor. But she did more than that. She also began to re-invent herself.

Margaret Marceau, the woman who wrote to me, remembered parts of that long ago story about the Kalmus legal battle with remarkable clarity. She was a student then, working towards an honours degree in English and history at the University of New Brunswick, and had read the item in the local paper. She remembered that Natalie had been a technical assistant to Kalmus, that they'd eventually divorced, and that the amount of money his ex-wife was seeking in the court case had prompted the local newspaper editor to observe in print; "Many people in New Brunswick will be surprised to learn that a former Douglas girl cannot live on $10,000 a month"!

What Ms. Marceau couldn't remember was Natalie's maiden name.

That part was easy, though. Consulting the Kalmus entry in film encyclopedias, I learned that Natalie's maiden name was Dunfee. I knew this was a common surname in Douglas, which happens to be directly across the St. John River from where I live, although the local spelling is Dunphy. But a bigger problem was that, in one instance, she was described as a native of Boston, and in another, of Norfolk, Virginia. There was no mention of either New Brunswick or Douglas.

Fig. 9.1 Margaret Marceau, long-time volunteer with the Grand Falls Historical Society and driving force behind the local museum, who brought Natalie Kalmus and the newspaper story of her dissatisfaction with her divorce settlement to the author's attention.

I let the story languish. Then one day I happened to mention it to a woman I knew, a Red Cross homemaker who assisted various elderly clients in the city, and she told me one of them was a Dunphy. A few days later, on the homemaker's recommendation, I went to visit the woman. Yes, she told me, "It was always a story in our family, about our Natalie. We thought in a way that it almost connected us to royalty."

Before I left her home, the woman gave me a copy of a Dunphy genealogy, which I presumed would reveal the definitive connection between "our Natalie" and the Dunphys of Douglas. Rushing back to my house, I eagerly went through the pages of the genealogy and was disappointed to find that, although there were Dunphys named Nancy and Nellie, I couldn't locate a single Natalie.

Again, there was a long pause in my research, until the late Winter of 2004 when, preparing for a trip to California, I called the Margaret Herrick Library of the Academy of Motion Picture Arts and Sciences in Beverly Hills with a list of people and subjects I was researching. Almost as an afterthought, I mentioned Natalie Kalmus. Just a moment, said the archivist, and then, coming back to the phone, she said, yes, they had some material about Natalie, but nothing about her beginnings. "Isn't that strange?" she added.

At the Herrick Library a couple of weeks later, Marion and I examined the Kalmus file. Its contents were interesting, but the archivist was correct, it contained no hints of Natalie's origins. Back home, we decided to try a different tack. I wrote to a state agency in Massachusetts, requesting a copy of the Kalmus marriage certificate. It yielded two important pieces of information. One was that, when they were married in 1902, she wasn't Natalie, but Nettie, and the other was that she had been born in "Houghton," Maine. There is no Houghton in Maine. There is, however, a Houlton. It is right on the border with New Brunswick.

So now we had Nettie/Natalie within a stone's throw of the province at a time when people moved fairly freely back and forth across the border, sometimes to marry (as my own great-grandparents had done), sometimes to give birth. We turned to the census and school records of the Provincial Archives in Fredericton, and it was there that we finally found what we were looking for—the beginnings of an ambitious country girl who, at the start of the twentieth century, had emerged from the unlikely surroundings of a farm home and a one-room schoolhouse in New Brunswick to be part of the grand adventure of bringing colour to the movies.

Born in 1881, she was named Nettie Maybelle Dunphy, the first name possibly derived from her great-grandmother's, which was the biblical Mehetabel, sometimes shortened to Hettie. The Dunphys, descended from the O'Donoghues of County Kilkenny, were among Douglas's first settlers, probably arriving in the eighteenth century. They seem to have done rather well, in time owning parcels of farmland all over Douglas and on the adjacent river islands.

One June day I drove over to Douglas to try and find the graveyard where Nettie's great-grandparents, Mehetabel and her husband Joseph, were buried. Following the directions of a teacher at a local school, I turned off the highway just past an old apple storage building and went a short distance up the side of the ridge, now sprinkled with the homes of Fredericton suburbanites. The cemetery, barely visible from just below, sat on a plateau, and my first reaction, as I took in its spectacular vantage, was that these oldtimers certainly knew how to pick their burying places. The view encompassed New Brunswick's great river as it flows down through a series of islands towards the provincial capital. The graveyard itself was neatly tended, with yellow swatches of hawkweed spreading across the mostly open spaces. A few white blossoms of wild blackberries peeked out from the surrounding trees. Here and there were clusters of gravestones, but the Dunphy stones, belonging to Joseph and Mehetabel, two of their sons and their wives, stood apart from each other, and slightly askew. Beside two of the stones, someone had placed sprigs of pinkish, artificial roses.

Joseph and Mehetabel had a grandson, George, who married Annie Grant, from the States. Their first child, William, was born in New Brunswick in 1872, but the next three, including Nettie, were all born across the border. According to census records, Annie officially immigrated to Canada in 1884 and had three more children, one of whom died shortly after birth.

In Douglas, George and Annie operated a farm, and the children went to school at nearby Mouth of Keswick, named for a tributary that enters the St. John at that point. In a schoolhouse that sometimes accommodated up to seventy pupils of various ages and aptitudes, a single teacher held forth. He was young Egerton Everett, who lived across the river and, for several months of the year, was able to paddle his canoe to and from school every day. Nettie, who began attending in 1887, the year she turned six, may have learned a lot about drive and ambition from him. At the very least, she availed herself of everything the school had to offer, remaining a pupil until 1897, and chalking up near-perfect attendance that final year, when she was fifteen.

Sometime after that, she made her way to Boston, one of the favourite destinations for young men and women from Canada's Maritime Provinces. Many found lifelong careers there, and some found romance, too. An exceptional case was that of Jeanette Amanda Stiles, from the New Brunswick village of Hillsborough. Moving to Boston with her father so that she could study music, she took a job at the Jordan Marsh department store. There she met James Clark Jordan, son of the store's founder, married him, and entered a life of wealth and comfort and such perks as having her portrait done by the artist John Singer Sargent.

Nettie Dunphy was working as a shop girl, too, when she met Herbert Kalmus. There was no Singer Sargent painting of her, but she did become the first woman to be photographed in Technicolor.

By 1917, the Kalmuses and their associates in the company, after long months of experimentation, were ready to make a full motion picture in colour. This, they hoped would capture the attention of movie companies, who so far had been largely indifferent to their efforts. They shot a one-reel feature called *The Gulf Between* amid the bright sun and lush surroundings of Jacksonville, Florida. Showings in New York and elsewhere were a failure, however, when a critical part of the projector—a device intended to bring the two coloured images into register—didn't work properly.

They continued their experiments over the next decade and a half, and, meanwhile, others entered the competition. In England, twenty-six-year-old Claude Friese-Greene, a cameraman whose father pioneered colour cinema but went bankrupt, sought to redeem the family name with a system that used alternate frames of film tinted red and green to create the illusion of colour. It was called the Natural Colour Process, and young Friese-Greene tried to publicize it by filming vignettes of British life during a sixteen-hundred-mile automobile tour in 1924. His travelogue, now the oldest surviving footage of Britain after the Great War, might have been a success, except that projection problems also sabotaged his effort.

In the early thirties, the Kalmus group finally produced a system that worked. Their so-called "subtractive" process joined three separate negatives, each registering about one-third of the colour spectrum, to reproduce all of the colours of the rainbow. Another young experimenter, Walt Disney, used it to make a cartoon called *Flowers and Trees*; it was a great success and Technicolor was finally on its way. Now there was a rush to make colour films, one of which, interestingly, was a remake of Ernie and Nell Shipman's *God's Country and the Woman*.

At the same time, the burgeoning interest in colour also revived an old concern. People remembered that the two-colour process had garishly assaulted their eyes and their sensibilities. A critic for *The New York Times* warned that, unless care and restraint were exercised, "color will fall into the hands of the unlettered and cause such a rape of the laws of color harmony and contrast, such a blare of outrageous pigmentations, that only the colour-blind will consider it safe to venture inside a motion picture theatre." Others insisted that movies were a natural black and white medium, and that anything else was a frivolous distraction.

This time, though, the Technicolor people anticipated the problem and in fact shared the critics' concern. They worried that, if Hollywood wasn't careful in its use of colour, the ensuing aesthetic disaster would stop the transition from black and white in its tracks. So Kalmus and his colleagues created a company offshoot called the Color Advisory Service to ensure that strict standards were applied in the use of colour. When contracting to use Technicolor's cameras, cameramen, processing and printing, a studio also had to agree to involve the Color Advisory Service in nearly every step of the production process. The Service's advisors had to be consulted on the script, the film's colour scheme, the hues of its props and sets, even the colour of the actors' clothing, and this strict vigilance would be maintained right through to post-production. It was a demanding, powerful role, and the person Technicolor put in charge was Natalie Kalmus.

In 1939, *The New York Times* ran a story about how Natalie had emerged from Technicolor's laboratory "into one of the biggest jobs in the motion picture industry." She was, said the newspaper, "a supreme court of expert opinion on what happens to any shade of the spectrum, once it is filtered through a camera lens." A glamorous photograph of Natalie accompanied the story, and under a headline that read;

Expert in Color Photography,
Woman Is Paid $65,000 a Year

The *Times* reported that she received this generous salary because the Technicolor company had been "developed largely with her assistance," despite many heartbreaking setbacks over the years. "If she is indispensable today on a movie lot where mistakes may cost many thousands," the paper said, "it is because she was diligent through the ordeal of selecting, rejecting, photographing and projecting, through substitution of photographic equipment and of manifold types of film, of discoveries of adaptable fabrics and forms and of the innumerable disappointments in finished products."

In a talk to a technical wing of the Academy of Motion Picture Arts and Sciences, Natalie described her mission as bringing "color consciousness" to filmmaking. To avoid vexing clashes of colour, she said, movie people should look to nature and "the iridescent brilliance of the butterfly's wing, the subtle tones of a field of grain, the violet shadows of the desert, the sun's reflection in the ocean." It wouldn't hurt, either, if they consulted the

Fig. 9.2 Natalie Kalmus in her Hollywood office. She was executive head of the art department of Technicolor and among her responsibilities were advising and assisting the art and wardrobe departments of the studio during the making of Technicolor productions.

works of the Old Masters. The aim should be to "make a coloured motion picture a work of art."

Fair enough, but exactly what qualified Natalie for the job? In a 1933 radio interview, a partial transcript of which showed up in her file at the Herrick Library in Beverly Hills, she related it to her close involvement with the development of Technicolor. She had been everything from a "dye mixer" to a photographic subject. "It was at once quite obvious," she said, "that an artist would be of considerable advantage in the working out of many problems, and my early training qualified me to act in the capacity of colour expert." More revealing still was Natalie's perception of herself. "If you are properly devoted to a career of any sort," she told *The New York Times*, "you won't have to seek advice about it. No one is going to be able to stop you anyway."

In 1945, the gossip columnist Louella Parsons got a scoop; Herbert and Natalie Kalmus had "been divorced for many months." As Natalie told

Parsons, "Our troubles happened when we went East last year. We both realized our life together had become deadly monotonous. When we were together, all we discussed was Technicolor. I guess it was my fault. I was never free to travel with Dr. Kalmus. My work kept me tied down in California. He, of course, was engrossed in his own business interests and I in mine."

Natalie wasn't telling the whole truth. She and Herbert had, in fact, been divorced for almost a quarter century, although apparently few knew about it. Moving to California, they had continued to live together, in an Italianate home in Bel-Air, outside Hollywood. They ate meals together, and when he entertained, she was a charming and lively hostess to their unsuspecting guests. They lived in separate wings of the house, but the invisible dividing line was crossed many times, including, so Natalie later claimed, for visits to the bedroom. She also continued to wield influence at the office, and if a contentious issue arose, Herbert, who always referred to her as "Mrs. Kalmus," invariably backed her.

The charade was remarkable—and it turns out not to have been their first.

At Stetson University in Florida in 1909, seven years after their wedding, they had presented themselves as *not* being married. She enrolled as Miss Nettie Dunfee, and he, in correspondence with university authorities, assumed the persona of a guardian or mentor.

This is revealed in letters in the Stetson University Archives at De Land, an inland town north of Orlando. One is a handwritten letter Herbert wrote from MIT to Professor A. L. L. Suhrie, the university secretary, in August 1909. Enclosing a postal order for ten dollars "to serve as deposit for a room for Miss Nettie Dunfee," Herbert says, "She is over 25 years of age, but will have to take largely high school work." He explains that the university has previously agreed that she could register as a special student without writing entrance exams. "All bills for her school year will be paid by me from here," he continues. "I should like her to have the best room and board obtainable which I judge from your catalogue to be in East Hall." He closes by asking the secretary for another catalogue "as I sent mine to Miss Dunfee." In a subsequent note, he clarified "that she desires a single room, that is a room alone."

Natalie's mother Annie participated in the pretense, too. A week before Christmas, she wrote to the university president, Dr. Lincoln Hulley, asking permission for "Miss Dunfee" to be allowed to leave the school on the morning of December 24 to meet her brother. She would then spend the holidays with relatives, whom Annie did not identify, and her brother would have her back in De Land for the opening of the next semester. She wrote the letter from 37 Harvard Avenue in Allston, a Boston neighbourhood close to MIT, and signed it, Mrs. G. K. Dunfee. Replying on December 22, Dr. Hulley told Annie Dunfee that her daughter and his, a freshman that year and not quite eighteen, had become good friends. "Your daughter's conduct," he added, "has been entirely praiseworthy as a student here, and she is held in high esteem by the teachers and students." Permission was granted for Nettie, now twenty-seven, to leave the campus.

She apparently enjoyed the year she spent at Stetson—her mother spoke of "happy messages" Nettie sent. One thing she didn't like, though, was dormitory life, and this prompted a letter from Herbert to Dr. Hulley in mid-February 1910 in which he told the president; "Miss Nettie Dunfee has my permission, and that of her mother, to take her meals and to room away from the University dormitories, as suggested in her last letter to me."

What was behind this subterfuge? A century later, it is difficult to know. Could it have been because they were trying to avoid criticism at a conservative, southern university of a woman leaving her husband to attend university? Or was it *his* idea that, if his wife wished to extend her formal education, which had effectively ended in a one-room schoolhouse in New Brunswick, she should do it quietly and semi-anonymously? A third possibility is suggested by the tone of the letters exchanged by the family and the university. They treat Nettie/Natalie as a teenager instead of an adult woman moving into her late twenties. Was she possibly ill? The answer may have been in an earlier letter Herbert wrote to the university, this one strangely missing from the Stetson files.

By the early nineteen-forties, Natalie's world was unravelling. Her job as colour advisor on movies, a function the Technicolor Corporation insisted on, had brought her into conflict on film sets. Louis B. Mayer's son-in-law, David Selznick, for one, threw her off the set of *Gone with the Wind*. (Her name did, however, appear in the credits for the movie, which became the first Technicolor blockbuster.)

Things were deteriorating on the home front, too. Herbert sent her to England, ostensibly to help solve problems at a British Technicolor plant, but just as likely, because he wanted her out of the country. There is an element of strain and foreboding in a letter she wrote, in June 1940, to Mary Hulley Beatty, a sister of her close Stetson friend, Harriett Hulley, recalling her days at the college. "I am most grateful," she said, "that, no matter what happens, such delightful memories can never be taken from me."

Then she received word that one of her sisters was dying.

Eleanor Dunphy, or Ella, was ten years younger. She had been still at home when Natalie moved to the States, but they had remained close. So now Natalie raced to her sister's bedside where Eleanor, near death, murmured about being able to see familiar faces. Smiling and stretching out her arms, she said, "I'm going up." Natalie later described the scene for the magazine, *Guideposts*. "Never again will death frighten me in any way," she wrote. "This was my sister's inheritance to me—her final beautiful gift. I had seen for myself how thin was the curtain between life and death. I had been privileged to glimpse part of the wonderful truth about everlasting life."

If this incident showed an ethereal side of Natalie, so too did her practice of paying astrologers for regular personal advisories. One of them, David Sturgis of Los Angeles, told her there were certain times of the year when "because of favourable Sun aspects to your birth sign Aries, you should make progress and profit in all major affairs." It may have been only coincidence, but in 1948, just as she was entering one of those favourable times, she started a California divorce suit against Herbert, beginning a series of court actions that took place over the next several years.

In the 1948 suit, Natalie admitted to the 1921 divorce, but claimed it had never become final. Besides, she said, they had remarried in 1923. She accused Herbert of cruelty, desertion and infidelity, alleging that he'd been intimate with five different women, a charge that inevitably inspired newspaper headlines about him being "too colourful" for his ex-wife. Natalie conceded that they had recently reached a new property settlement but said she'd only agreed to it under threat of "force and violence." Her situation was so dire, said her lawyer, that she'd been forced to pawn jewelry to meet expenses at the Beverly Hills hotel where she was living.

In response, Herbert said he'd been paying monthly alimony since early 1922, and that Natalie, in accepting those payments, had acknowledged the divorce. Her lawsuit, he contended, was just "one more in a series of threats and attacks" she'd levelled at him over the years.

When the California Superior Court continued the case to late October, Natalie fired her lawyer, hired a new one, and started another lawsuit. Early in the proceedings, she suffered a mild heart attack. Returning to the courtroom, she appeared wan and listless, but still managed to enlarge on her claims about a 1923 remarriage. It had taken place in New York, she said, shortly before she underwent an operation. "We put our arms around each other and sort of made a vow that in the eyes of God and in our own hearts we were still married." To support her argument, her lawyer introduced various letters, deeds, telegrams, and a copy of a 1939 *Who's Who*, which mentioned only their original marriage and naturally made no reference to the secret 1921 divorce.

But the state Supreme Court didn't buy it, nor did other courts in Massachusetts and California accept similar arguments she made until almost the mid-nineteen-fifties. When she lost a California suit for separate maintenance, she became hysterical. According to newspaper reports, she sobbed and shouted as yet another new lawyer led her from the courtroom; "Oh, God! Oh God! Won't any court dare give me justice"?

Meanwhile, Herbert, now in his late sixties, remarried, his bride a thirty-eight-year-old newspaper writer, lecturer on personal charm, and divorced mother of two teenaged daughters. Natalie wasn't happy about the marriage, but her only legal victory came when, after a hospital stay, she sued a California hospital for jabbing her in the behind with an infected needle and was awarded damages of three thousand dollars. She also was haled into court by a law firm that had once represented her and claimed it was owed thirty thousand dollars. On the eve of rendering his decision, the judge in the case received a letter from her. He promptly fined Natalie five hundred dollars and sentenced her to five days in jail for contempt. Another tearful eruption followed. "I'd like to go to jail so that I can publicize the injustice that's been done to me," she hollered to the courtroom. Her sentence was suspended after she apologized.

In the early nineteen-sixties, Herbert Kalmus decided to tell his story in a book. It was a detailed and sometimes engaging account of his early life and the development of Technicolor, but it had one perfidious omission. It made absolutely no mention of Natalie, his legal wife for nearly two decades, his colleague and sometime companion for years beyond that, and someone who was, undeniably, a part of his life and work.

The book remained unpublished for thirty years. Then his second wife, Eleanore, long after he had died, took it upon herself to add two chapters to the manuscript. Her reasons, she said, were "to fill in the missing pieces" and reveal "the torture of his first marriage."

This she did with a vengeance. Acting as a kind of posthumous amanuensis, she claimed that Natalie had begun behaving erratically early in her marriage to Herbert. She'd obtained an abortion in Switzerland, for example, without ever telling him she was pregnant, an act that caused him "devastating pain." Later, she'd returned home yearly, a pattern she repeated when they moved to Ontario, and indeed whenever she found herself in a situation that made her uncomfortable or unhappy. According to Eleanore, Natalie had suffered frequent emotional meltdowns and had been hospitalized several times, including at the Mayo Brothers Clinic. Eleanore didn't deny that Natalie had learned something about art and colour, and had made a contribution to Technicolor's success. But, said Eleanore, she was underhanded, aggressive and woefully under-educated, at times embarrassingly so. She had given Herbert "thirty years of grief." He had stuck by her only out of "sympathy and pity," and yet this "wrenching, treacherous woman" had in the end tried "to take over one of the biggest corporations in the United States."

Eleanore's additions to the book contain several factual errors. She got Natalie's age wrong as well as Herbert's graduation year, and the year they were married. A paragraph about Natalie in a *Time* magazine article is misquoted. And Eleanore incorrectly asserts that Natalie never attended any school "of which there is a record"—a claim I found easy to refute when I checked with universities like Queens and Stetson.

But a bigger problem is the inherent one-sidedness of Eleanore's depiction. The book, titled *Mr. Technicolor*, didn't appear until 1993, long after Natalie's death, when there was no one to defend her or present her side of the story. Certainly she deserved a more impartial assessment than that of her former husband's second wife. Relationships, after all, collapse for all kinds of reasons. To begin with, Natalie and Herbert came from very different backgrounds, he a city boy bred into surroundings of music and culture, a college man; she a girl from the country, with only a grade school education. What pressures did that impose, once passions cooled? Herbert, an obvious high achiever, was very focused on whatever he did. When they lived in Switzerland, he took long and exuberant trips by bicycle with friends, leaving his young bride alone, with time to contemplate her own insecurities. Later, he pursued the colouring of movies with a similar, single-minded dedication, admirable from afar, but hard on a marriage, and Natalie's 1940s complaint that all they ever talked about was Technicolor may, in fact, have been an echo from an earlier time.

In old newspaper and magazine descriptions I found, Herbert was invariably portrayed as quiet and publicity avoiding, a silver-haired patrician whom Hollywood movie people treated with a reverence that matched Eleanore's. (She never called him anything but "Doctor," she confesses in *Mr. Technicolor*.) But let us, in the interest of balance, place a small asterisk beside these wholesome depictions. As angry and embittered as he was about Natalie, his failure to include her in his autobiography was dishonest and indefensible. It may be also noted for the record that he eventually had a falling out with his long-time pal and colleague, Dan Comstock, and that a magazine article described labour relations at the Technicolor plant as "among the worst in Hollywood."

Unfortunately for Natalie, while she saw her various lawsuits as merely trying to get her fair share of the Technicolor spoils, she came across in the papers as a grasping harridan, seeking to rifle her ex-husband's pockets to sustain her high life in Beverly Hills. The story went over no better in Hollywood than it did when it landed on the desk of that bemused editor with the long memory back in New Brunswick. Natalie was left with few friends, and she eventually moved back to Massachusetts. When she died in 1965, *Variety* and *Film Daily* reported her death in the same minimalist way they record the passing of long-forgotten players from silent films.

In recent decades, however, academic researchers have occasionally revisited the graveyard of cinematic history and disinterred Natalie's contribution. Their forensics have led to some positive verdicts. Richard Neupert, at the University of Georgia, wrote; "The work of Natalie Kalmus and her consultants ensured Technicolor's future dominance by actively convincing critics and potential customers that in addition to being accurate and relatively cost efficient, Technicolor would also be aesthetically pleasing, consistent, and essential." The rules Natalie established for the use of colour on the screen, continued Prof. Neupert, "helped Technicolor grasp and maintain a profitable foothold within the industry, where other colour companies (and even the earlier two-strip Technicolor) had failed." Another article, in *Film History*, declared those "long-standing aesthetic criteria for the correct use of colour" to be Natalie's "legacy" to the motion picture industry. As well, a 1998 television documentary about Technicolor, aired on the Turner Classic Movies cable network, paid her a "touching, grudging respect."

But no one has ever mentioned her Canadian roots, and, with their discovery now, she becomes, strangely, an even more shadowy creature of the cinema, a woman who created her own mystery through personal reinvention; little Nettie Maybelle Dunphy, who disavowed her humbler beginnings on a farm in New Brunswick and became Natalie Dunfee of Boston, Massachusetts, and then Hollywood, California. The mystery is why she did it, and the best guess is that she thought it would enhance her acceptance and prospects in turn of the century America if she came from some place other than the Canadian hinterland. The irony is that her true and simpler origins merely enlarge her story and make it all the more remarkable—the woman who helped bring Technicolor to the movies and who, to her relatives far away in New Brunswick, always remained "our Natalie," the one who "almost connected us to royalty."

Figs. 10.1 & 10.2 Greer Garson and Ralph Bellamy in character as Eleanor and Franklin Roosevelt in the 1962 movie, Sunrise at Campobello.

Chapter Ten

The Sun Shines on Campobello

In 1960, sixty-five years after the industry came into being, a Hollywood motion picture company finally came to New Brunswick to shoot a feature film—well, at least some of it. The story was an American one, but an important part of it had taken place on an island that, while sitting just off the fabled coast of Maine, is actually New Brunswick territory. The island was Campobello, in the Bay of Fundy, and the movie was called *Sunrise at Campobello.*

Advertisements for the movie later portrayed Campobello as one of the more obscure places on the planet. "Who ever heard of a place called Campobello"? one ad would ask in print. In fact, the island was well known to a covey of wealthy Americans who, as long ago as the 1880s, had arrived each summer seeking relief from hay fever and city heat in the salty Fundy breezes. They included the Roosevelt family of New York, and young Franklin Roosevelt would spend many happy days on Campobello. It was also where, after sailing along its flinty, serrated coast one summer's day in 1921, he showed the first symptoms of poliomyelitis, the disease that would cripple him for life. His long and courageous recovery so that he could later run for President was an irresistible American story of triumph, and it became, first, a Broadway play and then a motion picture.

The film was shot in Technicolor because by then most Hollywood movies were in colour—but also because its locale insisted on it. Campobello's dominant colour is blue—the blue of the sea, the blue of the sky when the curtain of fog is drawn back, and the bluish hues of the lupines that, in June, gush along roadsides and run in rivulets down to the ocean's edge. It is a combination that makes June on the island memorable. And some Junes are more memorable than others—especially June of 1960.

That was when Hollywood came to the island with its glamour and convertibles, its busloads of extras and technicians, its panoply of lights and cameras and cables. Campobello had never seen the likes, and rarely had the rest of Canada, which is why two of the country's largest weekend newspaper magazines carried feature stories about it.

As a stage play, *Sunrise at Campobello* had been a Broadway success, opening in January 1958 and running for the next year and a half before going on the road. American Democrats, still in the grips of the Republican Eisenhower administration, found a particular comfort and succour in the play. A Democrat had written it, the former Hollywood scriptwriter and movie executive, Dore Schary. Just a year or two earlier, he had been ousted as studio chief at MGM, and suddenly finding himself "between things," he had gained the cooperation of FDR's widow, Eleanor, and, in a matter of a few months, dashed off his play. He originally considered calling it *The Roosevelt Story*, but then, deciding that Campobello was where Roosevelt had first demonstrated his powers of resurgence after being struck down, hit upon the *Sunrise* title, which simply, as he wrote in his autobiography, "came down my arm and onto the paper."

The transformation of the play into a film was more or less a natural progression. Americans love heroic stories, and this one certainly had its heroic dimension. Moreover, Roosevelt had died in office, after leading his country out of the Depression and up to the threshold of victory in the Second World War. So Schary had a popular subject to begin with, and he found his dramatic focus in that agonizing time between 1921, when the illness struck FDR, and 1924, when he signalled the start of his own political comeback at that year's Democratic convention by managing to reach the podium to nominate New York Governor Alfred E. Smith as the party's candidate for President. After that, the success of the play, and Schary's prior experience and connections in the movie industry, virtually guaranteed that it would become a film.

It didn't take long. On January 30, 1960, Ralph Bellamy, the veteran actor who played FDR in the stage play, gave his last live performance, in Atlanta, and then headed for Los Angeles to start the movie. Shooting would continue over several weeks, and it included the film's big climactic moment, a re-enactment of the rousing convention scene in 1924 when Roosevelt, on crutches, made it to the podium. As *The New York Times*

Fig. 10.3 Eleanor Roosevelt, Ralph Bellamy, and Greer Garson on the set filming Sunrise at Campobello *in Hyde Park.*

noted, this scene alone, which involved a rented auditorium and some three thousand extras, cost well over two hundred thousand dollars, more than twice the bill for the entire stage production.

By early June, cast and crew had moved on to New York, where they shot a scene in which Franklin and Eleanor and their son Jimmy emerged from their five-story brick house and climbed into a sparkling 1924 Packard touring car for the drive to the convention site, Madison Square Garden. Next, the movie company went to the Roosevelt estate up the Hudson River at Hyde Park, N.Y. And then they were ready for Campobello.

But was Campobello ready for them? For much of its nearly three hundred year history, its sparse population lived amid the quiet solitude of a place that might have qualified for the poet Emily Dickinson's searching phrase, "Where the place called morning lies." Captain William Owen, the first "Principal Proprietary of the Great Outer Island of Passamaquoddy," named it *Campo Bello* in apparent reference to its beauty and fertility.

He brought a shipload of indentured servants from Lancashire to help settle the island in 1770, and he made a personal statement about fertility by "bundling" with his housekeeper to produce a son; he liked to refer to the boy as "the Hereditary Prince of Campobello."

But a century or so later, when the American gentry discovered Campobello, it was still a thinly populated and somnolent place—which was exactly what these folks were looking for, as an alternative to the busier summer resorts found elsewhere on the coast and in the mountains of New England and New York. Of course, the island needed some amenities, and the Americans proceeded to create them. They built three large hotels, one of which was named "The Owen." James and Sara Roosevelt (he was a vice-president and major shareholder of the Delaware and Hudson Railway) came with their one year old son Franklin to the island in 1883 and fell in love with it. They bought ten acres of land overlooking the water and built a summer "cottage" of some fifteen rooms for themselves. Then, according to Alden Nowlan's fine book on the history of Campobello, other well-heeled Americans followed to establish their own summer places on the island, and presently it had a semi-permanent colony of seasonal residents.

It was a splendid time to be rich, preferably young, and on Campobello. The vacationers sailed, fished, hiked, had picnics and picked wildflowers. Or they lay in hammocks and sat in wicker chairs on broad verandahs and read the magazines, newspapers and letters that arrived daily on the mailboat from Eastport, Maine, just across the water. Many brought with them retinues of retainers, who stood by ready to assist whatever leisurely undertaking came into their employers' heads.

This happy time continued into the new century. And then, one summer in the early 1900s, a putrid cloud drifted over from a suppurating fertilizer plant in Eastport, and like a dark bird flying across the sun, it signalled the end of the hotel era on Campobello. Two of the hotels closed that year, and the third, The Owen, barely survived. They were victims, to be sure, of more factors than the fouling of the island's salubrious breezes. But, hastened by the smell, the bad weather, and the limping economy of that year, many of the summer visitors left Campobello, never to return.

But not all departed, and, most notably, not the Roosevelts, whose lives had become too intertwined with the island to leave. In fact, although James Roosevelt had died, the family would actually enlarge its stake on Campobello. In June, 1909, the Saint John newspaper, *The Globe*, reported;

The Sun Shines on Campobello

"Franklin Roosevelt, of New York, has purchased the Hartman Kuhn cottage and is expected with Mrs. Roosevelt in July." He hadn't actually bought it—his mother had, but it was for Franklin and Eleanor, his bride of four years. Meanwhile, the widowed Sara was staying put, too, and, as *The Globe* item noted, she would "arrive at the same time at the old Roosevelt summer place here."

So the Roosevelts remained, and over the following decades most of the occasional excitements on Campobello were their doing, Franklin's especially. When he was elected the American President in 1933, the quiet islanders went down to the shore and built a hellish big bonfire to celebrate.

And now it was 1960, and Franklin, dead some 15 years, was causing yet another stir.

As the movie people hove into view on the other side of the narrow Lubec Channel, a few islanders gathered at their Customs House. In those days, no high arching bridge connected Campobello to the Maine-land, as one does today. Instead, the link was a ferry, which was really nothing more than a boat pushing a scow. It presented a definite logistical challenge, but at least it ensured that Hollywood's arrival on Campobello would be measured and orderly.

The movie folk had apparently decided that they should land on the island in a style matching people's expectations. So the first car to pull up to the Customs House—a white convertible—carried Schary, the film's producer, and its director, Vincent Donehue. Nobody recognized *them*, but next came a brown convertible, and it contained the person the bystanders had really come to see—the famous actress, Greer Garson.

She was a beautiful English girl whom Louis Mayer had "discovered" on the London stage in the mid-1930s. As usual, he'd been smitten, in this case by Carson's lovely speaking voice and dignified manner in addition to her beauty. She, on the other hand, had been less impressed by him, and especially by his suggestion that she move to California and become a movie actress. The morning after their first meeting, Mayer went to her apartment and met her mother. Louis was always very good at handling mothers, and the next thing Greer Garson knew she was under contract to MGM.

More than four decades and many movies later, the roles that most people still remembered her for, on Campobello no less than anywhere else, were two she'd had back near the beginning of her career. One was as an English schoolmaster's wife who dies during childbirth, in the 1939 film, *Goodbye, Mr. Chips,* for which she received an Academy Award nomination. And the other was the title role in *Mrs. Miniver,* a 1942 picture set in wartime England that also starred Walter Pidgeon, and for which she did win an Oscar.

Her movie career continued on a generally high level through the forties, but, by the mid-fifties, it was definitely flagging. Taking stock, she had decided to join her third husband, a Texas millionaire named Elijah "Buddy" Fogelson, on his spectacular ranch in New Mexico, where she found a new interest in, of all things, raising beef cattle. By the time Dore Schary asked her to take the role of Eleanor Roosevelt in his film, she hadn't appeared in a movie for six years. When a cheeky reporter asked her about this on Campobello, she said, "I love to act, but my career comes second now. My role as Mrs. Fogelson takes preference."

Nevertheless, at age fifty-seven Greer Garson still had star power, as was evident when she arrived on the island. Wearing dark glasses and a broad-brimmed hat tied tightly under her chin, she quickly attracted most of the attention, leaving her fellow actors—Ralph Bellamy, who had the Roosevelt role, and Hume Cronyn, a distinguished Canadian performer who played FDR's loyal associate, Louis Howe—in her shadow. Bellamy and Cronyn were themselves quite splendid looking, wearing conservative blue and gray suits, each decorated with a carnation in his lapel. But this moment in the Campobello sun was definitely Miss Garson's.

As the little band of island onlookers slowly swelled, the customs officer politely asked them to keep their distance while he performed a cursory luggage inspection. Then everyone was allowed to come closer, and the three actors chatted and signed autographs. When they finally were allowed to move on, a woman remarked that Greer Garson was every bit as pretty as she had been in *Mrs. Miniver* almost two decades earlier. In that movie, she and Walter Pidgeon played Kay and Clem Miniver, a well-off and respectable English couple living in a village near London to whom the war comes home in sudden and expected ways. With their matching good manners and air of refinement, Garson and Pidgeon were so perfectly suited to their roles that it seemed as though they could have been married to each other in real life, too, and the film, intended to inspire the Allied war effort, became MGM's biggest money-maker to that point. As for off-screen romance, Garson later married the actor who played her son in the film (and was ten years younger than she). The marriage didn't last.

The Sun Shines on Campobello

There were no motels or hotels, not even a restaurant, on Campobello in 1960. So the moviemakers faced quite a challenge in housing and feeding a cast and crew of nearly a hundred for their ten days on the island. But at least there were people willing to help. They included a rich American family named Hammer, and *they* were so willing that a rumour got started that the Hammer family had put some money into the film, hoping that it would help them sell the Roosevelt home, which they now owned.

Armand Hammer, a name that today reminds people of baking soda and toothpaste was an American industrialist (chairman of Occidental Petroleum) and philanthropist. His brother Victor ran the prestigious Hammer Art Galleries in New York. In 1952, the Hammers had bought Franklin and Eleanor's Campobello cottage from the Roosevelt family, and Victor meticulously restored it to its turn-of-the-century elegance. That done, the Hammers kept it for a few years, vacationing and occasionally entertaining guests there, and then they decided to put it on the market. The asking price for the property, which included fifteen waterfront acres and the original furnishings, was $50,000; if items from Hyde Park were included, the price would be $75,000.

Despite these modest sums, *and* the historical aura surrounding the property, it remained unsold into 1960. Then along came this Hollywood movie that promised to feature prominently Campobello and the Roosevelt cottage, and the Hammers extended full cooperation. This included making the Roosevelt place available for filming, and also letting some of the cast and crew stay there. That was how Dore Schary, for example, came to sleep in Franklin Roosevelt's bed, an experience he would cherish almost as much as he did inserting himself into the movie—a brief and hammy turn as the moustache wearing Connecticut delegate who yields the floor to the New York delegation, represented by FDR, during the rousing 1924 convention scene.

Dore Schary had certainly had his ups and downs in the quarter-century or so that he'd been involved in the motion picture business. He'd first gained recognition as a scriptwriter on *Boy's Town*, a 1938 movie about a priest's work with troubled boys, the story that produced the line, "He ain't heavy, he's my brother." Later, Louis Mayer hired Schary and put him in charge of MGM's secondary or "B" pictures, one of which was *Lassie Come Home*, a huge wartime hit that did for collie dogs what Flipper did for whales. But Schary's liberal leanings soon clashed with Mayer's conservatism, and he quit. Then, in 1948, Nicholas Schenk, the head of the studio's parent company, Loew's, rehired Schary as vice-president in charge of production, Irving Thalberg's old job.

Louis Mayer saw this as a rebuff to himself and probably a sign that "Mr. Skunk," the name he sometimes used for Schenk, was planning to get rid of him. He was right. By 1951, he was gone, and he died a half-dozen years later. Dore Schary, meanwhile, rallied MGM from late-forties' doldrums and in the early fifties produced several notable films and some of the studio's most successful musicals. Then, as television grew, MGM stopped making big money, and in late 1957 Schary himself was fired.

Which was how he had come to write *Sunrise at Campobello* and get the chance to sleep in FDR's old bed.

On the island, the Hammer family also helped to find accommodation for other members of the movie party, including Greer Garson. An obviously appropriate place for her, the star whom Louis Mayer had once touted as the successor to Norma Shearer as MGM's preeminent female actor, was a 135-year-old home not far from the Roosevelt cottage. It had been the residence of Admiral William Fitzwilliam Owen, a son of old Captain William and the third Principal Proprietary of Campobello. (A nephew of the captain's had preceded him.). The property was now owned by a widow named Evelyn Morrell, whose late husband had bought it from H. Morton Merriman, owner of the Hemmingway silk company and New York's Knickerbocker Hotel, on 42nd Street. The Merrimans had been friends of the Roosevelts, and Franklin had once sponsored Morton for membership in the Century Association, the city's premier men's club. The Morrells had purchased the property in 1951, after seeing an advertisement in *The New York Times*, and they had subsequently become one of the very few American families to live on the island year-round.

Owen House sat on a promontory called Deer Point on the western side of the island, its many rooms filled with antiques and its grounds festooned with flowers and old trees that the admiral himself had planted. Victor Hammer suggested it to the production company, but Mrs. Morrell was cool to the idea. She worried about her liability, should something happen to one of the movie guests while in her care. In late April, however, one of the film's production people, Joel Freeman, wrote from Beverly Hills, assuring her that personal liability wouldn't be a problem. Meanwhile, some of her Campobello neighbours began urging her to show more community spirit. So that was how the first two floors of Owen House came to be taken over by the movie crowd, including Greer Garson and her personal entourage of a maid, two hair stylists, and two make-up artists. And how Evelyn Morrell came to have one of the great experiences of her life.

In June, 2002, having decided to try and learn more about those memorable few days on Campobello, I visited the island where one of the first people I spoke to was Evelyn Morrell's daughter, Joyce. She had been a college student in 1960, at Middlebury, in Vermont, with only a passing interest in the exciting events taking place back home, although she did return long enough to see Ralph Bellamy when he and Hume Cronyn dropped by Owen House. "I have this memory of him," she said, "sitting in this overstuffed Victorian rocker and practicing with this cigarette holder clenched in his teeth. 'Does this look, all right'? he said. 'How am I doing'?"

But the one who really came under the Hollywood spell was her mother. Evelyn Morrell died in 1982, and Joyce said to me, "It is too bad you can't talk to my mother. She was really into this. Oh, she had a wonderful time." When she learned that her guests would include Greer Garson, Evelyn had become an enthusiastic hostess. The actress made her feel like an old friend, and the pair chatted amiably. In the cool evenings, Evelyn built fires in the fireplace, and Miss Garson bathed by candlelight, because not all of the Owen House rooms had electricity. She also called her husband Buddy, back in the States, imploring him to join her on this beautiful isle. By day, Evelyn brought out her best china and served tea to her guests—one of Joyce's mementos is a photograph of her mother pouring while a smiling Jean Hagen, the pretty actress who played FDR's secretary, Marguerite "Missy" LeHand, looks on. On Sunday, Evelyn took Greer to the service at the island's historic little Anglican Church, St. Anne's (Admiral Owen had built that, too), which the Roosevelts had also attended. It was like a dream, the actress and her new island friend strolling to church together amid the blue and green of a June Sunday, while a fresh-faced group of island high school grads looked on—they happened to be having their baccalaureate service that morning. It was a moment Evelyn Morrell never forgot.

St. Anne's, in fact, became a focal point of the moviemakers' stay on the island. They had needed a place where everybody could be fed, and that had turned out to be the adjacent church hall. It was a fine serviceable building that, when it wasn't being used for church related activities, was a hotbed of quilting by the women of the congregation. It had, however, never been used as a regular dining hall for a small army of people.

Fig. 10.4 Filming of Sunrise at Campobello. *Ralph Bellamy as Franklin Roosevelt (centre), in sweater and hat; Greer Garson as Eleanor Roosevelt at right.*

So, with the church's permission, the movie people made a few changes. In the area surrounding a small stage at one end of the hall, a double sink was installed, along with hot and cold running water, a gas range, and baking racks. Then they hired a catering outfit from Bangor, Maine, to prepare the food, and they put out a call for islanders to serve and do the wash up. Thus had St. Anne's Church Hall become the site of daily gatherings of the movie folk, who ate good down-home food and bantered easily with each other and with the island ladies who served them. It had been like one long series of church suppers, and the church got to keep the kitchen equipment.

Filming got under way immediately, on the very night the movie people arrived, in fact, when they shot a spectacular sunset over the island. Why photograph a sunset for a movie called *Sunrise at Campobello*? It was because the Roosevelt cottage happened to be located inconveniently on the island's western side, which, of course, received the last, not the first, rays of the sun. So, to get the sunrise shots needed for the film's opening, the moviemakers merely rearranged the local meteorology—they filmed a sunset and then ran it backwards. It did the job, although whenever it was mentioned afterwards, the islanders always chuckled a little.

The Sun Shines on Campobello

Several locations were used for the film, both on Campobello and over in Eastport, where the Maine Central Railway furnished a steam locomotive and vintage passenger cars for a scene involving Franklin's departure from the area after being stricken. On the island, the main location was the Roosevelt cottage, where, except for removing telephone and electrical wires and taking down a television antenna the Hammers had put up, remarkably few changes were required to return the place to its appearance in 1921. The producers did decide that the Roosevelt's little

Fig. 10.5 Dore Schary (left), producer of Sunrise at Campobello and Fred Phillips, assistant director of the New Brunswick Bureau of Information (right), consult on the movie set.

boat dock—in back of the cottage on Friars Bay—wasn't up to snuff, and they built another in a more picturesque setting. And they rejected the somewhat nondescript staircase in the Roosevelt cottage in favour of a more photogenic one in another summer residence.

As the filming began, newspaper reporters and magazine writers showed up, and, looking for local colour, they sought out islanders who had known the real Roosevelts. Anecdotes were plentiful. Cleveland Mitchell, who ran a small grocery store on the island, remembered Franklin as a generous tipper when he caddied for him at the local golf course. Mrs. Dexter Cooper, a summer resident whose late husband had once promoted a tidal power project in nearby Passamaquoddy Bay, told how the future president, as boy, had regularly pilfered cookies and biscuits from one of the summer homes, despite its being locked. At the White House, years later, she'd asked how he'd done it. "We tunnelled underneath," he said, grinning. There was also the story about another island storekeeper, George "Judge" Byron, who had become so angry with young Franklin when he caught him stealing from a cracker barrel that he'd propelled the boy out the door with a kick in the pants. "I am the only man in the world," the "Judge" later bragged, after he had become New Brunswick's King's Printer, "who ever kicked the backside of a president of the United States."

But perhaps the islander with the most intimate knowledge of the Roosevelts was Linnea Calder. Her mother, Anna McGowan, had been in service to the family for about 40 years, first as a laundress (while her husband worked as caretaker) and later as their housekeeper, both on Campobello and at Hyde Park. Linnea, too, had worked for the Roosevelts, maintaining the same sense of loyalty and propriety as had her mother, and that included, while hanging out the family's washing, making sure that Eleanor's undies were discreetly placed inside a pillowcase.

"We were used very well by the Roosevelts," Linnea's daughter Vera told me, including by Sara who, as she is portrayed in *Sunrise*, had an upper-crust imperiousness that led her to meddle regularly in Franklin and Eleanor's marriage. But to the McGowans and the Calders, said Vera, she was simply "Granny" Roosevelt, for whom they had both respect and affection.

Linnea was one of a handful of islanders invited to appear as extras in the film. Her big moment came in a scene at Cleve Mitchell's store, which the film crew invaded early one morning and, in a matter of a few hours, magically transformed into the way it might have looked forty years earlier. It was understood that Linnea, who was rather attractive, would play the role of her mother, Anna McGowan. But, in the end, all that could be seen was Linnea's back as she and another woman passed Eleanor/Greer Garson on their way into the store. Never mind. Linnea did get an autographed photograph from handsome young Tim Considine, who played the Roosevelt's son Jimmy, and she gave it to her granddaughter, who was enchanted.

Vera, too, had kept a souvenir photograph from those golden days, and she remarked on how amazing it had been "to think you were standing there actually watching a film being made. I mean this was something you never expected to see on Campobello. It was quite thrilling."

But it hadn't been the only time the luminous glow of show business had briefly touched the island. There was also the time Faye Emerson had visited Vera's school.

Faye Emerson. I remembered her. She had been a glamorous and ubiquitous presence on the game and talk shows of American television in the 1950s. But what I most remembered from those adolescent years (of both TV and me) was the controversy she caused when she began appearing on those shows wearing designer clothes with deeply plunging necklines, something considered quite shocking for this new "family" medium, although those appearances were also credited with getting males to watch something besides wrestling on TV. So what was Faye Emerson doing on Campobello? It turned out she had once been married to another Roosevelt son, Elliott, and they had been staying at the family cottage. This was before her bosom started making headlines (she and Elliott divorced in 1950), and her appearance in Vera's Grade Seven classroom had been, presumably, more discreet.

I went to Campobello three times, and on my second visit I rode over on the small car ferry that runs from Deer Island, New Brunswick—the only all-Canadian route you can take to the island. It was a bright, early-summer day, and as we pulled away from Deer Island Point, I looked to my right across the water towards Eastport, which had once been a thriving canning centre. From this distance, it still looked like a classic Maine coastal town, with its whitewashed homes and church spires poking above the trees, and it struck me that being here, and sailing "where the place called morning lies," must have been inspiring for a rich young man who might reasonably think that he could someday be the American President. In fact, *Sunrise at Campobello* opens with high aerial shots of Franklin and his family in their sailboat, the *Vireo*, off Campobello.

Discovering the Movies in New Brunswick

That day, I called on Blanche Johnston, who, at eighty-eight, had lived on the island all of her life. "We think it's a good place to live," she told me as we sat on the small front porch of the white house where she'd lived since she was twenty. "The weather. The quiet. I would hate to live in a city." When I'd called a few days earlier and told her of my interest, she'd been a little hesitant, unsure of what she might add to my putative tale, and now she said, "I don't think celebrities have that much impact on this part of the world. We're just not that impressed."

But she'd kindly called in reinforcements, and presently they arrived in the persons of Blanche's neighbour, Alice Gough, and Alice's daughter, Mary Helen Robichaud. It was forty-two years almost to the day since the *Sunrise* crew had been on Campobello.

Some of the crew had stayed with her, Blanche went on, and that was convenient for them because St. Anne's Church Hall was right next-door. Others were billeted at the Gough's, across the road. Taking up the story, Alice said she'd waitressed at the hall and, some days, helped serve lunch at other filming locations on the island. Everybody had worked awfully hard, but it had been exciting and fun, too. She recalled Greer Garson sweeping into the hall "a little airily" for evening dinner, and one of the island's prominent female summer residents had shown up quite "soused." A few island wells went dry because of all the extra laundry, but, otherwise, things had gone just fine, and she remembered that on their last evening the movie folk had invited the workers at the hall to join them for dinner.

Alice's daughter, Mary Helen, had her own anecdote. One day she'd been walking along the road with her friend, Gwennie Cline, when Joel Freeman, who was Dore Schary's nephew and the production supervisor on the film, drove by in a white convertible. He stopped and asked the girls if they'd like a drive. Mary Helen was ten years old. She still remembered that convertible, and its red leather upholstery. "We thought we would die," she said. "It was so exciting. We thought, 'Oh, this is good'."

Later that day, I met Mary Mitchell, the wife of a fisherman. In 1960, she'd been Mary Chute, twenty years old, two years out of high school, working for twenty-five dollars a week at a summer job for some Americans on nearby Head Harbour Island. When the filmmakers arrived on Campobello, she'd come over to help serve the meals at St. Anne's.

One day, she was approached and asked if she would like to appear before the cameras. She would be a stand-in for Greer Garson, whom she resembled in height and build. The fit was good, and in more ways than one. Mary's grandfather, Erlon Cline, who'd helped raise her on a small island farm after her father left when she was just a baby, had known Franklin Roosevelt. And now here she was being asked to be a stand-in for FDR's wife in a big Hollywood movie. It didn't matter that it would be that opening sailing scene, and that it would be filmed from so high in the air that she would be barely visible. She got dressed up in Greer Garson's movie clothes, took to the high seas, "and felt like a million dollars."

Mary lived now with her husband, Stanley, in a modern home with a two-car garage. But it hadn't always been that way, and as we sat at a table she told me a little more about her grandfather. There was a picture of him, she said, in the Nowlan book. It was on page 116 and included an anecdote about a tangle he'd had one time with a presidential security man on the beach by the Roosevelt cottage.

For Mary, in those days when her grandfather was bringing her up, going to a movie over in Eastport or Lubec had been a very big treat. Life then was certainly more difficult—the farm had an outhouse, for example—but she thought she'd enjoyed it more, especially working with the farm animals, and nowadays she loved going to Kings Landing, the re-created New Brunswick historic farm settlement near Fredericton. She'd lived all of her life on Campobello, and never had the island looked any better to her than when she returned home after a one-time, big trip to Alaska. But back in 1960, she said, Campobello had been an even quieter place; before the bridge to Lubec was built, it had "seemed like the island was ours."

On the very day the *Sunrise* crew completed shooting and left Campobello, Canadian and American officials came to the island for the ceremonial groundbreaking that constituted the formal start on construction of that bridge. If one believed a story in *The New York Herald Tribune*, the event was the direct result of the movie. In fact, the islanders had been campaigning years for a bridge, sometimes joined by the summer colonists. One time, during an annual concert to support the local library, the summer people had sung a song they called, "Cross over the Bridge—If We Had a Bridge."

Sunrise at Campobello reached movie theatres in the fall of 1960 amid a huge publicity campaign. It included distributing ten million FDR campaign buttons bearing Ralph Bellamy's image, and arranging for the U.S. National Council of Teachers of English to produce a study guide to accompany the film, which meant, of course, that, in order for the

Fig. 10.6 Poster from the Sunrise at Campobello *press kit.*

guide to be used, students would have to go to the movie by the busload. There were also radio and television promos, and large newspaper ads. Among the latter was a five-column by nine-inch mat that might have nettled some of the islanders had they seen it. At the top was the line that read; "Campobello...whoever heard of a place called Campobello"? And another asking why anybody should care "about a sunrise over such a place with such a name." The ad said a lot about Hollywood attitudes toward the country next door.

After the film's New York premiere, *The New York Times'* movie critic Bosley Crowther wrote that Schary's story "has been reproduced on the screen with a photographic fervour that gives, for better or worse, a wider exposure and sharper focus than it had on the stage." Crowther had some misgivings about the Bellamy and Garson performances, but he thought Hume Cronyn's, as Louis Howe, was "brilliant." Overall, he said it was a "well-done, moving biographical film." Brooks Atkinson, *The Times'* renowned stage critic, observed that, with the film, Schary had "increased the stature" of his work. He liked how "the glorious blue of the limitless sea" in the opening scene had served as a prologue comparing "the unbounded world of the healthy and the constricted world of the maimed."

The film did well at the box office. Only in the Soviet Union did it bomb. Entered in a Moscow Film Festival the following summer, it drew an overflow audience—which began to leave a few minutes after the movie started; at the end, only a few people were left. The Russians had apparently expected a film about FDR's role during the Second World War. Now that the Cold War had set in, a story about personal American heroism wasn't of much interest. American writer and director Joshua Logan, a festival juror, said entering *Sunrise at Campobello* had been a mistake; "The United States did not put its best foot forward."

But, on Campobello, folks couldn't wait for *Sunrise* to arrive at theatres. The Gough family got into their 1960 Chevrolet and drove all the way to Boston. Alice Gough felt the movie "was all right. We liked the part about Campobello. I think everybody was pleased that we were getting a little attention."

The Hammer family was probably pleased, too. Now, with a land bridge to the island coming at last, they were advancing the idea of turning the island over to the governments of the United States and Canada to maintain as an historic site. And, sure enough, in August, 1962, Democratic President John F. Kennedy, visiting the Brunswick Naval Air Station in Maine, proposed that a park be established on Campobello that would serve as a memorial to President Roosevelt and strengthen the bond between Canada and the United States. Later that fall, the diligent Hammers published a guidebook called *FDR's Beloved Island*. The wife of the Hammers' brother Harry put it together. It consisted mainly of black and white photographs, many of which she had taken herself, not always successfully. Nonetheless, they'd been exhibited some years earlier at St. Anne's Church. "Now," wrote Mrs. Hammer, who called herself "bette e. barber" (e. e. cummings style), "we offer them to a larger audience in happy memory." Reproduced on the inside back cover was a newspaper story about the Kennedy proposal.

Less than two years later, the wives of the new American president, Lyndon Johnson, and Canadian Prime Minister Lester Pearson came to the island to dedicate the Roosevelt Campobello International Park. Also prominent in the proceedings was Armand Hammer, who presented the deeds for the property to the new park's commissioners. "It was here,"

Lady Byrd Johnson observed during her remarks, "that tragedy struck, and it was here that a man triumphed over adversity." It sounded like she'd seen the movie, too.

Way back, when the *Sunrise at Campobello* crew was breaking camp and heading for the ferry, the rector of St. Anne's Anglican Church, the Reverend Norman P. Fairweather, had surveyed his charge and declared, "Our future looks bright." He had been right, more or less. The movie came out, the bridge was built, the park was created. Eventually it would encompass hundreds of hectares, all of which, including the Roosevelt home, were preserved in pristine condition. Nowadays it annually attracts thousands of visitors, many of them in buses, to see the cottage, examine Roosevelt exhibits, view a film documentary or two, hike the park trails, and perhaps make a quick tour of the island before heading back over the Roosevelt Memorial Bridge. It is tourism in a very concentrated form.

Naturally, island life has changed in other ways over the years. "At night-time, everybody knew where their kids were in the days of the car ferry," resident Anne Marie (Calder) Young told me. She was the class valedictorian at Campobello Island Consolidated School in the June of *Sunrise at Campobello*. Livelihoods have changed, too. Traditional fishing isn't what it used to be. There is aquaculture now, its presence announced by droning feeding machines and booming predator-scaring devices at offshore sites, and with its economic benefits said to be concentrated on fewer people. Americans are back as summer residents, but they are not the post-Gilded Age crowd like the Roosevelts, and they spend their time rather quietly on the eastern side of the island. An interested party some years ago was James McDougal, Bill and Hillary Clinton's flamboyant old Arkansas friend, who bought property on the island and talked of building a modern resort. But he died in prison, after the Whitewater real estate scandal.

Occasionally, I suppose, somebody hauls out a video for another look at *Sunrise at Campobello*. Today it seems as much a museum piece as the Roosevelt cottage. The actors' performances are stagy and strained, and poor Greer Garson, fitted out with protruding false teeth and adopting an exaggerated, singsong voice in apparent imitation of Eleanor, sounds god-awful. The late *New Yorker* critic Pauline Kael once described Garson as "one of the most richly syllabled queenly horrors of Hollywood," which was surely no way to treat a lady, but perhaps she was thinking mostly of the performance in *Sunrise*.

The memories on Campobello are better. Alice Gough, recalling that her husband helped build the new dock for the movie, and that some of the filming was done from his boat, also remembered that she got a lace doily from one of the tables at the church hall, and Greer Garson autographed it for her. She took it home, framed it, and it hung on a wall in her home until it faded in the sun. Daughter, Mary Helen, never forgot that ride in the convertible with the red leather upholstery; "I think about it quite often," she said. "It was so perfect." Even Blanche Johnston remembered that the filmmaking "made us perk up for a little while."

On the morning she departed, Miss Garson arose before dawn and wrote a note thanking Evelyn Morrell for her many kindnesses and for the gift of a little silver box. It was a note, Evelyn said, she'd always treasure. Later, the actress sent a gift of her own, a Wedgewood piece she bought in New York, on her way home, and the two exchanged letters for the next year or so. In *her* home, Mary Mitchell kept another kind of souvenir; copies of a *Sunrise at Campobello* production book, and of *Weekend Magazine* and *Star Weekly*, the two big Canadian newspaper supplements which that fall ran stories on the filmmaking. The rest of her family sometimes chided her about hanging onto such things for so long, but after all, she said, the event was "a big highlight in my life." Not quite as big, though, as giving birth to a son on the mainland a couple of years later and coming home with him, the last baby, as it turned out, to be brought back to the island on the ferry. It stopped running when the new bridge opened, and Campobello became not quite an island anymore.

Chapter Eleven

Remembering the Movies

Until the arrival of television, the place where most people "connected" with motion pictures was at the local movie house. Not just an unprecedented entertainment venue, it was also the wellspring from which came all the related habits that people took up. It caused them to follow the stars' careers via fan magazines, newspapers, and radio. Sometimes it prompted those most enamoured to try and emulate this actor or that in appearance, style, and manners. The hometown movie house was an institution of considerable formative influence, but, unlike churches, schools, hockey rinks, and curling clubs, only rarely, I discovered, did it merit any mention in local histories.

This is why I decided to record some oral histories. Starting with two former school friends of mine who got into the moviegoing habit in the 1950s, when I did, I chose my interviewees randomly, although, in some instances, they were people I knew to have more than a passing acquaintance with the movie business. In all, I spoke to a dozen people, not a sample size big enough to prove anything, but one that did nevertheless yield a harvest of surprising variations on the theme of movie memories and effect.

1. Barbara Birkland (neé Bertelsen) and Madeleine Gallimore (neé Guimont)

It's easy to forget, in this televised and digitized age, the effect movies once had on small-town North American life. In the 1950s, just as television was arriving, Grand Falls, NB, had two movie theatres, the Grand (formerly the Opera House), and, just across the street, which, incidentally, was called Broadway, a newcomer, the Riviera. Good friends Barbara Bertelsen and Madeleine Guimont were schoolmates of mine, and both were movie fans. In fact, it was Madeleine's father Sylvio, aided significantly by his wife, Edna, who built and ran the five-hundred-seat Riviera.

Fig. 11.1 Going to the movies in Grand Falls.

BARBARA: When I was little, my grandmother would take me. She would buy me popcorn and a candy bar, and it was always a cowboy movie. (Laughs.) When I got older, I went a lot by myself, and I kind of went just to escape. I went once or twice a week and was always sorry when the movies ended, and it was time to go home. Going to the movies was like being in another world.

MADELEINE: My dad's older brother was a priest in Quebec, and when we went there to visit, and our cousins came from Quebec City and Montreal, we'd all meet at the rectory, and he always ordered movies for us to see, the Three Stooges and that kind of thing. The movies were very, very good. They had to be. (Laughs.) Because they were sanctioned by the priest!

BARBARA: I remember going to *Gone with the Wind*, and it was so long that I took a lunch with me to eat at intermission. But, whatever the movie was, I'd really get into it, and I'd come home and pretend that I was so-and-so (Laughs).

MADELEINE: Dad always loved the movies, and he thought movie theatres would go on forever, and that's why he decided to build one. Mom and Dad called it the Riviera because they associated entertainment with the French Riviera, and also because of the St. John River going around the town.

My mother was very involved with our theatre. The outside colour was a pale, pinkish peach, because peach was her favourite colour. She made the drapes for inside the theatre, with the help of two neighbours. She was a good seamstress and had a Singer sewing machine that she was very proud of.

And she had a sense of flare, a sense of style. I think she'd acquired this from working in New York City as a governess in a rich home.

BARBARA: When I went home from a movie, it would stay with me a couple of days, and I was always somebody different. For every movie I went to, I became that character. I would try to do something with my hair, because I wanted to look like Jane Powell so badly. I would try my hair this way and that way. I never quite got it, though, never quite made it.

MADELEINE: I used to put a book on my head. Leslie Caron, for one, had a real straight walk, because she was a dancer, and I used to try to walk straight and put a book on my head. I think I saw that in a movie—the actresses doing that to improve their walks. I think I did that throughout my teenage years. Isn't that awful?

BARBARA: The movies gave us a glimpse into Europe and other places that we wouldn't have had in any other way at that time of our life. I remember a movie about someone who lived in a basement apartment in New York, and I thought it would be wonderful to do that and hear the subway and have it shake that little apartment. It would be so romantic. (Laughs.) I eventually changed my mind about that.

MADELEINE: We must have had at least six usherettes. They were mostly my friends, including Barb. And, of course, we had to have uniforms

Fig. 11.2 Barbara Bertelsen and Madeleine Guimont, Grand Falls movie-going friends of the author, 1956.

because that was how Mommy saw us. They were off-white, cream, I would say, with a little vest and a pleated skirt, which had to be ironed to look good. It was not a very practical uniform, but they were pretty with a sheer blouse of pale green that matched the drapes. Mom was something else!
BARBARA: We were very young, thirteen or fourteen. But once I learned how to use the flashlight, it was fine. (Laughs.) It was a great first job.
MADELEINE: We could see who was sitting with whom.
BARBARA: In the back row. (Laughter)
MADELEINE: I think my father thought that, if he built a theatre, it would be something he could leave behind maybe for my brother to take on. But, of course, the timing was wrong, and we couldn't get the right movies. We started showing French movies once a week, and they kept us going for a while. And we could get English movies from the J. Arthur Rank Organization, and they had a different feel to them, less pizzazz, more substance. I liked the English movies, still do, because I grew up with them, but they were not as popular, because they just weren't advertised generally, and they didn't have big drawing stars. But, otherwise, we could only get second-line movies, while the Grand got the first-line ones. I'm not sure why that happened, but it didn't work out for our theatre.

2. Mitchell Franklin

Moving picture exhibition was the Franklin family business. Mitchell Franklin's father was, at one time, president of RKO Canada, and the family had a dozen theatres of its own in the Maritimes, including four drive-ins, in which it was a regional pioneer. Mitchell entered the business in the 1930s, in Saint John, where the chain (known for a time as Franklin-Hershorn) eventually operated the Mayfair and Regent theatres in the city and a drive-in in nearby Grand Bay. Not long after he started, it was arranged, through local connections, for him to visit Hollywood, where one day he was ushered into the largest office he'd ever seen, and found himself face-to-face with Louis B. Mayer.

He asked me some pertinent questions; among them was, did I know any of the Jewish population in Saint John? And I said, well, yes I did. I told him I was president of B'nai B'rith. Are you Jewish? he asked. I said, yes, and he didn't say anything. He reached for the telephone and made a call. "Ida? I've got a nice Jewish boy sitting here from Saint John, and he's taking Mitzi out for dinner tonight, and you tell her that I said so."

Fig. 11.3 Mitchell Franklin ca. 1937, in Hollywood for an introduction to movie making.

I could hardly believe my ears. I didn't know who Mitzi was, and I wanted to look at some of the young starlets. Well, it turned out it was just the luckiest break I could imagine. She was a lovely looking girl. She was the boss's niece, and she took me everywhere. We went to some well-known Hollywood place, and I was aghast at the menu prices and the liquor prices, and I was trying to act the debonair, young, internationally famous raconteur, whatever.

Mitzi ordered a Scotch, and I ordered a Scotch. Unbeknownst to me, the style of serving liquor in that particular restaurant was that they brought a whole bottle and put it on the table, and there was a graduated scale down the side of a bottle, and at the end of the evening the waiter would look at the scale, and you'd have to pay for what was out of the bottle.

Along came Cary Grant. He said, "Hello, Mitzi," and sat down and reached for the bottle and an empty glass and poured it, and I thought, gee, this is terrific. Well, after he reached for the bottle about the third time, I began to worry, and when Mitzi ordered pheasant-under-glass, at $7.50, I knew I didn't have the money. Well, in those days, a man never let a woman pay the bill. But it didn't bother Mitzi. She paid the bill, and I was mortified.

Ida Cummings. She was Mitzi's mother and Louis B. Mayer's sister, and she asked me if I would take her to the premiere of the biggest MGM picture of that season. Well, I had rented a two-seat Ford car with a rumble seat, it was broken down and abused, but it was the cheapest thing I could find. I told Mrs. Cummings this is what I had, but she wanted to come with me.

So now I am driving Ida Cummings to the studio for the first showing of this great picture, and it starts to rain. I lifted the top of this convertible, and there was no canvas on it. It was removed. There was just the skeleton. I'll never forget that. And the other thing I'll never forget is Ida Cummings, with the heavy rain bringing her hair down all over, the mascara and the make-up all going to hell, and her distancing herself from me as far as she could in this two-seater. And when we arrived at the studio, she flew out of the car as if I was non-existent.

I was staying at the cheapest hotel you could imagine, a dollar a night, and it was a crumb bum place. One day I went down to the lobby, and there was this big fella sitting there, and he hollered, "Franklin"! I went over and he said, "Sit down. I want to talk to you." You see, he used to check the hotel registration, and I had registered from Halifax, Nova Scotia, Canada, and he said, "I've been in Halifax a few times. I've boxed down there. I used to be a boxer." So he decides to take me under his wing. Well, I don't mean to be snobbish, but that wasn't my idea of being shown around. I told him about the incident with Mrs. Cummings and the car. "No canvas on the car?" he said. "I'm taking you back in that car. They're not going to get away with that." I said, "No, no, no, Bing." Bing Conley. I had visions of him murdering the guy. He went in, and the next thing

I heard, the fellow was half crying and Bing was dragging him out by the collar. "My friend is from Halifax," Bing told him. "Give him back his money." Well, I really didn't want any part of this (laughs). I just wanted to get out. And the fella was protesting, and Bing gave him a clip on the head, and he said, "If you don't do it now, I'll cut every goddamn tire off this car." Anyway, the fella forced the money back on me, and I fled Hollywood.

3. David Adams Richards

Writer David Adams Richards' family ran moving picture theatres for more than half a century in Newcastle, on New Brunswick's Miramichi River. Two of his novels, Nights Below Station Street *and* The Bay of Love and Sorrows, *have been made into feature films, and he adapted another,* For Those Who Hunt the Wounded Down, *for television. Earlier, he wrote the script for* Small Gifts, *which became a CBC Christmas special. As well, his 1997 novel,* River of the Brokenhearted, *is based in part on his grandmother's experience in the picture business.*

My grandfather moved to Canada from England in 1911. He was a pianist. He had his degree from the Royal Conservatory, and his big plan was to start playing in Halifax and play all the way across to Victoria. When he got to Newcastle, he needed someone to accompany him on the violin, and this young woman auditioned, and it was Janie McGowan, my grandmother. She said, " I don't play the violin, I play the fiddle." He said, "Can you read music"? And she said, "I can't read a note, but there is nothing you can play that I can't follow." So they fell in love and got married, and they started their theatre. Of course, it was a silent picture, so they played for silent pictures.

When he died in 1923, I think she gave it up for a while and then she went into business with certain other individuals in town who tried to take over her theatre. They tried to foreclose on her mortgage. Then finally she got the rights to the talkies in the Newcastle area and put other theatres out of business. So they tried to blow her up with dynamite, and that didn't work because my great-uncle found the dynamite taped to the maple or birch or whatever he was loading up the stove with that night.
FOLSTER: Did you see a lot of movies while you were growing up in the 1950s?
RICHARDS: Yes, every chance I could. I remember sneaking into *Psycho* and getting to the part just before the shower, and there was a hand on

Discovering the Movies in New Brunswick

Fig. 11.4 *The Opera House in Miramichi (Newcastle) was built in 1903 for the Loyal Orange Lodge with members meeting above the theatre where travelling entertainers performed and where movies were shown from 1909. Two generations of the Richards family, beginning with Janie McGowan and William Richards who started in the movie business in 1910, operated a movie theatre in the Opera House from the late 1930s until 1979. Theirs was the longest single family theatre business in the Maritimes having begun in another building in 1910.*

my shoulder. And it was my grandmother. She said, "You can't watch this movie"! I said, "Oh, gee." (Laughs).

When I was three years old I started to smoke because my favourite movies were Rory Calhoun cowboy movies and all the cowboys smoked around the campfire. And so me and Kenny Crockett stole cigarettes out his mother's purse and decided to light campfires and smoke.

I always liked movie *noir*. A movie that showed a person's character and generally people against the odds, because that's what it's all about.
FOLSTER: It almost sounds like you were headed in the direction of becoming a writer by watching movies.
RICHARDS: I may or may not have been. The thing about it is, there are various ways of becoming influenced by certain things and maybe movies compelled me, sometimes, to pick up a book. I mean, who knows? Certainly, I could not have become a novelist without reading novels.

My mother fell off the steps of her porch bringing in the clothes when she was seven months with me, and I was born that night. First of all, they didn't think I was going to live, and then, if I lived, they thought I would be completely retarded. Then when it became clear that I wasn't retarded they felt that I would never be able to walk. Well, I managed to walk, but my left side was damaged for my lifetime, and so that put me at a distinct disadvantage, in one way, to kids around me. It makes you an outsider, but it is wonderful in that you can gather information of what an outsider is and what an insider is. I think that has formed the basis of my work.

It also allowed me to watch a lot of movies, because I couldn't skate. So when the kids went skating, I went to the movies.

Oh God, I [still] watch tons of movies. But you know what? I don't go to theatres anymore. I'm getting too old and grumpy to go to theatres. The last time, kids were talking behind me, and I broke the seat in front of me, I was so angry.

My mother didn't live to see any of my stories become films. My father got to see some of them. I don't know how many he watched. He got a cameo in *Small Gifts*, a little Christmas movie I made. When little Nora is going in to count up her pennies to get the money, he was in the bank for that. He never got on set, which was too bad. I would have loved to take him on set and show him actually how they did it.

When I saw the first rushes from *Small Gifts*, I started to scream. It was because, when you write something, just like when you read something, you have it exactly in your mind what that person or that character is. And you see someone. And Nora, in *Small Gifts*, for me was this little redheaded kid about nineteen years old, with freckles over her face, just married to the love of her life who was out of work and trying to get money for Christmas. And she was just this skinny little sweetheart, you know, and not very pretty. And the first time I saw Jessica Steen walk on camera, this beautiful woman who had been down in Hollywood and had come back to Canada to do this movie, I just started to scream. I said (laughs), "Jesus!" Also, Jeremy Ratchford spoke like a working class kid from northern Ontario, not a working class kid from the Maritimes. And there's a real difference.

However, once I began to realize that it is an approximation, that the director, the producer, the amount of money, the actors—their own physicality, just the way they look—brings a certain tempo to the work—once I began to realize that and settle down a bit, then I began to see that they did a really fine job and they really put their hearts and souls into it, then I began to be less concerned and more able and willing to admire what they were doing.

FOLSTER: Why do you think Canadian movies don't have a large following?

RICHARDS: There are a hundred reasons. Most Canadian movies come out of the CBC formula in Toronto. You have to know the country you are writing about. Toronto is so terrified of not being liked by the United States, who we are a cultural slave of, it hasn't taken the time to know its own country. And people have to know themselves. That's why I can write about Miramichi, my fictional Miramichi. It's not because I know so much about the Miramichi, it's because Miramichiers know about themselves. That doesn't transfer to Toronto. It never has.

The second problem is the money. They pay more for a Coke commercial than they do for a Canadian movie. And, of course, you don't really let people know it's in New Brunswick, so you don't want them to see the trees and you don't want them to see the licence plates. Because you've really got to pretend that these are Americans, if you want to get a deal internationally.

How do we save New Brunswick culture? Well, the first thing you have to ask is, what is New Brunswick culture? New Brunswick culture is Oprah Winfrey and Dr. Phil as much as anything else. New Brunswick culture is going and watching NFL football at the local bar.

FOLSTER: Do you think it's too late to pull it back?

RICHARDS: I'm saying it's wonderful that we have been able to incorporate all this and still keep some sense of ourselves. But we are not the kind of province that can create a movie industry because of that. If we do, that will be great. I mean, I'd be the first to applaud it, but I don't think we can.

FOLSTER: Well, maybe the movie industry isn't where you start. Maybe you start by just creating an identity for yourself, and that can come from people like you and a whole lot of other. . .

RICHARDS: Well, it has. I mean Alden Nowlan is, to me, a cultural icon in this country. He is one of the greatest poets that ever lived in Canada, maybe one of the great poets of the twentieth century in North America, in the English-speaking world, but I'll guarantee you that every New Brunswicker that ever lived has been influenced more by Louis B. Mayer than by Alden Nowlan.

4. Hilarian Coughlan

In the late 1940s, Hilarian Coughlan's parents, John and Elizabeth, got into the theatre business in Tracadie, a village on New Brunswick's Acadian Peninsula. The theatre had an uncommon name for a motion picture house, although one with a certain majesty about it. And the name wasn't the only unique thing about moviegoing in Tracadie. Some of the practices also startled his future wife, Patricia, the first time she encountered them.

The theatre was called the Rex, and they told me it was because every letter in a name cost money, and they chose Rex because it was the shortest. (laughs)

There were other theatres around. There was one in Caraquet, which was about twenty-five miles away, and one as well, I believe, in Shippagan, about the same distance away. But, for some reason, the drawing card was Tracadie; and, I should tell you, they were all in English. They were American movies, with no subtitles.

Tracadie, let's say, was sort of known as being more English than Caraquet or Shippagan. Like, when we played ball against Caraquet or Shippagan, the Caraquet team always had a very French name, while it was always the Tracadie Eagles or a name like that. Even the old nuns who

Fig. 11.5 *Story from the* Moncton Times, *October 24, 1972, covering the fire at The Rex in Tracadie.*

established the lazaretto said—I read this recently—Tracadie's a place of mostly French-speaking, but they love to speak English.

We also showed movies on Sunday nights, but instead of an admission charge, a silver collection was taken, because movie theatres weren't allowed to be open on Sundays. So, nothing was done as long as we didn't sell tickets. And people would willingly give the cost, or price, of a ticket. That's what they would pay—and this money was set aside to buy a fire engine for the village, and then a heated garage for it, and, if I'm not mistaken, even the boots, hats, and the coats the firemen wore. That could have been another reason people came to our theatre, because the fire department serviced the surrounding area, too.

Something else that was interesting for Patricia, [Hilarian's wife] when she first came into the picture, was that, in Tracadie, on Christmas Day, we'd have a big family meal. We'd be, oh, God, twenty-five or thirty, at the oldest of my sisters Mae's place, and then, afterward, we'd go to a movie (laughs)—a movie or a dance. And everybody else did that, too. Well, not everybody, but a fair number. Patricia just couldn't get over that, because at her place, in Rexton, it would be strictly visiting family, you know.

5. Herménégilde Chiasson, Lieutenant-Governor of New Brunswick, 2003-2009

People sometimes dream of rising to prominence or of being in the cinema. But in the small Acadian village of Saint-Simon, where Herménégilde Chiasson was born, there were no such dreams—or prospects. Yet he achieved both, and more. He became internationally celebrated as a writer, poet, artist, photographer, playwright, and filmmaker, and in August, 2003, he began a six-year term as one of New Brunswick's most popular lieutenant governors ever.

Fig. 11.6 Herménégilde Chiasson

The closest cinema or theatre was in Caraquet. My brothers would go there, and they would tell me the story of what they had seen. The theatre showed American films. I remember I picked a flyer off a car window, and it was for *Quo Vadis*. That was so impressive. But I think the first time I saw a film, it was a missionary who had come to our church, and it was a sound film that they were projecting on a sheet. I was maybe six or seven, and it was just

Remembering the Movies

about a fight between a tiger and a lion, I think. I was there with my father, and it created a great, great impression on me.

Later on, I went to Saint-Joseph College in the early sixties, and they had a film club there, and this is where I saw my first Truffaut and Antonioni, people like that, Fellini. And I remember that I would look at those films, but it really didn't connect in my mind that these were art films, and that you would have films that were made just for entertainment, and all that. One afternoon, I was looking at TV, and I saw *L'Eclisse* by Antonioni. I started to look at the way the actors were behaving, and then everything sort of clicked in my mind. So, from then on, I started to get interested in film.

Fig. 11.7 Childhood photo of Herménégilde Chiasson, creased and torn as he remembers it. Courtesy of Herménégilde Chiasson.

I also remember seeing a documentary on TV by Pierre Perrault called *Au pays de Neufue-France Ka Ke Ki Ku* [*Au Pays de Neufve-France (1960)*]. In those days, everything was done in a studio, especially in Quebec, because the budgets were really small, and the lighting was crude, and the films weren't very polished. But Crawley Films produced Perrault's film, and it had real images shot outside the studio with the softer light that is available out of doors. I think that had an influence on me in terms of documentaries.

It's very strange, you know, because where I was born, there wasn't a camera, so there's no image of me before the age of sixteen except a photograph of me that was taken by a neighbour, and someone gave it to me a while ago, and it's all creased and broken and all that, and you look at that, and you say, well, this is me at a far-away age, but it's very strange because there's no photograph before that.

So maybe this is why, having been deprived of that for a long while, I got so interested in image-making. I've noticed lately that I've produced a great many self-portraits. And that probably came out of having no image for so long and then sort of recovering it.

The idea to do a film came, I believe, when the National Film Board established a studio in Moncton. Many of my friends or people I knew were working at that, and I thought, if they can do it, I can do it, as well. Probably I always wanted to do a film, but I thought you had to be in a school. I had never thought of the apprenticeship approach.

Now I do many things, many different forms of art, but all of these things sort of inter-influence each other. I know that filmmaking has had a great influence on my writing because now I sort of think in fragments, you know, just like a film, like a puzzle. One thing I've also noticed, in my work as a visual artist, is that I have a tendency to do a string of images or sequence of images.

6. JOCELYN LEBEL

In Saint-Quentin, a farming and lumbering village in the north of the province, the local theatre was the Roman Catholic Church hall. And the person who chose the movies was Jocelyn LeBel's father, a lawyer and trusted community leader. The seats were hard-backed folding chairs, and sometimes the film broke in the middle of a dramatic scene, leading to cries of dismay in the audience. But it was always repaired, and that was how the villagers got to see movies in the 1950s, including quite a few with an historical theme.

Fig. 11.8 Exterior of Théâtre Montcalm, Saint-Quentin.

Remembering the Movies

Fig. 11.9 Interior of Théâtre Montcalm, Saint-Quentin.

It was called the Theatre Montcalm, after one of the figures in French Canadian history. My dad ordered the movies for the theatre. I know that because he would get these little three-by-five cards, and they had descriptions of the movies and the lengths of them. They were all English movies. There weren't any French productions in those days, except a few from France.

I don't think the main purpose of the theatre was to make money. I'm sure they didn't want to lose money, but it was not a way to make the church richer, let's say. It was just an entertainment for the community. Movies existed, and it was decided people should see them, and so we had a movie theatre.

I think my father saw to the propriety of the movies. He was a churchgoer, and he knew his community well enough to know what was good and what wasn't. But I think in those days there weren't too many movies that were objectionable. There were nice love stories. And there were cowboy movies, maybe with a bit of violence in them, but not as bad as today's.

Usually there was a film on Saturday afternoon, and it was always an action film, and the good guys always won over the bad guys. We kids applauded and booed. (Laughs). We were part of the action.

I was also allowed to go to the movies in the evenings. My dad was a history buff, and he loved historical movies. So he would order all these movies with history in them, and we were allowed to go, provided we would read about whatever it was in the movie. If it was Alexander the Great, he would bring out his encyclopedia, and we had to read about Alexander the Great. Or if it was Cleopatra or Napoleon or whatever, we had to know. He insisted that we get some knowledge of the topic that we were going to see. I remember that as almost like a school assignment. I really liked history in school, and I think it must have come from seeing all these historical movies.

We had a maid at home. Well, she wasn't a maid. I guess my dad called her his eldest daughter. She came to work for us because my mom was secretary to my dad, who was a lawyer, and this lady looked after the kids. In her free time, she also ran the canteen at the cinema. She lived with us, and I remember her taking care of the canteen and cleaning up the cinema after the show. Because of her, and because of Dad ordering the movies, we used to get in free. When we came to the ticket counter—it had a glass window and a little hole at the bottom—we were allowed to just slip in. But we weren't allowed to tell anybody that.

7. Eva MacDonald

The railway centre of Moncton had four theatres in its downtown when Eva MacDonald grew up there. Early on, she became a big fan of movies. Her father worked nights for Canadian National, and sometimes her mother took her to the Empress, where they gave away prizes one night a week, and the Bunkhouse Boys performed country music between double features, one of which was always a Western. A lot of her cinematic nurturing, however, occurred at the Kent, just around the corner from her home, and when the theatre burned, in the late forties, she was present for that, too.

Back in the forties, when I was growing up, we spent a lot of time at the movies. It was pre-TV. I can remember going to the movies as a preschooler, going on Saturday mornings with my brother, who was six years older, to the Superman Club. My mother had boxes of Sunny Boy cereal because we needed a number of box tops to get in. They showed serials, and I remember the *Black Whip*, with a female cowboy whose brother was killed, and she had to take his mask and his cape and go out and save the world. Between that and the nuns, I learned to be a world-saver. (Laughs)

Later on, I usually went to the movies with a group of friends, but one time when I was seven or eight or maybe nine I had a quarrel with them, so I was there by myself, and the manager got up on the stage and said there was going to be a fire drill, and everybody was pushing to get out. I was going out the right-hand exit, and I remember tripping over this woman in a fur coat. She was lying on the floor. She had probably tripped, and everybody just went over her. But everybody got out in very quick time, and we watched from the other side of the street while the theatre burned down. It burned to the ground.

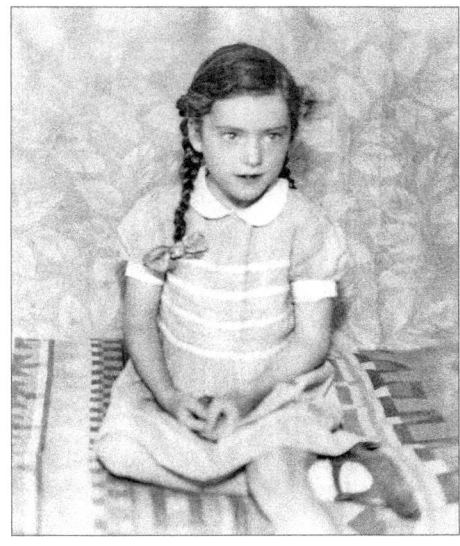

Fig. 11.10 Eva MacDonald, age 6.

It was a different world. We weren't protected the way they are now. I can remember my father had a railway pass. When I was probably around eleven, a friend and I would, on Saturday mornings, meet at two or three o'clock in the morning, and we'd each have our pass in hand. We'd walk through the streets of Moncton, down to the train station, and we'd get on the milk train to Saint John. It stopped at every farm on the way to pick up milk. We'd get into Saint John around eight o'clock, have breakfast, walk around, go to a movie, then take the train home, and get back probably at eight or nine in the evening. And we would do that by ourselves.

There's a scene in *The Bells of St. Mary's* when the girl doesn't pass because she's failed her exams, and then Bing Crosby [Father O'Malley] convinces the nun [Ingrid Bergman] that, really, the girl should have another chance. Well, I eventually became a teacher, and in my teaching career, I always gave them another chance. I thought this came out of my religious upbringing, but more likely it was the movies.

There was a book, *Rebecca*, by Daphne Du Maurier, and I don't know whether it was the book or the movie, but I almost married a guy just because he had an accent and looked older. In the book, Rebecca marries this older fellow with a British accent, and when I found one, I was real impressed. But then I found out he wasn't as old as he looked, and that was the end of that.

Names. All the Shirleys are of an age. They were born in the early to middle 1930s. Shirley Temple. And there was Linda Darnell. All the Lindas are of a certain age. All the Joans are from Joan Blondell and Joan Crawford. All the Joans are of an age. And those names have not come back into style again. In the 1950s, Debbies were pretty well born around 1956-57. Debbie Reynolds. Davids. When I was in high school, there were four Davids in my class. That was David Niven, who was very popular in 1939, when I was born. Now they take the names from TV, but then they took them from the movies.

8. Carolyn (Jamer) Campbell

I used to go up there [*the projection room at the Capitol Theatre in Perth-Andover*] and watch the movie, and I was always fascinated by the technicality of loading the projectors. There were two of them, and my boyfriend would start one film, and then he'd load the other projector, and there was some sort of little bell that jingled as it got toward the end of the reel. He would jump up and be ready to flip the switch to start the other projector. And I remember him watching for some little dots in the upper right hand corner of the screen. The dots were the signal to start the other machine and be ready to flip the switch to start projecting from the second.

Before that, I was still a little kid when I saw *Breakfast at Tiffany's*, and I remember being quite dazzled by it. I didn't come home and want to dress like the fashionistas, but I was fascinated by what I saw. And I did learn to whistle after I saw *Bridge on the River Kwai*. I loved the sound of whistling. I can't say I played cowboys, or anything like that, although growing up with a bunch of brothers, I could have been forgiven if I did (laughs).

There were a lot of churches in both Perth and Andover, and, yes, there was a Baptist Church on both sides of the river. There was quite a strong guidance by the religious people. We all grew up with it, and I think it certainly had a lot more influence on what happened in the community.

Fig. 11.11 The Andover Specialty Theatre opened in 1912 and reopened as the Capital after a 1921 fire.

I feel as if I lived a pretty insulated life there. If movies were controversial, they probably kept them to some of the larger centres. There must have been some local influence. You know, the owner probably felt a certain mandate from the people as to what he could and could not bring in.

I grew up going to the Baptist Church. I expect there was probably a certain amount of control on the part of my parents as to what I would have been allowed to go see. But, before I was a teenager, I don't think a lot controversial movies came to our village. You see them now, on television, some of the ones from that time, and it's hard to imagine what would have been controversial, based on what we're seeing today.

As teenagers, we used to hop in a car and go to the drive-in in Fort Fairfield, Maine. It was not too far, probably four or five miles to the border, and it was just over the border. A group of us would go in a car. I don't know whether we thought it was more economical, but it certainly was a lot more fun. I didn't go to the cinema over there, but I certainly did go to the drive-in.

9. Robert Michaud

When Edna and Sylvio Guimont decided to build their theatre in Grand Falls, the young man they chose to manage it was Robert (Bobby) Michaud. Although just nineteen, he already had business experience with his own men's clothing store in the town, and he loved movies. It looked like a dream job, but the venture would be plagued by bad luck. About a month after construction began, a fierce windstorm blew down the uninsured structure, destroying more than half the Western Redwood with which it was being built. And that, as it turned out, was only a prelude to the harsher lessons of the movie business that lay ahead.

About three months before the opening, Mr. Guimont and I went to Saint John to visit the distributors. We visited MGM, RKO, Columbia, Republic, six or seven of them. They all agreed to sell us movies. When we

Fig. 11.12 Riviera Theatre, Grand Falls. It operated for only 3 years in the mid 1950s falling victim to film distribution control that kept it from showing current and mainstream films.

Fig. 11.13 Norma Kertson at the Grand Theatre, Grand Falls with (according to her note on the photo) "devoted workers Lezotte (right), who ran the movies and the piano player (left)." Norma's father owned the theatre.

got closer to the opening, I went back to book them. The distributors told me what was popular, what would be the best movies to go with, and so on. I think I ended up with three months' bookings. Everything seemed okay. Then they told me to come back after lunch to confirm my bookings.

When I went back to MGM, I sat down in the manager's office, took out my calendar, and said, "Now, this is definite, we can book this and this"? And he said, "We've got a slight problem. I've booked these movies into the other theatre, the Grand, so I can't book them with you."

So I went to the next distributor, and the one after that, and so on. It was the same story at every one of them. They had booked their best pictures into the other theatre. As a result, we had to open with an American movie that was seven or eight years old, and we had a tough time from then on.

The other theatre in Grand Falls had been owned by the Kertson family. Ronnie Kertson ran it for a number of years. But by the time Mr. Guimont started construction, it had been sold to a movie theatre firm, Bernstein and Lieberman, of Saint John.

I think I went to see Mr. Kertson a few times during construction to ask his advice. He was very good to me, and he might have warned me about what could happen, but I never really paid attention. I had too much expectation, you know, that things were going to be so good.

We tried everything to draw people in. The biggest success we had was, we were the first to show a 3D movie. The competition didn't seem interested, but we were, and we bought it. Showing a 3D movie was different. We had to run both projectors at the same time, with the same reels, but with one offset from the other by about three sprocket holes to get the 3D effect. They were expensive movies, too, $120 or $130, instead of the $45 to $60 we paid for a regular movie. Plus you had to have those special glasses. But at least we filled the theatre when we had 3D movies, and we probably had six or seven.

Otherwise, we had to make money in front, at the confection stand, because we weren't making too much money in the theatre. So, on Saturday afternoons, for example, we'd stop the show between the serial and the main movie so the kids could go out to the canteen and buy popcorn, pop, anything, you know. (Laughs.)

The Riviera lasted two-and-a-half, three years. It was tough work, and I could see the heartbreak of my bosses, Mr. and Mrs. Guimont. They were good people, and they were devastated. Their life savings were tied up in that building, and they had a big mortgage after the storm. TV was coming in, a drive-in theatre was coming, and we couldn't get first-class movies. Everything just went wrong. Mr. Guimont finally sold the building to Bernstein and Lieberman. They stripped it, took all the projectors and the seats and everything and put them in their own theatre. Our building was rented a little while for a trade school, and then Irving bought it and tore it down.

10. Giles Walker, Conversation, April 9, 2007

Giles Walker, son of novelist, David Walker, was born in 1946 in Dundee, Scotland. He received a B.A in psychology from the University of New Brunswick and an M.A. from Stanford University Film School in 1972. He joined the National Film Board of Canada soon after, directing documentaries, then switching to dramas in 1977. Bravery in the Field *was nominated for a live-action short Oscar in 1979. The* Masculine Mystique, *the first of a trio of NFB movies dealing with issues of gender relations, was notable for its experimental approach, working with non-professional actors and techniques of improvisation. Walker's most successful fictional work is* Princes in Exile, *a film about a summer camp for children with cancer, notable for delicate but unsentimental treatment of the subject. Giles became a key figure at the NFB in the organization's development of dramatic storytelling that combined non-professional actors and documentary techniques. He is credited with being the producer of 39 films, the director of eight, and writer of six, including a variety of made-for-television films. His work has received numerous Genie and Gemini awards.*

Fig. 11.14 *The Walker family in St. Andrews ca. 1965: (left to right) Barclay, Julian, Willa (neé Magee), Giles, David Sr., David Jr. David Sr.'s novels (*Geordie *and* Harry Black*) were made into movies, Giles was one of Canada's most celebrated film directors of documentaries and dramas; and Julian, was Deputy Minister of the Department of Tourism, Municipalities and Culture during the period leading up to the establishment of the NB Film Agency.*

Giles said the film he made that stirs him with the most emotion is *Bravery in the Field* about an old World War Two veteran in Saint John who is set upon by punks. After making that film, he went on to make other types of films and didn't see it for about five years. When he finally saw it again, he said he was "very moved."

He remembers when they were filming the scene in a Saint John alley where the old man is being kicked and beaten up by three young punks, a woman happens by and charges in waving her purse, saying "You can't do that!" At which point Giles informs her they are making a film. She says, "Oh, I'm so sorry." "It was so New Brunswick," said Giles.

Looking ahead, Giles said he is hoping to make a film in the next year or so with Sam Granna called *Something to Hide*. The story comes out of a chance encounter he had with a long-distance truck driver one night in Fredericton. It will be a comedy set in Saint John. An American actor would play the truck driver, who was an American from South Carolina. The script is by a Fredericton writer, Chris Bruce. Giles thought the film could get theatrical release or it could go directly to video. [This film was apparently not made. It does not appear in Giles complete filmography as of 2011 when his last film, *The Way of Tai Chi*, was made.]

Another young New Brunswick scriptwriter whom Giles thinks has great promise is Jeremy John Bouchard, who wrote *Black Eyed Dog*. The script, says Giles, is better than the film.

Giles recounted a humorous anecdote from the past. The Walker family had a cottage on their property at St. Andrews where the actress Myrna Loy used to come and spend time in the summer. There was no telephone in the cottage, so when a call came into the main house for her somebody would have to let her know. A frequent caller was Louis Mayer. Carpenters were then working on the house. They had no idea who either Mayer or Loy were. So, when a call came in from Louis, they would shout, "Mr. Mayer for Myrna Loy." And she would shout back, "I don't want to talk to him." This apparently was not one of Mayer's attempted courtships of beautiful actresses, but rather a business matter. He could be very tough, but so, apparently, could Myrna Loy.

The novel, *Geordie*, written by Giles father, David Walker, was made into a successful and famous movie. Giles said his father had nothing to do with the filming. It was released in North America as *Wee Geordie*. When the movie came out, Giles remembered that Lady Dunn organized a showing for invited guests at the Marina Theatre in St. Andrews. It stood across from the Shiretown Inn and next to the building that houses the Sea Captain's Loft.

The Dunns had a full-fledged movie theatre in their home in St. Andrews—"Dayspring"— and would fly in movies from New York in their private jet, which would land at Pennfield. Guests were assigned seats, which they occupied at all showings.

When asked about New Brunswick's potential for making feature films, Giles reflected on this by estimating how many crews might be available to work on films at the same time. In NB, he thought only one.

By comparison there would be three in Halifax, forty in Vancouver, twenty-five in Toronto, and nine or ten in Montreal.

Recalling recent attempts, Giles noted that James Goldstone had planned to make a movie called *They Shoot Their Masters* in St. Andrews. Advance pictures had been taken and locations selected. Giles was to work on it, but it fell through.

And finally, Giles remembered a New Brunswick movie project about the story of people—a young woman in particular—who had smallpox that the British placed on farmlands occupied by Acadians before the Expulsion. The movie was to be titled, *In the King's Name*. The CBC rejected the idea and the film was never made.

Geordie Goes to the Movies

David Walker was once asked why the small seacoast town of St. Andrews, New Brunswick, suited him as a novelist. "I think it's better for a writer to be away from it all," he replied, "and anyway I just happen to be a country fellow." In 1950, Walker, who'd been born in Dundee, Scotland, wrote a novel that became a movie, about another country fellow—a frail laddie from the Scottish Highlands who builds himself into an Olympic champion. In a mid-century world primed for romantic tales with heroic and happy endings, the book, *Geordie*, and the film, called *Wee Geordie*, were successes.

Walker was a soldier-turned-writer. Trained as an officer at the Royal Military College, Sandhurst, he'd joined the British Army's Black Watch Regiment in 1931. After seven and a half years' service in India and the Sudan, he'd become *aide-de-camp* to Canada's Governor General, Lord Tweedsmuir, aka the writer John Buchan. Later, during the retreat at Dunkirk, Walker was captured by the Germans and, despite three escape attempts, spent nearly five years as a German POW. "I think those crowded conditions made me very uncomfortable in crowds forever after," he said.

He landed in New Brunswick after the war because, in 1939, he'd married Willa Magee, a Montrealer who'd spent many happy summer days as a child in St. Andrews, an old CPR resort community. Determined to be a writer, Walker began with short stories, some of them "the most ghastly tripe" that nonetheless helped support a growing family. He became a popular contributor to *The Saturday Evening Post*. In 1952, his novel, *The Pillar*, based on his POW experience, got the Governor General's award for fiction, and in 1953 he won again for *Digby*. Metro-Goldwyn-Mayer showed interest in *Digby*, but a film was never made. Another acclaimed Walker novel, *Harry Black*, did become a movie, *Harry Black and the Tiger*, but it got poor reviews.

Wee Geordie had the advantage of being a charming and warm-hearted story; a wee wisp of a boy, forced to endure the taunts of classmates, signs on for a long-distance body-building course. The efficacy of the instructions from "Professor Samson" is dubious, but Geordie does develop into a muscular giant whose sporting specialty is the hammer throw. After winning at the Highland Games, he proceeds to the Olympics in Melbourne, Australia. A possible complication develops when he meets Helga, an amorous Danish shot-putter, while back home his Highlands sweetheart, a lovely lass named Jean, wanders the hills and follows the Games on the radio. Reviewing the movie when it arrived from England, a critic for *The New York Times* liked its regional dialogue and humour, some of it rendered by the esteemed British actor, Alastair Sim. The reviewer also admired the Scottish scenery, which he said had been captured in Technicolor with particular artistry.

The team behind the film, the English duo of Frank Launder and Sidney Gilliat, knew not only how to make a movie, but also how to promote one. For *Wee Geordie*, it started with a well-publicized, Scotland-wide campaign to find the right person to play Geordie. He should be "an unspoiled Highland lad" of nineteen or so, at least six-feet, one-and-a-half inches tall, and weigh "not less than 13½ stone." Acting experience, they said, was not "an absolute essential."

Remembering the Movies

They did, however, in the end choose an actor, Bill Travers, who, although in his thirties, had the required features of a country lad, a height of six feet, six and a half inches, and a willingness to bulk up the rest of his frame. Travers gave a fine performance as Geordie, and the movie brought him international recognition. He and his wife, Virginia McKenna, later starred as the conservationists George and Joy Adamson in the popular film, *Born Free*.

Back in St. Andrews, two of the town's biggest movie fans were a multimillionaire businessman, Sir James Dunn, and Lady Dunn. They regularly held film nights for invited guests at their home, Dayspring. But when *Wee Geordie* came out, they took over a local theatre and invited an even bigger crowd for a special showing, a rare event in small-town New Brunswick.

Success did not derail David Walker. He continued to write, and when he died in 1992, his canon consisted of nineteen novels, a hundred or more short stories, and non-fiction that included an engaging autobiography. He was a writer of action who found a comfortable "at homeness" amid the countryside and people of New Brunswick. As he said in an 1977 interview, "If I lived with a lot of smart alecks, I wouldn't be very happy."

Epilogue

State of the Art

On a warm night in June, 1996, a large crowd came to the Lord Beaverbrook Hotel (now the Crowne Plaza) on the banks of the St. John River in Fredericton. "The Beaverbrook," named for a former New Brunswicker who became a British press baron and peer, stands opposite The Playhouse theatre and beside the Beaverbrook Art Gallery in a little cultural-governmental precinct surrounding the New Brunswick Legislature. The Hotel often hosts official events, but there had never been one quite like this. It was the formal launch of Film New Brunswick, a government agency created to promote movie making in the province.

The crowd had obviously come to celebrate. Standing with drinks and canapés in hand, the guests chattered so incessantly that they threatened to drown out the speakers as they came to the podium. "I feel as though I should call for quiet on the set," said New Brunswick raised, Montreal filmmaker, Giles Walker.

I can't say whether any of the speakers alluded to this—couldn't hear—but the occasion had a nice historical symmetry. Exactly one hundred years earlier, the first motion pictures had landed in Canada (and, just five months later, they came to New Brunswick). This time, though, New Brunswick was lagging; most other jurisdictions in North America had film promotion agencies by the time Film New Brunswick was formed.

An Acadian filmmaker from northern New Brunswick, Renée Blanchar, is generally credited with scoring the breakthrough that led to the creation of the New Brunswick agency. In a ten-minute 1990s meeting with Frank McKenna she managed to persuade the premier that having a film-nurturing unit could benefit the province economically. McKenna, whose enthusiasm for promoting New Brunswick helped gain him a national reputation (he later became Canadian ambassador to Washington), saw that making movies in the province might both raise its profile and create jobs.

Discovering the Movies in New Brunswick

* * *

David Folster's death prevented his completion of what was to be the final chapter of this book. This Epilogue was intended to update his story of New Brunswick filmmaking with current developments. But his more current research had only just begun. His files contain material on several issues that had been on his mind for a long time—for example, the benefit of movies to the locale where they were set or shot, and the chances of our own New Brunswick stories being made into films. He recorded interviews with additional New Brunswickers involved in filmmaking including Léonard Forest, who had a long and distinguished career with The National Film Board; Tony Merzetti and Cat LeBlanc, respectively Executive Director of the New Brunswick Film Cooperative and volunteer, then employee; Rodolphe Caron cofounder of the Edmundston film cooperative, Cinémarévie; and poet, artist, and filmmaker Herménégilde Chiasson. David also clipped and filed newspaper articles about places in North America, England and Europe where movies had been shot and the subsequent boost to their profile and tourism appeal. And he wrote to all the film agencies and commissions of the Canadian provinces for information on their programs of support for filmmaking.

Subsequent research would have provided a more fulsome background to filmmaking initiatives from the 1950s to the 1990s and to the decision of the provincial government to support film production with an agency dedicated to it. The summary that follows is in no way a substitute for what David would have written but it does fill in some of the details on the advance of filmmaking in New Brunswick during this period.

* * *

A newspaper article in the Saint John monthly community newspaper, Echo, in 1980 referred to New Brunswick being known as "the cinematic Boondocks of Canada—a few commercial studios making promotional and documentary films and the number of freelance independent filmmakers were few and far between." Prior to that date, most of the early activity in filmmaking resulted from the work of the National Film Board (NFB). Originally the National Film Commission, the NFB was established by legislation in 1939, in part to create propaganda films in support of the Second World War, but also to promote the production and distribution of films designed to help people in all parts of Canada understand the ways of living and the problems of Canadians in other parts of the country. The small number of films relating to New Brunswick is indicative of their lack of success in accomplishing this. Production was weighted heavily toward central Canada. Of approximately two hundred short films made in several series in the 1940s to the mid 1960s, eleven related to New Brunswick. Two of these films were on the Deichmann's pottery operation, two were on fishing, and two on Fundy National Park; subjects considered important or representative by the National Film Board. Kjeld and Erica Deichmann were again featured in a longer, quite delightful 1953 film, *The Story of Peter and the Potter*, shown each year to school students in the province.

In the mid 1960s the NFB began regionalizing its English production activities, opening production centres in cities across Canada with Halifax designated for the Atlantic Provinces opening in 1973. Rex Tasker, from Britain, became the first executive producer of the NFB's studio in Halifax.

Fig. 12.1 Invitation to launch of the NB Film Agency 1996.

The NFB wanted representative filmmakers from each province and Jon Pedersen was identified as a New Brunswicker who already had some involvement with film. Pedersen, among other pursuits, had been writing abstract poetry and wanted to add moving images to his poetry. While wintering in Greenwich Village in the late 60s, he had purchased a 16mm Bolex camera at a pawnshop and proceeded to experiment with visual poetry. Later, because of this previous experience with film, he was chosen by the NFB to be one of their trainees. Subsequently Pedersen began to learn the NFB's more professional production techniques, using the equipment they sent him and with the help of long, instructional phone calls with NFB employees in Montreal, who were some of the most experienced camera and sound experts in the country. But, the Halifax NFB office frustratingly dictated the subject matter of the NFB films he made. The first topic suggested was gardening, which resulted in an award-

Discovering the Movies in New Brunswick

winning film *Tara's Mulch Garden*. However, Pedersen was disappointed that they had refused his more socially conscious proposal to make a film documenting the last New Brunswick rural cheese factory, a familiar community icon that would, within weeks, disappear forever. After making four successful NFB films he tired of the government's bureaucratic limitations and, recognizing that he needed to learn more about the independent film industry, struck out on his own. He founded Pickwauket Films Ltd., which produced the award winning short film, *Ski Peru!* and later he founded a second company, Capitol Films Inc. to make feature films. In 1987 Capitol produced *Tuesday Wednesday*, the first feature film shot in New Brunswick since 1919. Although the film won acclaim in Canada and the U.S., Pedersen ultimately found the marketing challenges for his little companies insurmountable and eventually moved on to related ventures.

At one point, Pedersen was charged with finding other film talent in New Brunswick. He identified Charles MacLellan who was Production Manager of the newly established NB Filmmakers Cooperative in Fredericton and writer and director of the Coop's first production, which focused on the history of the St. John River through the eyes of Peter Paul, a Maliseet (Wolastoqiyik) elder, of the Woodstock First Nation community.

Fig. 12.2 Jon and Freda Pedersen and daughter Dawn-Aeron Wason in the midst of shooting Tuesday Wednesday *in Fredericton, May 1987.*

During this time Pedersen also met and began a long film partnership with Arthur Makosinski, a brilliant Polish/Canadian Engineer/Filmmaker from Fredericton. Makosinski, who had a day job running UNB's Department of Physics Technical Services and also had had a lifelong interest in film production, worked closely with Pedersen to direct and produce both of the independent films *Ski Peru!* and *Tuesday Wednesday*. Makosinski also wrote and directed a very popular NFB film, *Those Wild, Wild Mushrooms*, which Pedersen produced. Makosinski was also well known for his technological expertise as he often designed and built his own film gear (such as a film to video transfer unit) and had been known to repair complex NFB equipment in the field, avoiding the delay of returning the gear to the NFB for repair. During his years in New Brunswick, Makosinski also made many brilliant film shorts such as a beautiful time lapse film, *Fiddleheads*, and a drama, *Free the Meat*, featuring a very effective pixilation of a dancing, plucked chicken torso.

The New Brunswick Filmmakers Cooperative had come into existence in 1979 with encouragement from the NFB. Fourteen people interested in filmmaking, and, aware of film cooperatives in other provinces, signed the incorporation application. The NFB Atlantic Studio in Halifax helped the fledgling organization with financial assistance, lab services, training, equipment, maintenance, shipping, and mentorship. The NB Film Coop initially raised $11,000 to provide a pool of equipment that was too costly for an individual to purchase, particularly when they would use it briefly and occasionally. This has remained a valuable service. The output of Doug Sutherland, director, producer, writer, and actor, who has made over three hundred and fifty television, film, internet, and stage projects including fifteen features, bears witness to the importance of the support of the NB Coop of which he was an early member.

Fig. 12.3 Doug Sutherland, early NB Coop member, who went on to a career in film in New Brunswick.

The Coop provided workshops, advice, and mentoring with more experienced members helping those who were new to filmmaking.

Discovering the Movies in New Brunswick

A large part of the Coop's activity has been serving as an information clearinghouse, making filmmakers, actors, and technical experts aware of what shoots are scheduled and bringing people from one part of the province to another to assist in projects and also to learn and put important skills into practice.

The Coop also has helped identify sources of funding. One of the Coop's current programs, the Short Film Venture Program, which began in cooperation with Film NB, assists emerging filmmakers in completing a film to serve as a "calling card" to introduce their work to potential funders. The Coop has supported mid-level producers in making films of high enough calibre to get the attention of Canada Council and other granting bodies. NB Film Coop members have produced and continue to produce about 30 films a year. Some are by independent filmmakers who aspire to Hollywood status, but many others are motivated by the satisfaction of creating something on a subject about which they are passionate and perhaps seeing it on television or screened at festivals. Most importantly, the Coop has brought together a community of people interested in filmmaking offering each other inspiration and encouragement. Its initiatives continue as programs of the NB Filmmakers Cooperative under the leadership of Tony Merzetti, a filmmaker in his own right, who has led its activities since 1986.

Fig. 12.4 Rudolphe Caron and Helene Daigle of La Cinémarévie Coop Ltee., Edmundston, collaborate with Blair MacIntyre and Tony Merzetti, of the NB Film Coop.

A francophone Cooperative, La Cinémarévie Coop Ltee, began in Edmundston in 1980 owing largely to the efforts of Rodolphe Caron. Centred in Brayon country, it did not draw in Acadian filmmakers but it produced a number of excellent documentaries and several interesting fiction films. La Cinémarévie and the NB Film Coop kept in touch and worked cooperatively until La Cinémarévie officially wound up in 2012, Rodolphe Caron having moved to Moncton to continue his filmmaking.

Films on Acadian subjects were made in the 50s and 60s by Quebec filmmakers. However, it was pioneering filmmaker Léonard Forest who made sure that Acadians were given the support needed to create their own films. Forest grew up in Moncton and after working as a journalist in Montreal accepted a permanent position with the National Film Board of Canada in 1954. He was involved with 150 productions and co-productions as director, producer or scriptwriter but only a small number of these films are about Acadia.

Léonard Forest made a major contribution to Acadian filmmaking by successfully encouraging the establishment of Studio Acadie in Moncton in 1974 as part of the decentralization of the NFB (ONB in French). Studio Acadie became the centre for Acadian film production and provided training, equipment and facilities for many Acadian filmmakers. When budget cutting at the national level closed the Moncton centre, Acadian filmmakers lobbied strenuously to keep it open and also started the first independent Acadian film-production companies. These included Les Productions Godin, Les Productions L. LeBlanc, Les Productions Cine-Baie and others. Independent Acadian film companies have continued to be established. Their films deal with themes important to Acadians such as culture, history, religion, and the working lives of the Acadian people.

Fig. 12.5 Léonard Forest, Acadian filmmaker, poet, and essayist.

Fig. 12.6 NB Film Coop Board of Directors 2001, early and long-time volunteers, and staff of the Coop. Back row, left to right, Glen Ross, Cat LeBlanc, Rodrigo Gutierrez, John Christenson, Pat Toner, Peter Lockhart. Front row, left to right, Tony Sekulich, Tony Merzetti, Lloyd Salomone.

In addition to Jon Pedersen's Capitol Films, several other anglophone film studios were set up in Fredericton in the mid-80s, including Atlantic Mediaworks (Bob Miller and Daphne Curtis) and Fiddlehead Films (Frederick Clarke). They did film projects for government departments and for private corporations. Several companies from outside New Brunswick filmed at Kings Landing during this time and a highlight in 1984 was the Hollywood film *Children of a Lesser God* shot in Saint John and Rothesay that involved some local people with film making experience.

The NB Filmmakers Coop launched an annual film festival in 2001, at first named the Tidal Wave Film Festival and, in 2005, renamed Silver Wave Film Festival. The Festival was created to provide an opportunity for filmmakers in the province to gather and see the work that others had produced. It engendered a shared sense of purpose and encouraged people to keep producing new work. The Festival has provided important networking opportunities for filmmakers to connect with people who might help them on a future project, and it connects them with key industry stakeholders, funders, distributors, and service suppliers. The Silver Wave Awards are another important aspect of the festival. This kind of recognition helps advance filmmakers as they continue their work.

State of the Art

In 1987 the International Francophone Film Festival in Acadie (Festival international du cinéma francophone en Acadie), or FICFA, was founded in Moncton with the objective of screening films from French-speaking countries worldwide and promoting Acadian films to French-speaking communities in Atlantic Canada and beyond. These festivals help to some extent with film distribution, which remains a problem for filmmakers in New Brunswick. However, the attendees at the Festivals are mainly those who already have a vested interest in Acadian films.

Having films screened has been a problem for all Canadian films. Canadians see very few Canadian films in their local movie theatres because of the control of the vast majority by US interests. There are two principle domestic Canadian theatre chains, Cineplex (75% share with 165 theatres), and Landmark Cinemas (10% share with 44 theatres). They get most of their content (big budget Hollywood films) from 6 foreign owned distribution companies in Canada who monopolize screens to the detriment of Canadian film content. By not being initially screened in a movie theatre, Canadian films lose out on box office revenue as well as opportunities for secondary distribution through pay-TV broadcast license fees and other platforms. A strong American lobby has prevented any change in this situation although both Canadian producers and governments have tried to deal with this problem.

Funding for film production has been and is problematic. Over the years modest levels of support and assistance have been available to filmmakers, although the sources, programs and funds available have changed. Major sources of support have been the Canada Council, the National Film Board, and Telefilm. Telefilm began in 1967 as the Canadian Film Development Fund/Corporation with ten million dollars to support the Canadian feature film industry and revitalize Canadian television. It was renamed Telefilm Canada in 1984.

The Arts Branch of the Government of New Brunswick initially provided small grants for travel and training. One-time

Fig. 12.7 Phil Comeau is a Maritime film and television director and scriptwriter who has received numerous awards for both his documentaries and drama feature films. Much of his work is about his Acadian culture.

funding was provided by the Department of Economic Development and Tourism for individual projects such as the highly successful *Le Secret de Jérôme*, the first feature length Acadian film produced in 1994 by Phil Comeau.

In the light of agreements between the provinces and federal government for cost sharing the funding of arts and culture projects, including film making, advocacy for government support of film production in New Brunswick increased. Several provinces that had provincial film agencies, and were providing matching funds, were successfully nurturing their filmmaking industries.

Fig. 12.8 *Lloyd Salamone, researcher, writer, and film maker, was author of a report on the development of a film industry in New Brunswick, background to the eventual formation of the NB Film Agency.*

In 1991 The Board of Directors of the NB Filmmakers Co-operative commissioned a research project on Film Industry Development. Cultural management specialist, Lloyd Salomone, prepared a report that recommended the development of a strong film, video, and TV production industry in New Brunswick. It identified four weaknesses that hampered NB's filmmaking capacity: the lack of provincial funding, the absence of an investment tax program, the lack of training programs for the industry, and the absence of a film commission office with a strong mandate and adequate resources.

The formation of Film-Video NB, an industry association representing directors, producers and others working in film, led to lobbying activity and meetings between film promoters and the provincial government, which laid out the consequences of New Brunswick being the only province in Canada without a film office. Pressure increased on government for the establishment of NB Film. The case was made that a strong film industry had the potential of employing several hundred people year round at professional salary levels, generating millions of dollars within the NB economy directly through employment of filmmakers and technicians, capital investment in facilities and equipment, and spin off benefits from hotel rooms, restaurant meals, car rentals, and personal purchases.

The economic benefits may have sold the government of the day on a film agency but, equally, Premier Frank McKenna's desire to create a positive self-image for New Brunswickers, and an enhanced image beyond its borders, played into the decision. Films would give the province a higher national and international profile and would help New Brunswick promote itself as a tourist destination.

Bruce Dennis, who was employed as a cultural officer in the Arts Branch of the provincial government, recalled in a May 30, 1998 Daily Gleaner interview that McKenna drew a comparison to Nova Scotia's film industry that was getting under way. It had garnered $50 million in its third year and McKenna wanted to develop a similar industry in New Brunswick.

This is the point—as David Folster was writing the introduction to what is now this Epilogue—that Renée Blanchar, chosen to be spokesperson by English and French producers who had met to discuss working together to lobby government to support film, successfully caught the ear of Premier Frank McKenna. The NB Film agency was launched in 1996 with programs fully underway in June 1997. Its support for film production included a tax credit to professionals in the industry from outside the province who agreed to mentor local filmmakers. Other incentives included an Equity Investment program with the provincial government investing up to 25 per cent of a film or television show's production costs, Development Loans of up to 40 per cent of the costs of developing a project, a Co-production Project in which support was given for producing a film as long as one of the partners was from New Brunswick. In addition to this direct financial support, aid was available for developing an infrastructure—people trained to work in the various aspects of film production.

In a government press release in 2003 the Film NB mandate was summarized as establishing an economically stable, viable, and vibrant film and television industry in the province and to increase opportunities for residents to work in the province's film and television industry. Film NB was set up as a business unit of the Department of Business New Brunswick to support production of film by New Brunswickers and to attract filmmakers from other parts of Canada and internationally to locate their films in New Brunswick.

The agency was well staffed at the outset. Sam Grana, hired as the first Executive Director, was a former NFB producer and well connected with the film industry in central Canada. He attracted Toronto and Montreal producers to come to New Brunswick and partner with local filmmakers as co-producers. The fact that many of the projects were headed by outside production companies could be seen as a necessary rite of passage to develop the skills of local producers so they could eventually lead projects of their own. However, some NB producers felt too much money was going to external film companies, and that the artistic was being sacrificed to the commercial. There were also complaints that experienced local technicians were not being hired by the external companies and had to work out of province to sustain a reasonable income.

Film NB had successes. The industry seemed to be growing. Local producers got valuable experience and mentorship. Financing was made available to support the development of New Brunswick based film and television projects. A number of notable films and television programs were produced: *Starhunter*, a $22 million television series shot in Minto; *In Her Defence*, a full-length murder mystery; *At the End of the Day: The Sue Rodriquez Story*; *This Matter of Marriage*, a Harlequin romance movie.

Documentary series found support too, including *Turning Points in History*, which featured interviews with real characters of the past. Two training programs were established to meet the growing labour demands of the industry; a Film Studies Program offered by the English Department at the University of New Brunswick in Fredericton, and a Certificate in Film and Television in Fredericton offered by the NB Film Coop. It consisted of introductory and advanced workshops and a training TV series of three episodes was produced with mentors attached.

With Sam Grana's controversial departure from NB Film in 1998, Ray Wilson, senior financial management advisor for culture and tourism in the Department of Economic Development, became the acting Executive Director of Film NB and was later confirmed in the position. The budget was reduced despite Grana having given an inadequate budget as his reason for leaving Film NB. Wilson was an effective leader and, even though working with a smaller budget, many projects were carried out, particularly through the assistance of the tax credit program. In recent years, the government downsized NB Film to two employees. And then, in a government reorganization, NB Film was moved to the Department of Tourism, Heritage and Culture signifying that filmmaking was seen more as an artistic than a commercial pursuit. The film tax credit program was cancelled in 2011 and replaced with a Film Production Program and a Film Development Program that provide incentive grants.

Raising the funds for a film or television production remains a challenge. Existing funding is project based, not company based, so there is no continuity and there is an unproductive lull between film projects. New Brunswick is not the only province where support for filmmaking has lost ground. Both Alberta and Nova Scotia have seen substantial cuts to government programs for filmmakers with the predictable results of jobs lost and production diminished.

The optimism David Folster expressed when he attended the launch of NB Film was not fulfilled. Without adequate funding to support the writing and development of scripts, production and post-production, and marketing and distribution, filmmakers will continue to struggle. However, there may be hope on the horizon as advances in technology could help New Brunswick filmmakers gain a foothold in the film industry. Digital technology is making film production less costly. Smartphones and YouTube are creating credible production and screening options, although this advantage may be offset by the quest for higher and higher levels of quality achieved through more expensive equipment. On the distribution side, streaming on various specialty channels—Netflix, Disney, and Amazon Prime—is providing opportunity for viewers to personalize what they watch from a wide sampling and permitting content to be widely accessed. This will lead to an increased demand for content and New Brunswick filmmakers can contribute to meeting it.

Fig. 12.9 Poster for Festival International du Cinéma Francophone en Acadie, *2018.*

David Folster was convinced that New Brunswick stories offered New Brunswick filmmakers the opportunity to create excellent movies, whether documentaries or creative narratives. He had a good sense of what it took to create the compelling images of good story telling. And he had a knack of knowing where to look for inspiration. In the essay, "I Am a St. John River Person," he put it like this:

> A true image, whether for a person or for a geographic area, comes not from the drawing board but from the soul. The collective soul of the St. John River is our shared history and culture, and it is rich. From where I am writing this, I can see just a small stretch of the St. John, and yet my vista is filled with cultural and historical icons.

The cultural and historical icons that filled David Folster's vista from along the St. John can be multiplied over the whole of New Brunswick. They await the soul of the storyteller with a camera to bring them to life and to our attention.

Dr. David Frank told his "Canadian History on Film" students at the University of New Brunswick that film is the language of the twentieth century. And, of course, it will continue to be for the twenty-first. Dr. Michael Higgins, former President of St. Thomas University and film critic, agrees with Professor Frank. Movies create incredibly powerful images of people and places. Films that portray regions are important as each has its own stories particular to its own circumstances. The filmmakers of New Brunswick can be confident in the stories they have to tell about our region. Although particular in the realization, local stories, well told, can become universal in their scope and appeal.

* * *

This Epilogue has summarized recent efforts to bring New Brunswick to a point where its filmmakers are telling their stories. Had David Folster been able to continue his research, he may have felt the increased activity and volume of production in the period leading up to 1995, and then in the years following, warranted a separate book. He may have identified individuals and episodes as he did for the chapters of this book and hung the ongoing chronology of filmmaking in New Brunswick on these stories.

Examples come easily to mind: for example the story of Jon Pedersen's amateur crew charging expenses to his credit card as they headed to Peru to follow and film the ski descent of two Fredericton adventurers from one of the highest peaks of the Andes, the 22,000' Mt. Huascaran, and of how they got lost on their way to the base camp, were stricken with altitude sickness, and made the acquaintance of three American skiers who later died in their pursuit of the high peak. And then there's the story of the labourious work of editing and syncing the sound in their eventual production of *Ski Peru*. There are numerous stories around the life and times of Frederick Clark, known as Fiddlehead Fred, the driving force of Fiddlehead Films, and of Sam Grana, the first Director of Film NB, both larger than life characters. And there are tales to be told about on-location incidents during the filming of mainstream movie successes such as *Children of a Lesser God* and B-Movies such as *Hemoglobin*, the Gothic thriller shot on Grand Manan.

Many other stories of the film industry as it has recently developed in New Brunswick are, no doubt, waiting to be told, and another book could be written bringing this latter part of our province's filmmaking history to light. Meanwhile, we can be thankful that David Folster, out of personal interest and with an unflagging commitment to telling New Brunswick's stories, carried out the research and the writing that has given us *Discovering the Movies in New Brunswick*.

Publisher's Afterword:

A Salute to David Folster

When David Folster showed me early drafts of the first chapters of his book about the movies in New Brunswick, I was a bit puzzled about what sort of book it would be. My interest was mainly as a friend and sometimes colleague who had an implicit faith in David's instinct for a good story and his devotion to elevating New Brunswick stories to a new level of interest and appreciation. Although I had a history in the book business, I hadn't yet become a publisher, so my interest was as a reader and supporter of David's work.

In the 1970s David and I worked off and on for a couple of years on a publishing project that was aimed at enlarging and advancing a general appreciation of the natural beauty and cultural life of New Brunswick. We decided to develop a magazine that would feature the best in visual presentation and cultural storytelling. We had a model in mind that inspired us—*Vermont Life*.

Vermont Life was the kind of magazine that did not require living in Vermont to appreciate the beauty of its graphic presentation and to be fascinated by the stories of living and working in the Green Mountain State. We saw the potential of a similar publication for showcasing New Brunswick.

Our province has a similar mountain and river valley terrain, equivalent towns, villages, and rural settlements, and a comparable tradition of small businesses, working farms, and community based art and craft producers. In addition, New Brunswick has a significant Indigenous population, three small cities, a landscape of lakes, a wilderness terrain, and a maritime economy on the Bay of Fundy and along the East and North Shores of the province—an abundant potential for good stories and visual art.

We developed a mock-up issue and David went in search of funding. Our hope was to secure financial support that would enable us to produce the magazine without advertising, or, if needed, to confine it to the final few pages. David made application to Canada Council for the Arts and opened conversations with key figures in large New Brunswick business corporations with whom he had personal contact.

None of these potential funders responded positively to our initiative, which was probably a good thing for us, although we were disappointed at the time. This was before the digital era and the production costs for the kind of magazine we had in mind would have required a steady flow of grants or an "angel" able and willing to underwrite the project. As a business proposition, it probably would have failed. Since no Canada Council grant was forthcoming and no "angel" appeared with chequebook in hand, we shelved this project but not our commitment. We both continued working in various ways to strengthen the appreciation of New Brunswick's natural environment and cultural heritage.

In addition to his journalism, David went on to become the founding president of the St. John River Society and the Executive Director of the Canadian Forestry Association of New Brunswick. In this capacity, he initiated the creation of a wall size map of the St. John River Watershed. This striking map of the Wolastoq bioregion is a notable expression of the sense of place that underlies much of the work to which David was devoted.

In 2014, through a combination of family circumstances and the advent of digital technology, my son, Brendan, wife Ellen, and I approached this commitment in a new way and established Chapel Street Editions (CSE). This was four years after David's death. Had he still been with us, he would have been a primary advisor for our book publishing business; it's likely he would have become involved in even more creative ways.

The values, commitment, and mission we shared in dreaming up a magazine to make New Brunswickers proud of their home place are also what prompted us to launch Chapel Street Editions. In this very real sense, David Folster, is still with us. I think about him and his contribution to this mission every time I open the computer to edit a new manuscript.

David had a way of encouraging fruitful conversation and discussion. Numerous times in the course of working through ideas or technical details, he would respond to suggestions or particular angles of vision with an acknowledgement; he was quick to say, "Good point." It sometimes meant "a point well taken" that was a helpful guide for further exploration. Or, it could mean a point at which further discernment was needed. But the confirming acknowledgements and positive manner with which he carried on such communication made working with him an intellectual pleasure and emotionally smooth sailing at every turn. I have never forgotten his example and have tried to make it my practice as well.

When the opportunity came to publish *Discovering the Movies in New Brunswick*, I saw it as way of paying forward something of what working with him contributed to the development of CSE. We are pleased and honoured to be the publisher of David's capstone contribution to New Brunswick cultural history. Presenting this final example of David's attachment to his home place, his devotion to telling New Brunswick stories, and the creative expression of his research and writing is a high point for Chapel Street Editions.

Marion Beyea, former Provincial Archivist, worked closely with David as he continued his research and writing. She retained the manuscript and all the associated documents that have been incorporated in the book. The publication of *Discovering the Movies in New Brunswick* at this time is due to her meticulous attention to detail and to the additional research she undertook in preparing the manuscript.

This whole effort has been a labour of love; from David Folster's persistence to Marion Beyea's diligence, from Brendan Helmuth's design of the book to its publication by Chapel Street Editions, the whole project is in the nature of a gift; creative work in arts and culture is usually in this mode. With *Discovering the Movies in New Brunswick*, David Folster has created an especially notable gift for the cultural history of the province to which he was devoted.

Keith Helmuth
Publisher & Managing Editor
Chapel Street Editions

David Folster. Photograph by Glen Ross.

About the Author

David Folster (1937-2010) grew up in Grand Falls, NB, was a graduate of the University of New Brunswick, and lived in Fredericton, NB. He had a long and distinguished career as a journalist. He got his start writing essays for *Sports Illustrated* about fondly remembered childhood baseball rivalries and hockey games in his hometown of Grand Falls. He went on to write for *Time Magazine*, the *Globe and Mail*, the *Christian Science Monitor*, *Canadian Geographic* and *Maclean's*, among other publications.

David was a reporter for CBC TV and Radio. His skillful storytelling earned him many listeners as host of CBC Radio's NB Folio, Neighbourly News, and as a regular contributor to Information Morning and other CBC programmes.

He had a deep and abiding affection for his home province and took every opportunity to promote its natural beauty and distinctive culture. He was the founding president of the St. John River Society and served as the Executive Director of the Canadian Forestry Association of New Brunswick. In this capacity, he established The Tree House, an environmental education organization that thrived under his leadership.

The common thread of his work and David's lifelong passion was telling the stories of New Brunswick and its people. He pursued this theme through meticulous research and with great skill, enjoying the hours spent talking to people and telling their stories. Researching and writing *Discovering the Movies in New Brunswick* was a decades long project that exemplifies his skill as a cultural historian and journalist. Its publication stands as the capstone achievement of his career.

In 1995, David Folster published a celebrated credo, "I Am a St. John River Person," in the *New Brunswick Reader*, a *Telegraph Journal* magazine. This flagship essay on his sense of place was included in *The STU Reader* [St. Thomas University], edited by Douglas Vipond and Russell Hunt, and published by Goose Lane Editions (2010).

David Folster is also the author of *The Great Trees of New Brunswick* (1987), *The Chocolate Ganongs of St. Stephen New Brunswick* (1990), shortlisted for the National Business Book Award, and *Ganong: A Sweet History of Chocolate* (2006), finalist for the Best Atlantic-Published Book at the Atlantic Book Awards.

Acknowledgements

In preparing the manuscript of *Discovering the Movies in New Brunswick* for publication David Folster had not yet composed the acknowledgments page. The following acknowledgments have been compiled from his research files, correspondence, and appointment diaries. They include persons and organizations he consulted in his research. The result is missing the reflections and comments he would have likely included on his association with some of the persons named, which would have added a personal dimension to the story of his relationship with those who assisted him. It will also likely be missing names of some people who helped him.

As his research spanned many years, some people will have retired and others, sadly, have died. David relied greatly on archivists, librarians and people with knowledge and experience related to the topics he was researching. He greatly appreciated their expertise and assistance, which ranged from suggesting sources to directly contacting colleagues in other research institutions with his questions.

David's first thanks would, undoubtedly, be to his daughters Tracy, Natalie, and Andrea for their assistance and support, and to his sister and brother-in-law, Ann and Rod Elkin. Natalie Folster assisted with editing an early version of the manuscript and organized and edited the interviews in Chapter 11.

The following institutions and their personnel were of assistance in research for this book.

Provincial Archives of New Brunswick: Marianne Arseneau, Twila Buttimer, Elena Cobb, Janice Cook, Elizabeth Diamond, Allen Doiron, Fred Farrell, Rob Gemmill, Joshua Green, Judy Hiscock, Jules Keenan, Heather Lyons, Wanda Lyons, Tom McAffrey, Luis Nadeau, Denis Noel, Julia Thompson.

New Brunswick Legislative Library: Janet McNeil, Margie Pacey, Carol Sears, Eric Swannick, Jean Weisserhorn-Delong.

University of New Brunswick Harriet Irving Library and Archives: Linda Baier, Pat Belier, Mary Flagg, Christine Lovelace, Leah Grandy.

New Brunswick Museum: Janet Bishop, Peter Laroque, Jennifer Longon, Felicity Opsechuk.

Discovering the Movies in New Brunswick

Academy of Motion Pictures Archives, Margaret Herrick Library. Center for Motion Picture Study: Barbara Hall.

Archives of the Roman Catholic Archdiocese of St. John's, Newfoundland: Larry Dohey.

Cinématèque Québécoise Montreal: Pierre Veronneau.

Film New Brunswick: Margot Flewelling, Ray Wilson.

Grand Falls NB Historical Society: Patrick McCooey, Margaret Marceau.

George Eastman House: Todd Gustavason.

Iowa State Historical Society: Beci Plunkett, Jeffrey Dawson.

Library and Archives Canada: Rosemary Bergeron, Greg Eamon, Bill O'Farrell.

Library of Congress: Rosemary Haines.

McCord Museum: Nora Hague.

Oakland Museum: Maria Eyemann.

Portland Public Library: Abraham Schechter.

Queens University Archives: Paul Bamford.

Saint John Jewish Historical Museum: Katherine Briggs-Craft.

Stetson University Archives: Gail Grieb.

University of California Los Angles, History & Special Collections for the Sciences, Louise M. Darling Biomedical Library: Teresa Johnson, Katharine E.S. Donahue.

Yale University Archives Beinecke Rare Book and Manuscript Library: George Miles.

In addition, the following people assisted in various ways.

Ray Anderson, Joan Beveridge, Vera Calder, Gary Campbell, Margaret Conrad, Ernie Dick, Don and Hisai Dickey, Cyril Donahue, Mary Doughty, David Frank, Beverley Franklin, Graham Garnett, Hoyt Golding, Alice Gough, Dorothy Hanscom, Michael Higgins, Richard Jamer, Blanche Johnson, Jocelyne LeBel, Sherry Little, Roger McGregor, Ron Magliozzi, Norma Martin, Tony Merzetti, Bill Miller, Alice Gaunce Miller, Mary Mitchell, Patty Moore, Paul Moore, Joyce Morrell, Louise Spruance Morse, Jon Pedersen, David Adams Richards, Cecil Ryder, Lloyd Salomone, Giles Walker, Julian Walker, Harold Wright.

Bibliography

Allen, Robert C. *Vaudeville and Film 1895-1915: A Study in Media Interaction.* New York: Arno Press, 1980.

Babbitt, George W. *Fredericton in the Eighties. With Glimpses of Saint John, Moncton and St. Andrews.* Fredericton. New Brunswick Travel Bureau, n.d.

Bardwell, David et al. *Film Style and Technology Part 6: Technicolor.* New York: Columbia University Press, 1985.

Balshofer, Fred J. *One Reel a Week.* Berkeley: University of California Press, 1967.

Bellamy, Ralph. *When the Smoke Hit the Fan.* Garden City, New York: Doubleday & Company, 1979.

Belton, John. "The Origin of 35 mm Film as a Standard," *SMPTE Journal,* August 1990.

Berton, Pierre. *Hollywood's Canada: The Americanization of Our National Image.* Toronto: McClelland and Stewart, 1975.

Bitzer, G.W. *Billy Bitzer: His Story.* New York: Farrar, Straus and Giroux, 1973.

Boisnier, Alicia. "*Movie Going Experiences of People of French-Canadian Descent Who Went to the Movies in the Burlington [Vermont] Area Between 1920 and 1950.*" Berkley: Student Paper, University of California. Walter A. Haas School of Business, 1993.

British Columbia Trade Development Corporation. *Hot Property.* Vancouver: British Columbia Film Commission, 1990.

Brown, Clare. "Management of the New Brunswick sport fishery during the 19th century," *Proceedings, 5th Canadian Symposium on the History of Sport and Physical Education.* Toronto: University of Toronto, 1982.

Browne, Lina Fergusson, ed. *J. Ross Browne: His Letters, Journals & Writings.* Albuquerque: University of New Mexico Press, 1969.

Buckbee, Edna Bryan. *The Saga of Old Tuolumne.* New York: The Press of the Pioneers, 1935.

Burke, Billie. *With a Feather on My Nose: Billie Burke Memoirs.* New York: Appleton-Century Crofts, 1948.

Burns, E. Bradford and Eadweard Muybridge. *Eadweard Muybridge in Guatemala 1875: The Photographer as Social Recorder.* Berkeley: University of California Press, 1987.

Cameron, Evan William et al. *Sound and the Cinema: The Coming of Sound to American Film.* Pleasantville, New York: Redgrave Publishing Co., 1980.

Canada, Statistics Canada. *Motion Pictures Theatres Film Distributors.* Ottawa: Dominion Bureau of Statistics, Industry and Merchandising Division, 1959.

Ceram, C.W. *Archaeology of the Cinema.* London: Thomas & Hudson, 1965.

Clark, Ronald W. *Edison: The Man Who Made the Future.* New York: Putnam's Sons, 1977.

Coe, Brian. *The History of Movie Photography.* New York: Eastview Editions, New York Zoetrope Inc., 1981.

Coit, Margaret L. and the editors of LIFE. "The Sweep Westward," *The LIFE History of the United States* 4. New York: Time Incorporated, 1963.

Collier, James Lincoln. *The Rise of Selfishness in America.* New York: Oxford University Press, 1991.

Comeau, Phil. "Acadian Cinema," *The Canadian Encyclopedia.* https://www.thecanadianencyclopedia.ca.

Cook, Samantha, ed. *The International Dictionary of Films and Filmmakers, Volume IV: Writers and Production Artists.* Chicago: St. James Press, 1994.

Cornwall-Clyne, Adrian. *Colour Cinematography.* London: Chapman and Hall Ltd., 1957.

Cox, Kirwan. "Canada's Theatrical Wars: The Indies vs. the Chains," *Cinema Canada,* June/July 1979.

_____. "Hollywood's Empire in Canada: The Majors and the Mandarins Through the Years," *Cinema Canada 22,* October 1975.

_____ "Rocca's big fight," *Cinema Canada,* February 1976.

Crapsey, Edward. *The Man of Two Lives.* New York: American News Company, 1871.

Cronyn, Hume. *A Terrible Liar.* New York: William Morrow and Company Inc., 1991.

Crowther, Bosley. *Hollywood Rajah: The Life and Times of Louis B. Mayer.* New York: Henry Holt & Company, 1960.

Donahue, Suzanne Mary. *American Film Distribution: The Changing Marketplace.* Ann Arbor: University of Michigan Press, 1987.

Doyle, Billy H. *The Ultimate Directory of the Silent Screen Performers.* New York: The Scarecrow Press, 1995.

Elder, R. Bruce. *Image and Identity: Reflections on Canadian Film and Culture.* Waterloo: Wilfrid Laurier University Press in collaboration with the Academy of Canadian Cinema & Television, 2006.

Fielding, Raymond, comp. *A Technological History of Motion Pictures and Television: An Anthology from the Pages of the Journal of the Society of Moton Picture and Television Engineers.* Berkeley: University of California Press, 1967.

Fetherling, Douglas, ed. *Documents in Canadian Film.* Peterborough: Broadview Press, 1988.

Folster, David. *The Great Trees of New Brunswick.* Fredericton: Canadian Forestry Association of New Brunswick, 1987.

Fuller, Kathleen H. *At the Picture Show: Small Town Audiences and the Creation of Movie Fan Culture.* Charlottesville: University of Virginia Press, 1996.

Fulton, Albert Rondthaler. *Motion Pictures: The Development of an Art from Silent Films to the Age of Television.* Norman, Oklahoma: University of Oklahoma Press, 1960.

Gabler, Neil. *An Empire of Their Own: How the Jews Invented Hollywood.* New York: Crown Publishers Inc., 1988.

———. "Early Takers in Atlantic Canada," *Photographic Canadiana* 23 no 3, November/December 1997.

———. "The Graves & Prudd Daguerrotype." *The Daguerreian Annual,* 1991

———. "Photography in Canada 1839-1841 A Historical and Biographical outline," *Photographic Canadiana* 21 no. 5, March/April and May/June 1996.

———. "Canada's First Daguerrerian Image," *History of Photography* 20 no.2, Summer 1998.

Gish, Lilliam. *The Movies, Mr. Griffith and Me.* New Jersey: Prentice Hall, 1983.

Goetzmann, William H. and William N. *The West of the Imagination.* New York: W.W. Norton & Co., 1986.

Gregory, Tappan. *Deer at Night in the Northwoods.* Baltimore: Charles C. Thomas, 1930.

Haas, Robert Bartlett. "William Herman Rulofson, Pioneer Daguerreotypist and Educator," *California Historical Society Quarterly* 35 no. 1, March 1955.

Halliday, S.D. "Ruloff, the Great Criminal Philologist," *DeWitt Historical Society of Tompkins County Publication* 1, 1906.

Harper, J. Russell. "Daguerreotypists and Portrait Takers in Saint John," *The Dalhousie Review* 35, Spring 1955.

Hendrichs, Gordon. *The Literature of Cinema: Origins of the American Film.* New York: Arno Press, 1972.

Herman, William. *The Dance of Death.* San Francisco: Henry Keller & Co., 1877.

Hoffman, Charles. *Sounds for Silents.* New York: DBS Publications, 1970.

Hutchison, Bruce. *The Unknown Country: Canada and her People.* New York: Coward-McCann Inc., 1942.

Irland, Frederic. "Sport in an Untouched American Wilderness," *Scribner's Magazine* 20, September 1896.

———. "Trout of the Nipisquit," *Scribner's Magazine* 35 no. 6, May/June 1904.

Josephson, Matthew. *Edison: A Biography.* Toronto: McGraw Hill, 1959.

Kalmus, H.T. Technical Adventures in Cinema Land," *Journal of Motion Pictures Engineers* 31 no. 6, December 1938.

——— and Eleanor King Kalmus. *Mr. Technicolor.* Chesterfield, New Jersey: Magic Image Film Books, 1993.

Kalmus, Natalie. "Color Consciousness," *Journal of the Society of Motion Pictures Engineers* 25 no. 2, August 1935.

Kindem, Gordon. "Hollywood's Conversion to Technicolor: The Technological, Economic and Aesthetic Factors," *Journal of the University Film Association* 32 no.2, Spring 1982.

Klein, Jonas. *Beloved Island: Franklin & Eleanor and the Legacy of Campobello.* Forest Dale, Vermont: Paul S. Eriksson, 2000.

Koven, Marcia. *Weaving the Past into the Present.* Saint John: Saint John Jewish Historical Museum, 1989.

Kula, Sam. "National Image, National Dream," *Cinema Canada,* February 1976.

Lee, W. Storrs, ed. *California: A Literary Chronicle.* New York: Funk & Wagnalls, 1968.

Lindsay, Nicholas Vachel. *The Art of the Moving Picture…Being the 1922 revision of the book first issued in 1915.* New York: Liveright Publishing Corporation, 1970.

MacBeath, Dr. George and Capt. Donald F Taylor. *Steamboat Days on the St. John.* St. Stephen: Print'N Press Ltd., 1982.

MacKay, Donald. *The Lumberjacks*. Montreal: McGraw Hill Ryerson Limited, 1978.

MacNutt, Stewart. *New Brunswick, a History: 1784-1867*. Toronto: MacMillan Company of Canada, 1963.

MacNutt, Stewart. *New Brunswick and Its People*. Fredericton: The New Brunswick Travel Bureau, n.d.

McCullough, David. *The Path Between the Seas*. New York: Simon and Schuster 1977.

Maine. *The Way Life Should Be*. Augusta: The Maine Office of Tourism, Dept. of Economic and Community Development and the Maine Tourism Commission and The Maine Film Commission Annual Report, March 1990.

Malkames, Karl. "The 35-mm Motion Picture Camera from the Beginnings to the 1920s," *SMPTE Journal,* June 1981.

Manvell, Roger, ed. *The International Encyclopedia of film*. New York: Crown Publishing, 1972.

Millard, Andre. *Edison and the Business of Innovation*. Baltimore: The Johns Hopkins University Press, 1990.

Michaud, Paul, ed. *The American Movie Reference Book: The Sound Era*. New Jersey: Prentice-Hall, 1969.

Moore, Paul. "Burton Moore: A Unique, Clever Man," *The Tobiquer* 5, 1979.

Morris, Peter. *The Film Companies: A Comprehensive Guide to More Than 650 Canadian Films and Film Makers*. Toronto: Irwin Publishing, 1984.

_____, *Embattled Shadows: A History of Canadian Cinema 1895-1939*. Montreal: McGill-Queens University Press, 1978.

Musser, Charles. *The Emergence of Cinema to 1907*. Farmington Hills, Michigan: Cengage Gale, 1990.

Nason, David. *Railways of New Brunswick*. Fredericton: New Ireland Press, 1993.

New Brunswick Department of Crown Lands. *Annual Reports*. Fredericton: Queen's Printer, 1900-1917.

Neupert, Richard. "Technicolour and Hollywood: Exercising Color Restrain," *Post Script* 10 no. 1, 1990.

Niven, Kemp R. *Early Motion Pictures*. Washington: Paper Print Collection, Library of Congress, 1985.

Palmquist, Peter. "Photography in the West," *The Daguerreian Annual,* 1993.

Paquet, Andre, ed. *How to Make or Not to Make a Canadian Film.* Montreal: Le Cinemateque Canadienne, ca. 1967.

Phillips, Fred H. *Fredericton, Centennial City.* [Reprint from *The Canadian Geographic Journal,* February 1948. Provincial Archives of New Brunswick MC300 Ms 49.]

Pierce, Margaret. "Making Films People Want to See," *Atlantic Advocate,* October 1979.

Postman, Neil. *Enjoying Ourselves to Death.* London: Penguin Publishing Group, 1986.

Pratley, Gerald. *Torn Sprockets: The Uncertain Projection of the Canadian Film.* Newark: University of Delaware Press, 1987.

Pryluck, Calvin. "The Itinerant Movie Show and the Development of the Film Industry," *Journal of the University Film and Video Association* 35, no. 4, Fall 1983.

Ramsaye, Terry. *A Million and One Nights.* New York: Simon and Schuster 1926.

Risteen, Frank H. *The Celestial City: Fredericton New Brunswick, and the St. John River, For the Tourist and Sportsman.* Fredericton: Fredericton Tourist Association, 1898.

Roberts, Lawrence J. "Camera and Systems: A History of Contributions from the Bell and Howell Company (Part 1)." *SMPTE Journal* 91 no. 10, October 1982.

———, Lawrence J. "Cameras and Systems: A History of Contributions from the Bell and Howell Company (Part 2). *SMPTE Journal* 91 no. 11, November 1982.

Roske, Ralph J. *Everyman's Eden: A History of California.* New York: The MacMillan Company, 1968.

Richmond, Neal W. "A Reference Collection on the Moving Pictures," *Bulletin of The New York Public Library* 53, June 1949.

Ryan, Pat. "A River Running out of Eden," *Sports Illustrated* 32 no. 21, May 25, 1970.

Salomone, Lloyd. "Film Industry Development Research Paper." Fredericton: New Brunswick Filmmakers, unpublished, 1993 [Courtesy of the author.]

Schary, Dore. *Case History of a Movie by Dore Schary as Told to Charles Palmer.* New York: Random House, 1950.

Schatz, Thomas. *The Genius of the System: Hollywood Filmmaking in the Studio Era.* New York: Pantheon Books, 1988.

Sclanders, Ian. "Rich Man's River," *Maclean's*, April 15, 1947.

Shaw, Marilyn. *Mount Carleton Wilderness: New Brunswick's Unknown North.* Fredericton: Fiddlehead Poetry Books and Goose Land Editions Ltd., 1987.

Schickel, Richard. *Movies: The History of an Art and an Institution.* New York: Basic Books Inc., 1964.

Selznick, Irene Mayer. *A Private View.* New York: Alfred A. Knoff, 1983.

Smith, Mary Elizabeth. *Too Soon the Curtain Fell.* Fredericton: Brunswick Press, 1981.

Solnitt, Rebecca. *River of Shadows: Eadweard Muybridge and the Technological Wild West.* New York: Viking, 2003.

Shore, M.C. *Two Months on the Tobique. An Emigrant's Journal, 1851.* London: Smith, Elder & Co. 1866.

Smith, John M. and Tim Cawkwell. *World Encyclopedia of Film.* New York: Galahad Books, 1974.

Steven, Peter. "When the Movies Came to Canada: Living Pictures," *The Beaver*, April/May 1996.

Swanberg, W.A. "The Case of the 59-Ounce Brain," *True*, May 1953.

Taylor, Frank J. "Mr. Technicolour," *The Saturday Evening Post*, October 1949.

Taft, Robert. *Photography and the American Scene.* New York: Dover Publications Inc., 1974.

Telefilm Canada. *Annual Report 1991-1992.* Montreal: Telefilm Canada Communications Department, 1992.

Thompson, Gerald. *Edward F. Beale and the American West.* Albuquerque: University of New Mexico Press, 1983.

Vinson, James, ed. *Twenty Years of Silents.* Chicago: St. James Press, 1987.

Wallace, Frederick William. *Blue Water: A Tale of the Deep Sea Fishermen.* Toronto: Musson, 1907.

Ward, Charles. "Caribou Hunting," *Scribner's Monthly*, December 1878.

Wenden, D.J. *The Birth of the Movies.* London: Macdonald and Co. Ltd., 1975.

Wright, Harold E. "Saint John & The Movies: A Research Report." Saint John, unpublished, 1987.

Newspapers

Boston Transcript

Calais Advertiser

Campbellton Graphic

Daily Gleaner, Fredericton

Moncton Times

New Brunswick Courier, Saint John

New York Times

Moncton Times

North Shore Leader, Newcastle

St. Croix Courier, St. Stephen

St. John Globe

St. John Progress

St. John Record

Telegraph Journal, Saint John

Victorian News, Perth-Andover

Union Advocate, Newcastle

Periodicals

Canadian Film Weekly

Film Daily Yearbook

Motion Picture Review Digest

Moving Picture World. New York

Year Book Canadian Motion Picture Industry

Illustration Credits

Fig. 0.1 (pg. 5) Ski jump scene. Scanned from film at Provincial Archives of New Brunswick.

Fig. 1.1 (pg. 8) Rulofson Obelisk. Citation: Folster fonds MC1233. Folster fonds MC1233.

Fig. 1.2 (pg. 19) William Rulofson. Bradley & Rulofson, San Francisco. Creative Commons Attribution 2.5 Generic license. https://commons.wikimedia.org/wiki/File:Picture_of_William_Rulofson.jpg.

Fig. 1.3 (pg. 24) Muybridge's arrangement of 24 cameras. Public domain image from Creative Commons, Internet Archive Book Images from: *The Horse in Motion* by Jacob Davis Babcock Stillman, 1882.

Fig 1.4 (pg. 26) Eadweard Muybridge image. Creative Commons Attribution 2.5 Generic license. https://commons.wikimedia.org/wiki/File:Muybridge_race_horse_gallop.jpg.

Fig. 1.5 (pg. 29) Zoetrope. Creative Commons Attribution-Share Alike 4.0 International Leonardo da Vinci National Museum of Science and Technology, Milan. https://commons.wikimedia.org/wiki/File:Zootropio_-_Museo_scienza_tecnologia_Milano_05899.jpg.

Fig. 1.6 (pg. 30) Hartland covered bridge. Interior image title: Inside of Hartland Bridge, in New Brunswick. Photographed by Konstantin Ryabitsev. Creative Commons Attribution-Share Alike 2.0. https://commons.wikimedia.org/wiki/File:Tunnel_vision_(Hartland_Bridge).jpg. Exterior image: https://pixabay.com/photos/covered-bridge-world-longest-2397031/

Fig. 1.7 (pg. 31) *Dance of Death*. Folster fonds MC1233.

Fig. 1.8 (pg. 33) Edward H. Rulloff, formerly Rulofson. Creative Commons Attribution 2.5 Generic license, Nation Park Service. https://commons.wikimedia.org/wiki/File:EHrulloff-drawing-1871.jpg.

Fig 1.9 (pg. 35) Muybridge's zoopraxiscope and disc from the collection of the Kingston Museum in Kingston upon Thames, southwest London, England. Photographed 4 June 2013, Creative Commons Attribution-Share Alike 4.0 International. https://commons.wikimedia.org/wiki/File:Muybridge%27s_zoopraxiscope_and_disc.jpg.

Fig. 2.1 (pg. 37) Cinematographe Camera. This file is licensed under the Creative Commons Attribution-Share Alike 3.0 Unported license. Scanned from LE MAGAZINE DU SIECLE (year 1897) Modified by Mcapdevila. https://commons.wikimedia.org/wiki/File:Cinematograf-Project3.jpg.

Fig. 2.2 (pg. 39) Opera House in Saint John. Provincial Archives of New Brunswick Isaac Erb fonds P210-962.

Fig. 2.3 (pg. 43) "The Kiss" Public domain image from Creative Commons, A frame enlargement from Thomas Edison's 1896 silent film "The Kiss" featuring May Irwin and John C. Rice reprising the controversial final scene of the play "The Widow Jones" in which they had starred in 1895. https://commons.wikimedia.org/wiki/File:May_Irwin_John_C._Rice_Kiss_1896.jpg.

Fig. 2.4 (pg. 45) Walter Pidgeon with Greer Garson in Mrs. Miniver. Museum of Modern Art Film Stills Archive.

Fig. 2.5 (pg. 47) Walter Pidgeon, Greer Garson, & Margaret O'Brien. Public domain image from Creative Commons, Life magazine, Volume 16, Number 14 (page 90)AuthorTime Inc.; photograph by Metro-Goldwyn-Mayer. https://commons.wikimedia.org/wiki/File:Madame-Curie-LIFE-1944.jpg.

Fig. 3.1 (pg. 53) William Ryder and James Ryder. Provincial Archives of New Brunswick Folster fonds MC1233.

Fig. 3.2 (pg. 57) *Moncton Transcript*. Provincial Archives of New Brunswick F3260.

Fig. 3.3 (pg. 58) Jane the Moose. Provincial Archives of New Brunswick P350-504 Fred Phillips Collection.

Fig. 3.4 (pg. 59) G. W. "Billy" Bitzer. Provincial Archives of New Brunswick Folster fonds MC1233.

Fig. 3.5 (pg. 60) G. W. "Billy" Bitzer and D. W. Griffith. Public domain image from Creative Commons. https://commons.wikimedia.org/wiki/File:Billy_Bitzer_D_W_Griffith_1920.jpg.

Fig. 3.6 (pg. 63) Lakestream Lake, Cannan Woods. Provincial Archives of New Brunswick Folster fonds MC 1233.

Fig. 3.7 (pg. 65) Cover of Crown Lands pamphlet. Provincial Archives of New Brunswick RG 617 – A2/b1919.

Fig. 4.1 (pg. 68) Gas illuminated camera. Provincial Archives of New Brunswick. Folster fonds MC1233.

Fig. 4.2a & 4.2b (pg. 69,70) Teddy Voye handbills. Provincial Archives of New Brunswick Folster fonds MC1233.

Illustrations and Credits

Fig. 4.3 (pg. 71) McAdam Theatre. Provincial Archives of New Brunswick P140-28.

Fig. 4.4 (pg. 74) Handbill from the Nickel. Folster fonds MC1233.

Fig. 4.5 (pg. 79) Projection room at the Lyric Theatre. New Brunswick Museum – Musée du Nouveau-Brunswick, www.nbm-mnb.ca 989.74.

Fig. 4.6 (pg. 82) Fire at the Kent Theatre. Provincial Archives of New Brunswick P913-1.

Fig. 4.7 (pg. 83) *New York American*. Public domain image from Creative Commons. https://commons.wikimedia.org/wiki/File:Stanford_White_33.jpg.

Fig. 4.8 (pg. 84) Evelyn Nesbit Thaw. This work is from the George Grantham Bain collection at the Library of Congress. https://commons.wikimedia.org/wiki/File:Evelyn_Nesbit_Thaw_by_Bain_News_Service.jpg.

Fig. 5.1 (pg. 87) Roseberry St., Campbellton. Provincial Archives of New Brunswick P170-10.

Fig. 5.2 (pg. 91) Carl Nelson's truck. Provincial Archives of New Brunswick Folster fonds MC3339 Courtesy Dorothy Hanscom.

Fig. 5.3 (pg. 93) Fredericton's Opera House. Provincial Archives of New Brunswick Folster fonds MC1233.

Fig. 5.4 (pg. 93) Poster for shows at Fredericton's Opera House. Provincial Archives of New Brunswick Folster fonds MC1233.

Fig. 5.5 (pg. 95) Imperial Theatre opening in Saint John. New Brunswick Museum – Musée du Nouveau-Brunswick, www.nbm-mnb.ca X13447

Fig. 5.6 (pg. 98) Sandford Jamer, Sadie Romans Parker. Provincial Archives of New Brunswick Folster fonds MC1233.

Fig 5.7 (pg. 100) Exterior of the restored Imperial Theatre. Public domain image from Creative Commons. Photographer: DDD DDD~commonswiki. https://commons.wikimedia.org/wiki/File:Saint_John,_New_Brunswick_Imperial_Theatre.jpg.

Fig 5.8 (pg. 101) Interior of the restored Imperial Theatre. GNU Free Documentation License from Alexvye at English Wikipedia on Creative Commons. https://commons.wikimedia.org/wiki/File:Imperial_Theatre,_Saint_John_03.jpg.

Fig 5.9 (pg. 102) *The Unemployed Taxi Driver*. Design by Brendan Helmuth, copyright 2017 Jack MacDougall.

Discovering the Movies in New Brunswick

Fig. 6.1 (pg. 106) New Brunswick guides. Provincial Archives of New Brunswick Folster fonds MC1233 P589-2.

Fig. 6.2 (pg. 107) Adam Moore. Provincial Archives of New Brunswick Folster fonds MC1233 P589-1.

Fig. 6.3 (pg. 111) Red Brook Lick. Provincial Archives of New Brunswick Folster Fonds MC1233 Courtesy Donald Dickey Jr.

Fig. 6.4 (pg. 112) Donald R. Dickey's photograph. Provincial Archives of New Brunswick Folster fonds MC1233 Courtesy Donald Dickey, Jr.

Fig. 6.5 (pg. 115) Burton Stanley ("Bert") Moore. Provincial Archives of New Brunswick Folster fonds MC1233.

Fig. 6.6 (pg. 116) Bert Moore with Donald R. Dickey. Provincial Archives of New Brunswick Folster fonds MC1233.

Fig. 6.7 (pg. 118) Promotional brochure. Provincial Archives of New Brunswick Folster fonds MC1233.

Fig. 6.8 (pg. 120) Intertitles. Provincial Archives of New Brunswick Folster fonds MC1233.

Fig. 6.9 (pg. 121) Donald R. Dickey, Florence Dickey. Folster fonds MC1233 Courtesy Donald Dickey Jr.

Fig. 7.1 (pg. 126) Ernie Shipman. Library and Archives Canada. C-05217.

Fig. 7.2 (pg. 136) Advertisement for *Blue Water*. Provincial Archives of New Brunswick Folster fonds MC1233.

Fig. 7.3 (pg. 138) Norma Shearer. Museum of Modern Art Film Stills Archives.

Fig. 7.4 (pg. 141) "Telling the Truth," Ernie Shipman advertising. Provincial Archives of New Brunswick Folster fonds MC1233.

Fig. 8.1 (pg. 153) Louis B. Mayer, A.A. Dysart. Provincial Archives of New Brunswick P350-278 Fred Phillips Collection.

Fig. 8.2 (pg. 155) Walter and Lillian Golding. Provincial Archives of New Brunswick Folster fonds MC1233 Courtesy Hoyt Golding.

Fig. 8.3 (pg. 158) Cartoon by Ed Sotto. *Citizen and Cheriot Chatter*, Culver City, California April 9, 1948 Loyola Marymount University.

Fig. 8.4 (pg. 163) Mayer Memorial Chapel. Provincial Archives of New Brunswick Folster fonds MC1233.

Fig. 8.5 (pg. 164) Mayer Memorial Chapel detail. Provincial Archives of New Brunswick Folster fonds MC1233.

Illustrations and Credits

Fig. 9.1 (pg. 167) Margaret Marceau. Provincial Archives of New Brunswick Folster fonds 1233.

Fig. 9.2 (pg. 172) Natalie Kalmus. Library of Academy of Motion Picture Arts and Sciences.

Figs. 10.1 & 10.2 (pg. 180) Greer Garson and Ralph Bellamy. Provincial Archives of New Brunswick Folster fonds MC1233 from the *Sunrise at Campbello* media kit.

Fig. 10.3 (pg. 183) Eleanor Roosevelt, Ralph Bellamy, and Greer Garson. Collection FDR-PHOCO: Franklin D. Roosevelt Library Public Domain Photographs, 1882 - 1962 By Unknown author or not provided - U.S. National Archives and Records Administration, Public Domain, https://commons.wikimedia.org/w/index.php?curid=16542410.

Fig. 10.4 (pg. 190) Filming of *Sunrise at Campobello*. Provincial Archives of New Brunswick Folster fonds MC1233. Courtesy FDR Library.

Fig. 10.5 (pg. 191) Dore Schary and Fred Phillips. Provincial Archives of New Brunswick P350-37 Fred Phillips Collection. Department of Tourism photo.

Fig. 10.6 (pg. 196) Poster from the *Sunrise at Campobello* press kit Provincial Archives of New Brunswick Folster Fonds MC1233.

Fig. 11.1 (pg. 202) Going to the movies in Grand Falls. Provincial Archives of New Brunswick Folster Fonds P615-17.

Fig. 11.2 (pg. 203) Barbara Bertelsen and Madeleine Guimont. Provincial Archives of New Brunswick Folster fonds MC1233.

Fig. 11.3 (pg. 205) Mitchell Franklin. Courtesy Beverly Franklin.

Fig. 11.4 (pg. 208) The Opera House in Miramichi. Courtesy of Tracy Waye Kelly.

Fig. 11.5 (pg. 211) Fire at The Rex. *Moncton Times*, October 24, 1972. Courtesy Moncton Times & Transcript.

Figs. 11.6 & 11.7 (pg. 212, 213) Herménégilde Chiasson. Courtesy of Herménégilde Chiasson.

Fig. 11.8 (pg. 214) Exterior of Théâtre Montcalm, Saint-Quentin. Courtesy Lionel Castonguay.

Fig. 11.9 (pg. 215) Interior of Théâtre Montcalm, Saint-Quentin. Courtesy Lionel Castonguay.

Fig. 11.10 (pg. 217) Eva MacDonald. Folster fonds MC1233. Courtesy Eva MacDonald.

Fig. 11.11 (pg. 219) The Andover Specialty Theatre. Provincial Archives of New Brunswick P194-689.

Fig. 11.12 (pg. 220) Riviera Theatre. Provincial Archives of New Brunswick Folster fonds 1233.

Fig. 11.13 (pg. 221) Norma Kertson and co-workers. Provincial Archives of New Brunswick Folster fonds P615-19 Courtesy Norma Martin.

Fig. 11.14 (pg. 223) The Walker Family. Courtesy UNB Archives and Special Collections David H. Walker fonds MG L 35, Series 5, Item 2.

Fig. 12.1 (pg. 231) Invitation to launch of NB Film Agency. Provincial Archives of New Brunswick Folster fonds 1233.

Fig. 12.2 (pg. 232) Jon and Freda Pedersen and daughter Dawn-Aeron Wason. Courtesy Jon Pedersen.

Fig. 12.3 (pg. 233) Doug Sutherland. Courtesy Tony Merzetti, NB Film Coop.

Fig. 12.4 (pg. 234) Rudolphe Caron, Helene Daigle. Blair MacIntyre, and Tony Merzetti. Courtesy Tony Merzetti, NB Film Coop.

Fig. 12.5 (pg. 235) Léonard Forest. Creative Commons Attribution 2.5 Generic license. Rodolphe Caron, 6 August 2014. https://commons.wikimedia.org/wiki/File:L%C3%A9onard_Forest.jpeg.

Fig. 12.6 (pg. 236) NB Film Coop Board of Directors. Courtesy Tony Merzetti, NB Film Coop.

Fig. 12.7 (pg. 237) Phil Comeau. Public domain image from Creative Commons. https://commons.wikimedia.org/wiki/File:PHIL_COMEAU_film_director.jpeg.

Fig. 12.8 (pg. 238) Lloyd Salamone. Courtesy Tony Merzetti, NB Film Coop.

Fig. 12.9 (pg. 241) Poster for *Festival International du Cinema Francophone en Acadie*, 2018. FICFA Marketing. Creative Commons Attribution-Share Alike 4.0 International license. https://commons.wikimedia.org/wiki/File:FICFA.png.

www.ingramcontent.com/pod-product-compliance
Lightning Source LLC
Chambersburg PA
CBHW071428070526
44578CB00001B/36